Ladder to the Moon

❖ ❖ ❖ ❖ ❖

Allegra Taylor

Ladder to the Moon
A Woman's Search for Spirituality

ILLUSTRATIONS BY ELSA WARNICK

INDEX COMPILED BY MARY KIRKNESS

SAFFRON WALDEN
THE C.W. DANIEL COMPANY LIMITED

First published in Great Britain in 1999
by The C.W. Daniel Company Limited
1 Church Path, Saffron Walden,
Essex, CB10 1JP, United Kingdom

ISBN 0 85207 313 5

Produced in association with Book Production Consultants plc
25–27 High Street, Chesterton, Cambridge, CB4 1ND, UK
Designed by Tina Ranft and set by Cambridge Photosetting Services, Cambridge
Printed in England by Hillman Printers (Frome) Ltd, England

Dedication

To my grandchildren
Jay, Maddison, Jake,
Harrison, Sean, Freya,
Zoë, Rafael and Kalila
And
For R., my life's companion, with my love.

Acknowledgements

I would like to thank all those who generously gave me assistance,
hospitality and encouragement while working on this book in particular
Dr. Soraya Tremayne and the Centre for Cross Cultural Research on
Women, Oxford; the Lebanese writer, Hanan al Shaykh; Ólàlèkán
Bàbálòlá; Jean Sayre-Adams; Dr. Jenny Goodman of Ruach Chavora
in London; Margot and Alex Forbes; ALEPH, The Jewish Spiritual
Renewal Movement in Philadelphia; Sharon and Darleen de Vida in
Washington; Marina Ricciardi, Lucy Rush and Cecelia Hurwich in
San Francisco; Jan Wheatcroft in Los Angeles; Sue Morrow Flanagan in
New York; Peter Clarke, Gemma Walker and Fania Mahony in Ireland;
Tess and Dara Molloy on Inishmore; Geri Mitchell in The Gambia; the
Polish writer Felix Scharf; Joachim Russek and Robert Gadek of the
Centre for Jewish Culture, Cracow; the Zen Peacemaker Order for their
beautiful 'Bearing Witness' work; Ben Haggarty and The Company of
Storytellers for my title. Thanks also to my publisher Ian Miller for his
trust and good humour; to my editor Rosanne Hooper for her valuable
comments and suggestions; to all the wonderful women who have been
my teachers and my travelling companions on this journey for sharing
their stories and most of all to my beloved husband Richard and our
children Ben, Tim, Femi, Matt, Francesca and Fauzia for believing in me.

Contents

❖ ❖ ❖ ❖ ❖

Chapter 1

❖ ❖ ❖ ❖ ❖

'Let the beauty we love be what we do.
There are hundreds of ways to kneel
and kiss the ground.'

RUMI

Leaving home is a physical odyssey, but it is also a state of mind to journey far from everything that's safe and known. Setting off to follow a spiritual quest is an honourable tradition in many cultures so I know I am in good company, but that doesn't make it any easier. Although I have travelled alone before it's never without a certain amount of trepidation. I'm not that fond of staying on my own in anonymous motel rooms or eating alone and I don't like being lost. Yet, on a pale-washed English morning with a thin spring sun leaving ghostly negatives of unmelted snow like paper cut-outs on the grass beneath the bare cherry trees, I began my journey. The first rung of my ladder to the moon. Some ancestral thread keeps reeling me out.

My father, a refugee from Poland, once wrote a little memoir which he entitled *'The Wonderings of a Wandering Jew'* and I think I have inherited his shoes. Being Jewish seems to carry with it a built-in obligation to gather up the many scattered fragments of the Diaspora, of the holocaust legacy, to understand the restlessness, the rootlessness. An inherited condition of exile, generations of homelessness, a childhood constantly on the move have bred in me a need, periodically, to collect bits of myself from significant locations around the world. And so it was time for another journey. A quest. In fact, three quests in one: a challenging menopausal adventure – leaving myself open to wherever the tides took me; a survey of some current developments in the field of women's spirituality built up from interviews and conversations with many different women; and, perhaps most importantly, a profound inner journey in search of wholeness, in search of a spiritual centre within myself. It became a journey that was to change me more deeply than I could have imagined, more deeply than any growth workshop or packaged adventure tour ever could. I had chosen to begin my search by 'wondering' around America because the yeasty ferment of women's spirituality has had a twenty year head start there. In England there is much questioning and longing but women are still struggling to find an authentic spiritual voice, struggling to find acceptance in positions of spiritual leadership. I wanted to see what I could learn and bring it home – home, that evocative word with its multiplicity of meanings. Home, as journey's end, as a spiritual destination, as coming to rest in my own heart. The end of exile.

On the plane my eyes closed and I had a vivid dream ... I was a bird, a giant condor. My six-foot wing span stretched across the huge uplifting thermals like a ship on the high seas. Sailing, sailing in the thin Andean air I could see to infinity in every direction. Above me the glare of a hard, bright moon. Below me the pointy, unforgiving peaks of the jagged mountains. A chain of them – a spiny dragon's back – lay treacherously, in a pretence of sleep, only waiting for someone to step inadvertently, unsuspectingly on his tail to lash and thrash with storms of terrifying intensity. The land beneath my gaze was unfinished as if the Gods had left their toys scattered about, haphazard, capricious. I searched for a place to rest, to nest but I could see only barren black granite and bone-chilling winds driving Patagonian snows into furious drifts and eddies. I seemed to be doomed, like the Flying Dutchman, to wander forever.

I knew there was some task I had to perform but I didn't know what it was. Some magical items, perhaps, that I must collect to break the spell which had cast me in this lonely role. I could hear the mournful whistle of the wind in my wing feathers bearing me aloft. I could hear the beating of my own warm-blooded heart – the only living thing in an eternity of ice and rock. I could hear the cut-glass splintering crack and creak of a glacier moving its ponderous way, one millimetre every thousand years, towards its transformation. What would be my transformation? Was I to be forced to learn about loneliness? About homelessness? About clear-seeing? I was so tired. It felt good to lie on the wind, surrendering to the currents taking me where they willed. Even in the midst of my isolation I knew that in some way I was fortunate to be there. Very few other eyes had ever seen this view of the earth's curving horizon. It was a summer night and the sky was a luminous cobalt scattered with diamond-bright stardust. A sense of completion came over me. I slept, born

aloft with the music of the spheres ringing in the crystal air. I knew I was only half of this planet. Where was my true home?

The dream was so clear and detailed it felt like a real happening. Jung called dreams 'the small hidden doors in the deepest and most intimate sanctum of the soul, which open into that primal, cosmic night far beyond what a conscious ego could ever reach'. I woke startled and had to look at my arms to check they weren't covered in feathers. The symbolism was almost too obvious and for the rest of that long, long surreal flight, changing planes in Dallas with minutes to spare, looking out on the stark contrast of a flat, brown Texas landscape where a pall of nicotine-stained smog hung over the city like a shroud, I felt disorientated and subdued.

I read the newspaper on the plane and my attention was suddenly caught by an extremely relevant news item. For the first time in its history the part of God, in the ancient, medieval York Mystery Play, was to be played by a *woman*. This, of course, had caused a furore with the venerable Archdeacon of York, thundering that, "A woman playing God is just another example of the rising tide of feminism which overturns the biblical understanding of God and will split the church." His tirade was swiftly countered by The Reverend Joy Carroll, a newly ordained minister from London, who argued, "Of course, God can be portrayed by a woman. God is neither male nor female, but since He has been portrayed as a man for centuries it can't hurt God to be played by a woman for a few hundred years ... the fact that men in the Church are frightened of the notion of God being portrayed by a woman is down to a deep-seated fear that they might lose control." The incident illustrated with great clarity the rival passions in this whole women-in-the-church debate, of how so many men feel threatened and women are strengthening their resolve to fight back and to claim, once and for all, a position of spiritual equality. What is being raised, to quote Roger and Jennifer Woolger in *The Goddess Within*, is the question of "the whole psychospiritual imbalance in our culture" – a profound disharmony between the masculine and feminine life forces.

I remember feeling furious with the rigidity and conservatism my non-Jewish mother had to deal with when she wanted to convert to Orthodox Judaism in order to join my father in his final resting place. She found the synagogue a very forbidding and unwelcoming place, a men-only club – the women were relegated to second-class status, hidden by screens, not allowed to touch the holy scrolls, regarded as 'unclean' during menstruation and forbidden from entering the temple until they had taken a ritual bath. She eventually triumphed and won the right to call herself a Jew just in time to be buried in the plot next to the love of her life, but that's about the only good it did her. Another nail in the coffin of the Patriarchy as far as I was concerned and the incident added to the long list of reasons why I feel estranged from patriarchal mainstream religion.

A good, simple definition of *patriarchy* offered by Gerda Lerner in her fine book, *The Creation of Patriarchy* is 'the institutionalisation of male dominance over women both in the family and in society in general'. It implies that men hold power in all the important institutions in society and that women are deprived of access to such power. Where religion is concerned, many women feel that a great wounding has been perpetrated upon those of our sex for far too long and the reason why the York incident is so significant is that it clearly illustrates a built-in assumption about the nature of the Divine. It is about centuries of the elevation of the masculine and the devaluing of the feminine.

The meaning of the word 'religion' – re-ligio – is to re-tie the bonds, to reconnect with the source but wherever I look it connects to a male God. The four-letter name YHWH, usually pronounced Yahweh or Jehovah, was deliberately meant to be unpronounceable. What it actually represents is, 'That which was and is and will be, formless, *genderless*, being and becoming – ONENESS.' but it is invariably translated as 'Lord', 'King' or 'Father'. I want to know how the Source got hijacked by one half of the human race and how we can get it back? In company with a growing number of women, Jewish, Christian, Muslim, I feel wounded and cheated by the centuries of exclusion. And now many of us are trying to find a way to visualise anew what religion could be and how we could become whole. In turning to the myths and stories of the ancient goddesses, in exploring Wicca and Paganism, in searching for something meaningful amongst the sacred traditions of other cultures, women are recognising that the Divine is not only 'out there' but is in us and we can reclaim it. As Simone de Beauvoir once said, "This has always been a man's world, but none of the reasons hitherto brought forward in explanation of this fact has seemed adequate."

In antiquity the goddess was a valid image. Her priestesses were respected. Women had an equal part to play in the spiritual matters of their communities. But the world turns. Things change. The new monotheistic religions founded by men had an exclusively male priesthood and by the Middle Ages the wise woman had metamorphosed into the wicked witch.

The terror of the Inquisition reigned for over 200 years. In relatively permissive England alone 30,000 witches were tortured and killed between 1542 and 1736. Unbelievably, Witchcraft Laws were still on the statutes until *1951*. The Inquisition outlawed and demonised the ancient wisdoms of women and cut them off from their own direct experience of spirituality. Denied any form of spiritual authority until the year 1992 when the Church of England synod finally granted them the right to become priests (not priestesses, mind you, and still serving the Father rather than the Mother), women have been conditioned to have little confidence in their own spiritual vision. Prejudice against women in the church is rife and a legacy of fear still haunts those of us who seek to reclaim the mystery, power and magic of the feminine.

But slowly, slowly in the wake of the women's movement, the New Age movement and the ecology movement there has been a growing recognition in the West that, although the word still carries a frisson of alarm, 'witches' were, and still are, none other than wise women who preserve in their collective unconscious the remnants of an older religion based on worship of nature and the feminine principle. It is an interesting observation that as the churches are getting emptier there is a simultaneous gathering groundswell of interest in ancient pagan traditions, Celtic and other European folk traditions, and Native American traditions. Within mainstream religion, feminist scholars and theologians (or should that be thealogians) are reinterpreting sacred texts, reclaiming the women who were bulldozed out of history. Things are on the move again. It is an exciting time to be alive. Part of the purpose of my quest is to get a better idea of the choices women are making in the closing years of the millennium. I am no scholar or expert myself but in common with many ordinary women I share a vision of the feminine becoming truly integrated into a rich and varied spiritual palette in which sexism plays no part. Patriarchy also hurts men.

I arrived at last in Portland, Oregon to find my friend Elsa's laughing, loving face waiting for me at the barrier. One of life's greatest pleasures is to be met. Especially at strange airports. To be expected, looked for, waited for is such a blissful contrast to the usual chin-quivering bleakness of facing a forest of hands waving for other people when nobody knows you or knows you're there or cares at all.

Elsa is an artist – a painter and illustrator. We have known and loved each other for many years. Lifetimes. As soon as she heard I was writing a book about women and their search for an authentic spirituality, she launched into a bracing defence of atheism, and of autonomy and creativity as the only spiritual path worth taking.

"Then and now I wanted none of it!" she said. "My Jewish upbringing had nothing to do with spirituality – only 'supposed-to's', like washing your hands after going to the toilet, like making your bed. You *did* all that Jewish stuff but it was meaningless to me. Sunday school was boring and stupid, unnecessary, repetitious. In the synagogue everybody was pretending, watching each other, watching the clock. It was like a dysfunctional family where everybody says everything is fine. I thought it was all bullshit. Only the music was beautiful and transcendent. But the rituals! The repeat-after-me stuff, the walking round the Torah – pure hypocrisy! People were sweating, yawning, bored to death. And since then, all the religions, the isms, the retreats, mantras, deep breathing, chants, systems and processes that are supposed to avail you of a spiritual experience – none of those things ever spoke to me. They bothered me. Embarrassed me. I thought it was all lies. I never could open my arms to that stuff. It pushed me away because it was all unrelated to *my* spiritual experience which seemed to come from inside me. It was directed from within, not something imposed from outside – not a stand-up, sit-down, clap-your-hands ritual. And anything to do with a special place of worship – I winced at that.

"To me, spirituality has nothing to do with the rational mind. It is an ability to *be* without self-consciousness. You simply *are* – fully alive, engaged, integrated. That, to me, is a spiritual state and my first real memory of it is not, in fact, related to art but to being in nature. The first time I was able to come down out of my busy brain, out of my physical awareness into a condition of connectedness was in nature. I was always a very driven person when I was a child. Very perfectionistic. Very self-conscious. Always in control, analysing, describing, labelling. Never relaxed, never at peace. I performed very well but I was just 'on' all the time. Then I went to Copenhagen when I was 20. I sensed a joy of life there – beautiful flowers, great butter. I was ready. Walking one day on a vast green lawn with sunlight on it, I just remember coming out of that state and recognising where I had been – at peace, in harmony. No tension. No anxiety. It was almost like a levitation. I was not conscious of my physical body. I was just utterly light, free, unencumbered. Once I'd experienced this I recognised it as the state I was supposed to feel when all my friends in college were chanting and talking about unconditional love. But that had meant nothing more to me than the 'supposed-to's' of my childhood. It did not give me any altered state of being in any way. It was *busy* work.

"That 'ah ha!' experience was rather like my first orgasm – 'so that's what they meant! Now I know!' Once I had had that, I was open to it and began to sense the components that could make it happen – learning to relax, to turn off my brain, to get rid of the critical, analytical head stuff. When everything is integrated like a brilliant athlete or musician then there is a coming together, a flow, a sublime dance of all your parts.

"I have trouble with the God word. People have told me that it's arrogance, lack of humility, but I can't bow down to 'It', the Big Thing Out There. It just doesn't do it for me. It doesn't compute. I don't care what you call it – all this Higher Power stuff – I don't relate to that kind of language. That is hierarchical thinking, pleasing-the-boss thinking. It's just somebody's intellectual notion. I care about the quality of what happens. When I'm in a completely altered state, engaged, in harmony, I'm in the 'Mozart place' – a place of unbridled passion married with exquisite discipline. That's art. It's so sublime, so utterly perfect that you almost *die*. We are as expansive as we want to be. I do what I do with a full heart because that's what I've got to do. I don't cheat and I don't trick. I don't want a ticket to anywhere. I just want to do it for and of itself. The best I can. Autonomy. It comes from within and if that makes me a bad person and not humble then somebody better explain why."

Elsa was on full throttle and when she paused for breath I could only say that although I might describe it differently, we were not actually in disagreement. The nature of the transcendent experience is pretty much the same however you may arrive at it.

"This Big Daddy in the Sky, this Almighty Father, this being in thrall to a male authority figure whom you are supposed to please … No!" Elsa continued. "I'm not interested in doing it for 'other', only for itself. I like personal responsibility, not doing something for a reward, for approval, for salvation. Not 'advance three squares and you'll get a bigger ice-cream cone'. 'Spiritual', to me, is when I feel whole and guileless and free from mental constructs – soaring, weightless, a joyful dance of all my parts. Spirituality is the place where the real moment of your experience is *embodied* so that whatever *is* – peeling a carrot, putting on a band-aid – you are utterly present and engaged. Attentive. Respectful. You don't compromise. You're not trying to get away with giving a mediocre version. No matter what you are doing you attend to it with care. Nobody has to be checking up on you. No God has to be watching. It's an internal imperative and that, to me, is a state of grace.

"I'm in awe of the ocean, the stars, the sky, the Spring, the overwhelming mystery and power, the unfathomable magic. I want to swim in it, dance in it, rejoice in it, extract from it, use it – but I don't need answers. I just want to be *present*. The idea that there is a 'truth' is absurd. There are only points of view. Love is carried on down from generation to generation. The genius and deeds of those who have gone before are sprinkled like stardust on those who are not yet born. In me there is the drive to create. I am turned on and elated by visual harmony. I am excited by life and I want to capture that feeling. I swoon and rejoice when it works."

I love Elsa. More than anyone I know she has retained into her 6th decade a sense of childlike wonder and innocence. In her marvellous picture books for children everything comes alive. Salt and pepper pots have personalities. Tubes of toothpaste offer opinions. Boxes of matches sing and dance. She once sat for days sketching old vacuum cleaners in a museum because she fell in love with them. She faxed me her drawings. Her excitement and enthusiasm were so infectious I fell in love with them too. Her delicate, meticulous water-colours transport you instantly into the world of her imagination. Over the years, Elsa and I have always hoped that synchronicity would provide an opportunity for us to work on a project together. This seemed to be it so I was absolutely delighted when she agreed to design the cover and do the text illustrations for this book. Here are two of her poems. I think they capture her well:

> SWEET MYSTERY OF LIFE
> *I might be weak, but I am also strong.*
> *Such degrees of each make me laugh.*
> *How can I, who foul up so many things*
> *Be able to perceive so much?*
> *Are we all like this, incredible?*
> *A mixture of the most unexplained, undefined glory?*

ON OCCASION
Once in a while
The stuff in my head
And the stuff in my body
Are the same

There's a place
Where nothing asks
For anything at all,
Where whatever's there fills all the cells
And dances.

I was in buoyant mood as I left Elsa's sanctuary and headed north to the Eleventh Annual Spring Mysteries Festival – a gathering of pagans from all over the United States. I was on my way to the Olympic Peninsula, driving up the old Highway 101 – the Pacific Coast Highway. In my borrowed Cherokee jeep I hurtled past dense forests, past little logging towns and immense bodies of water – past inlets and islands and distant shipping lanes in the fine, sunny weather.

It seemed a good idea to start with Paganism, a much-maligned and misunderstood spiritual path and one which continues to attract many women by its gentle, nature-based teachings. It all came about because I had seen an advertisement for the Center for non-Traditional Religions and written to them telling about my quest and asking for suggestions or contacts in the American Northwest. I received an immediate warm and friendly response inviting me to attend the festival as an 'honoured guest' thereby having "a real opportunity to meet with many more Pagans and Wiccans while in Seattle than you might otherwise expect." You bet.

My first tentative encounter with a pagan philosophy of life had taken place not long before in the magically named little town of Stepaside in Wales. Hidden from view in an overgrown field was the Mother Nature camp to which I had come to spend a week learning about 'magic in the European tradition'. The camp, consisting of several large teepees and a couple of round straw-roofed hogans dotted about in the long grass, was the brainchild of a delightful woman called Anna Humming Earthworm Hawthorn. I had visited her stand at the Mind, Body and Spirit Festival a few weeks earlier and been attracted to the gentle, friendly ambience. On an impulse I enrolled. I had no idea what to expect but if there was a continuing tradition of European magic, I reckoned that a search for spirituality should include an acquaintance with it.

When I arrived I confess my heart sank a bit. I am the complete town mouse, I've never been camping and I was useless at it. It had looked easy enough when I watched one of the camp inmates split kindling with an axe and start a merry blaze but now everything was damp and I was nearly in tears. Then, what triumph! What pride when eventually a little plume of smoke arose from my teepee and the big iron kettle was steaming on the grate. I made myself a bowl of exquisite porridge and a pot of tea. All this took two hours. No place here for the pace and preoccupations of city life. Only the present moment.

Teaching sessions were held in the straw hogan. Anna, a shy, diffident woman who calls herself "a not very charismatic witch" was so unassertive and apologetic as a teacher that a couple of times during the course of that first morning I found myself looking at my watch and wondering what on earth I was doing here in a wet field full of slugs sitting round a smoky fire, smelling like a kipper.

I was feeling decidedly bolshie about going out in the rain on a 'pathwalking meditation' to test an analogy between the pathways we walk in the world and the pathways in our nervous systems, but once I'd put on my wellies and started wandering about in the woods it suddenly began to seem much more profound. The symbolism came thick and fast; how much I tend to depend on the pathways other people have already made; how hard it is for me to venture into unknown territory; how frightened I am of becoming lost; how important ancient paths are for knowledge, safety, trade, communication, survival; how exciting to cut a brand new trail where no one had ever been before; how easy to hack your way insensitively rather than to go with care and consideration. Yes, the paths we create in our minds – ways of thinking – are like the external pathways of the world. Circuitous routes are often better than straight ones, especially uphill, and different perspectives are visible from different paths. In the multiplicity of spiritual paths to choose from there is no one right way – only different approaches to developing awareness, loving-kindness and compassion.

Anna's main point had effectively been made: that metaphors have always been the best way of teaching the pathways of knowledge and that apprentice-ship to the mysteries of ancient wisdom begins with putting your feet on the path. Some of the places you go will be very old tracks laid down since the Dreamtime, others will be your own. All are valid.

At the end of the session I felt my senses were sharper and my awareness keener than before. I also felt humbler and more receptive. There is something about modern life that makes us think we can learn everything quickly, greedily – get a video, have a briefing, hire an expert – but taking time to do things slowly alters your perceptions and creates the possibility for the unexpected to slip in between your heartbeats.

Anna calls herself a witch only because she feels it is important to reclaim the word from the fear and loathing where it has languished since the Middle Ages. She is "dancing the dream awake" as she says. I came to admire her tremendously. Her quietness is deceptive – a great strength, in fact – and her teaching style organic rather than didactic. You suddenly make connections, uncover things for yourself that were there all along. She is an enabler; a flame from which others can light their tapers. She is a qualified psychotherapist and medical herbalist. In ancient times she would have been a priestess.

Anna took on her whimsical name a few years ago. "It started as a joke," she said. "People were starting to adopt all these American Indian names; Dancing Sun Bear, Yellow Moose Woman or what have you. I wanted to be a 'workshop' person too but I had never seen any of those animals so I chose Humming Earthworm Hawthorn. 'Humming', to stay in tune with changing energies and to enchant the mind into harmony. 'Earthworm', the only creature which eats earth and creates fertile topsoil. 'Hawthorn', the witches' tree. Its thorny branches and bushy habit create a protective environment for the seedlings of larger trees, it provides the hottest firewood known and its berries make medicine for the heart."

I was very lucky. There could be no one better from whom to learn about magic. "Magic", said Anna, "is not about tricks. You have to train yourself to see again the miracles around you." Magic is about watching, being aware, being awake; a ceremonial acknowledgement of the cyclical changing of the heavens and an understanding that the movement of the earth and the heavenly bodies affect the affairs and progress of humankind. Hence her insistence that we spend a lot of time in nature just pondering and meditating upon the elements. They help us to uncover and recognise the connections between things and the way that nothing happens on its own but creates a chain reaction. We spent hours on our own walking in the countryside thinking about the properties and characteristics of water or air, fire or earth.

I was fascinated by the connections and similarities between our ancient European traditions of 'magic' and the medicine wheel traditions of the Native Americans. Their medicine wheel is a tool for fine-tuning our relationships with the natural world, with the cycles of birth and death, with the 'four directions'. As I understand it: The east is the place of the sunrise and new beginnings, of the Spring equinox. It is associated with birth and the element of air which is breath, life and inspiration. A feather or a stick of incense is often used to represent the east. The south is the place of the noonday sun, of the Summer solstice. It is associated with the intensity of youth and the element of fire which is love and growth and purification. Its symbol is a candle. The west is the place of the sunset, of transition and introspection, of the Autumn equinox. It is associated with our middle years, of harvest and healing. Its element is water and a chalice is often used as a symbol of the west. The north is midnight, darkness, the place of the elders and the age of wisdom. It is the time of the Winter solstice – the shortest day – when we celebrate the return of the light. The element of the north is earth and it is usually represented by a crystal, some salt or grain. Calling on the four directions with their associated elements and their animal totems, aligning ourselves with their energies and their rhythms opens the door and invites the benevolent forces from other realms to come to our assistance. That's magic.

Anna spoke very informatively about the pagan festivals – the ancient precursors of the holidays we observe today. In addition to the solstices and the equinoxes there are the 'cross-quarter days' in between. Samhain, for example, which became Hallowe'en is a time when the veils between this world and the Other World get very thin. One cycle is dying while another is beginning. Everything is returning to the earth, the leaves fall, the sap retreats, Persephone makes her journey to the Underworld. It was the time of the burning of the 'green man', the corn king who must die in order to be reborn the following spring. It is the festival of wholeness and of the soul, associated with apples – the symbol of eternal life. It is a time to honour the mysteries, a time of transformation, purification and bonfires. The origin of the pumpkin jack o' lantern was a candle in a skull honouring the seat of consciousness. It is a time for ghost stories and fortune-telling games – releasing the ghosts and ties of the past that bind us. A time for witches to practise their craft – Wicca, the craft of the wise.

The other cross-quarter days are Imbolc on February 2nd., which became Candlemas, a fire festival with its emphasis on emerging after the darkness of winter and rekindling the inner fire, a festival of germination and the stirring of the seed. This was the time of the goddess in her maiden aspect – the Bride, Birgitta. The time of Shrove Tuesday, Carnival, sexual freedom before Lent, Valentine's Day (originally in honour of the God Pan). Then there is Beltane on May Day – a time of the sacred marriage of the God and the Goddess, a time for courting and flirting. Time to dance the dance of life with wild desire and sweet delight, to celebrate fertility and abundance. A time for celebration of relationships which bring forth life. In olden times, all fires were extinguished and lit anew from the Beltane fire built on the top of a hill. And, finally, Lammas or Lughnasa on August 1st – the time of the corn mother, of ripeness, lushness and maturity. But the descent into the dark has begun and the cycle comes round again.

A witch was a shaman, a healer, a wise one, symbolically 'riding' the transforming powers, disappearing into different dimensions. (In Mexican, Native American, African or Amazonian Indian societies today, such gifted people are much revered). She might well have used hallucinogenic plants for far-seeing, hence the stories about flying and broomsticks. Her sign was the hexagram, the six-pointed star, which signified perfectly balanced energies. The original meaning of a 'hex' was a witches ability to restore balance. Her cauldron was the symbol of transformation. She was the repository of ancient wisdom (even the word 'wisdom' in its original usage meant 'possessing powers of magic'). And what is meant by magic? "It is to be mindful of the forces of nature," said Anna, "and to call upon their help thereby enhancing your own power – the power of thought to create energy and reality." This doesn't seem any more illogical to me than a belief in God.

Magic is art. It has to do with forms, with structures, with images that can shift us out of the limitations of everyday reality, with visions that can hint at new possibilities. Magic is also will – action, passion, choices, faith. When you consciously direct energy by the images in your mind, by your speech, by your actions you cause changes to happen. This is no different from prayer. Having integrity as a witch or as anything else means recognising that your choices have consequences and that you are personally responsible for what happens.

Occult shops are full of books of spells and incantations – how to get your lover back, how to get revenge, how to win… These are the obvious traps waiting for angry people who are longing to make their lives different without taking responsibility. But magic is not about power over other people, said Anna, "It is about calling forth your own autonomous power from within."

Anna's teachings are based on a world view of 'immanence', a pantheistic conception of the Divine being present throughout the universe; of spirit and transformative power being embodied in the natural world. Her creed has *nothing whatsoever* to do with Satanism, a post-Christian perversion of the occult, although this, of course, was the propaganda put about by the Inquisition which still sticks to this day. From this came the ill-informed bandying about of the emotive words 'black magic' and the great misunderstanding that has arisen around the concept of pagan rituals.

"It is a shame that 'black' has become associated with evil," said Anna. "Black magic is really about letting things grow in the warm, dark places. It is slow, nurturing women's magic (which is why it became damned). Like the womb, it is a place of growth; it is the symbolic fertile earth where the hidden seed lies unfolding; it is the ocean's depth; it is the netherworld where we go for our visions. We shouldn't be afraid of the darkness. It is the place where we dare to close our eyes, to rest, to sleep, to dream."

She talked about the exciting new area where science and spirituality meet, where scientists have begun at last to recognise what shamans and healers have always known; that matter and energy are not separate forces but different forms of the same thing – like water, ice and steam. A younger generation of writers and thinkers from the scientific community such as Gary Zukav (*The Dancing Wu Li Masters, The Seat of the Soul*) and Fritjof Capra (*The Tao of Physics, The Turning Point*) have broken new ground in the last decade or so. Capra tells of his revelation while travelling in India on the hippy trail. Contemplating an image of the dancing multi-limbed Shiva surrounded by a ring of fire he understood for the first time that mystics and physicists were both trying to illuminate the same basic fundamental truths about the nature of the universe. Miracles are merely the clever handling of energy in all its manifestations. Divine intelligence may be as small as an electron.

Albert Einstein once said; "A human being is part of a whole called by us, 'universe' – a tiny part limited in time and space. We experience our thoughts and feelings as somehow separate from the rest – a kind of optical delusion of our consciousness. But this delusion is a prison of our own making, restricting us to our personal desires and to affection for a few persons nearest to us. Our task must be to free ourselves from this prison by widening our circle of compassion to embrace all living creatures and the whole of nature in its beauty."

Since Einstein formulated his theory of relativity in 1916, physicists have discovered that the human organism is not just a physical structure made of molecules. At the most basic sub-atomic level, we are also composed of *energy fields*. We are constantly changing, ebbing and flowing, affected by what goes on around us. Scientists are learning to measure these subtle changes with more and more accuracy – for example; electrical currents from the heart (ECG), electrical currents from the brain (EEG), lie detectors which measure electro-potential of the skin, devices which can measure magnetic fields around the body without even touching it.

This knowledge is growing all the time and we are more able to see the connections between objective scientific descriptions and the world of our own subjective human experience. We now know that sub-atomic particles are affected by the energy being directed at them in the form of thought. In other words, *thought forms have energy.* Thought forms have the power to heal. Imagery and the spirit play a central part in the process of the transformation of both physical and emotional life. It has taken science a long time to come up with subtle enough instruments with which to measure what, in our collective unconscious, we have always known. Fairy stories and folk tales are full of curses and blessings which are no more nor less than thought forms, negative and positive. When the witch doctor points the bone at an Australian Aborigine and tells him he will die, he will. When our parents or our religious leaders bestow blessings upon us, they give us comfort and courage. We are made stronger. Wicked trolls, with a mumbled spell, can turn a princess into a block of ice, a bird, a seal. She can be redeemed by the power of love. At a deep level we know this to be true.

Our old solid world of concrete things is surrounded by an invisible, fluid world of radiating energy, constantly moving, constantly changing. This is what spiritual healers have been saying all along – the deceptively simple yet striking fact that *thought influences matter;* that the mind and the emotions have a profound effect on the body for they can alter the behaviour of the minutest components – the sub-atomic particles, the very building blocks which go to make up its structure and compose its intricate, interrelated systems.

We cannot cause change without changing ourselves, said Anna. "It's not so much 'how can I get others to do what I want?' but 'what is preventing me from owning my own power?' In shaping energy we take on the shape we create, we become the power that we call forth. If we can see ourselves as part of the whole we can affect the whole. If I am only concerned with myself, that is 'wave consciousness' and eventually I will crash on the beach and that's the end of me but if I can see myself as connected to all things then I become the ocean. I believe that all of us have the ability, given sufficient dedication, to gather knowledge, magic, power and wisdom by getting in touch with our own deep core and tuning in to natural cycles."

Demons, she said, were nothing but our own fears. They can be conquered by naming them. They lose power when they are called by their true names (envy, insecurity, jealousy, lust). We need to take the horrible vibe out of the occult and re-own it. It is not to do with having control over other people, it is about being an instrument in the Divine orchestra.

"A ritual is a state of openness and total attunement where you become one with the natural forces around you. It should be creative and sensitive like the lovemaking between two people. There is nothing sinister or particularly dangerous about rituals. Like any other useful tool or technique, it can be irresponsibly misused but the laws of karma ensure that any evil eventually rebounds on the perpetrator, rendering it ineffective in the long run. The first principle of magic is that all things are interconnected. All is relationship. You can't do any lasting magic without love."

Most of the people I met at the Mother Nature camp were travellers. I was profoundly moved by their yearning to find another way to live – by the Utopian dream of a fair, loving non-hierarchical community where people heal and encourage one another and take care of the Earth. People who have been deeply wounded by our alienating culture – poets, mystics, misfits, dropouts – are attracted to the vision being nourished there. A place to be safe and loved. A tribe. The beautiful thing about a real community is that it counters estrangement and isolation. People are connected to one another and to nature. Alas, the thrust of Western culture has been to destroy little communities who reject mainstream living. For some reason conventional society feels threatened by the travellers and teepee dwellers. On a personal level, the whole notion of homecoming and belonging touched me very deeply. I thought of Wordsworth's extraordinary poem *Intimations of Immortality*:

> *Our birth is but a sleep and a forgetting*
> *The soul that rises with us – our life's star -*
> *Hath had elsewhere its setting and cometh from afar.*
> *Not in entire forgetfulness and not in utter nakedness*
> *But trailing clouds of glory do we come*
> *From God who is our home.*

Maybe we are all longing to go home to some place we remember but have never been.

The neo-pagan movement with its re-discovery of the goddess seems to offer a real alternative to the masculine symbolism of the great monotheistic religions. The whole idea of 'dominion over' is anathema. It encourages a respect for the feminine, a reverence for the cosmic forces and a love of the natural world. Its rites are full of dance, poetry, laughter and music. It is no coincidence that the movement is growing while the churches are emptying.

With its focus on the natural world, the elements and the seasons, Anna's teaching gently illustrated how everything is in a constant state of flux, forever flowing. Magic is about transformation but it is happening around us all the time. Our bodies, in a continual cycle of dying and renewing, are magic. All of creation is an open system into and out of which flow constant streams of energy. "Once you begin to see things as *processes* rather than fixed *things* then you can begin to affect the flow," said Anna. "You can re-balance; put things back in harmony."

I feel perfectly happy with this concept. Everything I have learned about healing in the ten years I have been actively practising accords with this definition of magic. Until I met Anna my rather dismissive image of modern pagans had been formed by a couple of quick browses round my local New Age shop which has a whole section on Wicca complete with pointed hats, cloaks and bottles of All Night Long Oil. Its easy to scoff but beyond the fantasy and the fancy dress, the promises of a never never land and the longing for a potion to make your dreams come true lies a philosophy infinitely more profound. Through all the centuries of persecution it has lain low but never completely disappeared.

So now, I was on my way to the furthest, Northwestern corner of the United States to an American pagan gathering and the re-enactment of an ancient rite. Trains laden with huge felled trees wound their way along the water's edge on their way down to the paper mills on the Columbia river. I was feeling quite intrepid as I drove along; an adventurer, a seeker, a pilgrim. Then just as suddenly my mood changed and I found myself experiencing a sharp pang of homesickness. Home seemed very far away.

I found myself thinking, too, of my beloved friend Marie. When her teenage daughter, Pascale, was killed in a freak accident Marie was drawn to undertake a Native American 'vision quest' in an attempt to make some sense of the tragedy. She wrote a beautiful book about her journey called, *A Healing Quest*, but there were countless times when all she could do was howl with loneliness and grief wondering what in heaven's name she was doing so far from home. Maybe we are seized by this implacable, intractable need to undertake a spiritual search when there is a yearning for connectedness, when we are homesick for the light, when we are gripped by the pain and grief of loss (of a child, of a relationship, of youth.) I haven't been prompted by anything as terrible as the death of one of my children but like many other women today, I am grappling with a way to redefine what spirituality means to me and the ways in which I can tap into it. I am trying to 'walk through the open gate', in the writer, Kimberley Snow's phrase. Looking for authentic ways to invite and maintain a feeling of connection with something larger than myself.

"I've suddenly realised something! I see what it is", said one of my healing clients, sitting bolt upright on the treatment table back home. "I've been looking at things all wrong. I've been angry and frustrated by all the difficulties in my life instead of seeing them as a gift. It's been under my nose the whole time. I've been asking God to show me then not listening to the answer. The things which I have been trying to get rid of – the domestic challenges, the health problems – are the very things which are forcing me to make changes and ask questions". Our gentle healing session had brought her mind, body and spirit into balance and enabled a moment of clarity. She had begun to trust her connection to the Divine. On this journey I am hoping to do the same. To see the difficulties and challenges as gifts. To surrender and open myself to those shafts of light that illuminate the space where maybe I stand in my own shadow.

The combination of our materialistic, consumer culture and the atheistic, scientific ethos of our times has conspired to make us doubt such moments of insight and revelation, to doubt the very existence of our place in the sun. We have lost the tools with which to cultivate the health of the spirit or our connection to the sacred. As women oppressed by a patriarchally dominated religious tradition we have lost confidence in our instincts.

As a way forward, I personally feel the need to explore and experiment with many sources – from Buddhist teachings to Wicca rituals – to create a synthesis, a wholeness that will nourish the indwelling spirit. I want to know what it would feel like to wake up, to come alive, to dance and sing, to chant and drum, to fill up with wonderment at being a woman, to celebrate the divine energy of my spirit, to connect with all women, with all beings, with the earth, the sky, the trees and the rocks.

I finally arrived on the tip of the Northwest peninsula for the Pagan celebration of the Eleusinian Spring Mysteries of Greek mythology. Fort Flagler National Park is a most beautiful spot overlooking the Puget Sound and the Straits of Juan de Fuca with the Canadian Rockies gleaming, dramatically snow-clad and majestic in the far distance across the water. I was one of the first to show up at the rather incongruous setting of an old de-commissioned army barracks where the Pagans had booked in for the Easter Week to perform, as they do every year, the ancient Mysteries.

Gradually people started to appear. A battered old van bearing the bumper sticker, 'Isis, Isis, Ra! Ra! Ra!' disgorged three baby witches – shaven headed, pierced young women in Addams Family clothes with black lipstick and purple talons. There were bikers and hippies and middle-aged grannies – one drove up in a red sports car. 'Life's a witch and then you fly!' said her bumper sticker. There were also plenty of ordinary families with children who unpacked picnics on the grass. There were two stout lovebirds from Idaho, arms entwined, who met here at a previous event and have been together ever since.

As each new batch of arrivals turned into the carpark dressed for the occasion in various merry interpretations of fancy-dress witchery – a dazzlement of bizarre inventions gradually took shape. There was an ancient crone who hobbled about in fringed Indian buckskin with beaded moccasins and a tall staff with a crystal ball embedded in the tip; a saturnine gent dressed head to toe in black leather with a pentacle tattooed on his forehead; an elderly man in a long black cloak with a long pointy hood; a baby with her own special little sky-blue hooded cloak. There were bards and healers, artists and musicians, covens and communes. A motley crew they were with as many non-conformists, misfits and oddballs as you would expect. Trailing velvet abounded. People came in Robin Hood and Maid Marion outfits. There was a weasely chap in a fur hood with antlers and a group of enormous ladies in spectacularly plungy laced-up bodices.

Watching all these colourful folk arrive I felt somewhat detached to begin with – an outsider looking in. And, it's true, I am an outsider but I am also a spiritual traveller with an open heart trying to understand the deeper meaning beyond the external trappings which, it has to be said, can look a bit weird. Gradually, as I listened to their strongly held views, a deep respect grew in me. Theirs is a spirituality with immense power and depth as valid as any other and often misunderstood. In fact, after a short while, in such a festival atmosphere I began to feel rather dull and boring by comparison. I wished I had brought my purple feathered cloak which hangs in a garment bag in my attic – bought in a moment of madness years ago and just waiting for an occasion such as this. At least I had great kudos because I'd come all the way from England. 'The Holy Land', they wrote on my name tag. Everyone wants to go there – to Glastonbury, to the great standing stones, to the ancient Motherland.

I got talking to a tall, regular-looking old ex-naval officer in his seventies wearing a baseball cap who came to the 'craft' a couple of years ago through his pagan daughter when he realised that the general precepts coincided precisely with his own views and the way he'd always tried to live his life – namely, that you create your own reality, that you envision an ideal and move along towards it, that the energy you put out is what comes back to you. "I thought pagans were people who had no religion", said the ex-naval officer, "but I now believe that the main task of the Pagan movement as a whole is nothing less than to save the planet. Pagans consider nature to be sacred and that we human beings need to be mindful of our impact on it. I believe that we can lead the way to a more peaceful future."

A woman named Ivy was feeling a little anxious, not knowing what she had let herself in for. She knew only that she has slowly and with gathering conviction found herself drawn to Paganism and Wicca by a deep yearning for meaningful ritual in her life. She told me about a special ceremony that she and a group of friends had invented to mark the menopause. "None of us really knew what we were doing," she said, "but we closed our eyes and we *remembered*. I believe in ancient memory and that we all have, buried within us, all the knowledge and wisdom of our fore-mothers." The ceremony had come together spontaneously and they were all moved by its power and beauty.

Over the past few years, even in England, where we tend to be reticent about these things, women are joining together more and more frequently, in large groups and small ones, to create meaningful rituals and symbols, to mark important rites of passage. Battling against a legacy of fear and negativity deep in the collective unconscious, starting up a circle or a coven requires a lot of courage, creativity and imagination. Ever since Anna's Mother Nature Camp in Wales where I first learned about it, I have come to love ritual. I love the transformative potential of it. I love the powerful drama of it. I love the way it helps me to *embody* experience and deal with it physically. I need it in my life and for the past few years, like Ivy, I have been inventing and 'remembering' rituals to mark significant events for myself and others – the birth of a grandchild, the beginning of menstruation for a young woman friend – or rituals to heal emotional trauma – unfinished business with a parent who has died, unresolved grief over an abortion or miscarriage. It is a tremendously exciting process and seems like important work. Ritual allows us to act out our myths and stories – to share and to witness, to experience directly archetypes of symbolic transformation.

When we had all registered, an opening circle was held outside in the magnificent natural theatre of sea and sky by the last light of the dying sun. The casting of a circle always begins a ritual and serves to bring everyone together for a common purpose. It serves as a transition into an expanded, non-ordinary state of consciousness. It defines a safe and magical space within which the power and the energy are contained – preventing their dissipation and focusing on the intentions for the days to follow.

Starhawk, the author of several influential books on the subject of ritual and women's spirituality believes that there is a crucial transformation of our culture taking place, away from patriarchal violence, towards love of life, of nature, of the female principle. In our opening circle we praised the Great Mother, we invoked the animal spirits, we invoked the powers of the four directions and of the elements. Pagans stand in a circle to celebrate roundness, to look inward at the face of the Divine in each other. In the hopes that she would bless our gathering, Goddess songs were sang, ceremonial tasks were performed and a spiral dance was danced. This was not an exclusively women's event but women were taking most of the leadership roles. The impression I got was that the Goddess is alive and well and making her presence felt in the world today.

Bear Arms would be a pub if it were in England but in the nearby little town of Port Hadlock it is a gun store. There are some pretty conservative, not to say redneck, folks around here and Pete Pathfinder's injunction "not to wear your cloaks in the town" was a sensible precaution against provoking any unnecessary aggravation. Pete is the founder and Arch-priest of the Aquarian Tabernacle Church – one of the many pagan groups in the United States. He is also the initiator of this annual festival and my host.

Back at the camp, the morning began with a symposium – "What sort of leadership do we want?" It was open to everyone but mostly those who came were already practising as priestesses or priests. Pagans, modern ones at least, are an anarchic bunch all of whom have come out of some other religious background because they detested the tyranny of the orthodoxy. Any kind of structure is deeply mistrusted because of its tendency to solidify into a hierarchy and everyone agreed that there was more likelihood of a potential Pagan leader becoming a target for anti-authoritarian aggression from within the movement than there was any danger of gurufication. People project all the authority issues that they might have had with their parents, catholic nuns, teachers etc. onto whoever stands up and takes on the mantle. I very much liked a High Priestess from Florida, the Reverend Jacque, whose full-time job it is being a Wiccan minister. When she goes into prisons or hospitals to do her pastoral work she wears a dog collar "because you don't get a second chance to make a first impression".

A friendly, pretty woman, Jacque spoke about the long-running battle for freedom of worship she has fought with her local City Hall. Florida, often known jokingly as South Georgia, is Bible Belt Country – a stronghold of evangelical, fundamentalist Christians. When the Unitarian church finally agreed to rent her little group some space to hold meetings a neighbour started rumours saying they were dancing naked, wielding knives, killing babies and all kinds of other preposterous lies! A local newspaper printed her photo and ran an article next to it entitled; "Is there a link between the rise in abortion and the number of witches?" It went on about witches being mad for ritual and constantly needing a supply aborted foetuses. People moved into the area from the Right to Life group to spy on them. There were death threats and once a carload of young men drove by shooting at them. In the end Jacque had to appeal to the Federal Court in order to force the city to hear the case. They just didn't want to know.

"Luckily, if you dig deep enough, the law is there", she said. "Familiarise yourself with it. Get to know the law librarian. Use all your charm. Once you've decided to take the path, don't be intimidated. Stand tall. Worship outside if you want to. People gain strength from your commitment. Say proudly, 'I am a witch. I am a priestess. I'm in an earth-centred religion and we believe the Gods and Goddesses are everywhere. It's called Wicca.' Stand up and tell the world our religion is first class. Our children learn what they see, not what they hear. Teach them to be assertive. What kind of example are the fundamentalists teaching their children? I thought Jesus preached about replacing hate with love." In the end Jacque was found totally innocent of all the trumped up charges and won the right to practise her religion unmolested. Now, more and more frequently, her presence is requested as a minister in hospitals and prisons.

"There are probably more than 100,000 active pagans in the United States alone", she says. "If we are going to change public misconceptions about us we have to be seen to be valuable to the community. You can't get caught speeding or avoiding your taxes. Help out at the animal shelter. Run a soup kitchen for the homeless. Your first line of defence is a list of your good works."

"What should I say If someone asks me if I am a witch?" asked one young woman. "If I say yes I get into all these arguments about Satanism with stupid, ignorant people who have already made their minds up. If I don't say yes I feel a coward."

"Answer a question with a question," said Jacque. "Ask them, 'What do you mean by witch?' Explain your question. If you mean am I interested in herbal medicine? Yes. Am I a hands on healer? Yes. Do I worship outdoors? Yes. Am I a Pagan? Yes. Do I believe in the old Gods and Goddesses? Yes. Do I have a deep spiritual commitment to the Earth? Yes. Tell them that Satanism is a Christian concept. It is a perversion of Christianity. In a pre-Christian religion, how could there be an Anti-Christ? If someone asks me what constitutes a wiccan I say, 'Why don't you watch one for a while and see how they are living?'"

When the discussion ended we all gathered outside for the start of the great sea ritual. Three aspects of the Goddess – The Maiden, The Mother and The Crone – symbolising the major phases of a woman's life, danced in our circle, the old dying and becoming the new. According to ancient tradition, the Great Goddess was always triple, representing the phases of the moon waxing into fullness, waning into darkness, becoming renewed in tranquillity and wisdom. Representing also the upper world, the earth and the underworld, the flower the fruit and the seed. Blue and shivery in their diaphanous Greek costumes, the performers bravely recreated Eleusis and the Aegean Sea in the Northwest corner of Washington State.

We were each given a daffodil and a small pink pig made out of baked dough to represent symbolically the real sacrifice of a real pig. In ancient times this would have been part of the purification process which had to be gone through in preparation for initiation into the mysteries and may have had something to do with the shedding of blood into the earth and its menstrual symbolism of cyclical renewal. Then we all filed down the road to the sea in a long procession chanting, 'The river is flowing, flowing and growing. The river is flowing down to the sea. Carry me tenderly, a child I will always be. Carry me tenderly down to the sea'. In a trice, the 'sea priests and priestesses' had disrobed and stood naked on the shore. White as alabaster and covered in goose pimples they heroically collected our flowers and plunged into the freezing sea to offer them. Then we all 'sacrificed' our pigs, hurling them into the waves to symbolise that which we would like to cast off. There was much laughter and exhuberance and more chanting. I loved the air of creativity and freedom and was aware that we have a lot to be thankful for living in a society where the laws and the constitution are actually on your side if you're prepared to stand up for your rights.

After dinner there was a women's circle around a nice, crackling bonfire. Fifty women drumming and hollering is an awesome sight. People took turns, as the spirit moved them, leaping to their feet for an impromptu solo dance in the firelight while the rest of us clapped and cheered them on, ululating shrilly like an encampment of Bedouins. Sparks flew in the night air. The nearest we came to debauchery were the ritual paper cups of Ribena and chocolate chip cookies passed round! On the other side of the woods, the sound of the rival men's circle rending the air could be heard through the trees – celebrating the hero, the warrior, the hunter – asserting their masculinity in all its innocent strength and virtue, cleansed and reborn in the atavistic ecstasy of dancing and drumming in the moonlight.

The forum next morning was on the subject of "What is a pagan?" I was astonished at the wide range of backgrounds represented by the participants; a landscape artist, an architect, the mayor of a New York suburb, a Ph.D. in Anthropology, businesswomen and men, sex therapists, counsellors, teachers, a moose-jaw carver, a classical cellist, an airline caterer … the same cross-section you'd find anywhere, in fact. The point is, you probably wouldn't recognise a pagan if you saw her or him in the street. Some are wandering pilgrims, some read the Wall Street Journal and have investments. Some throw their bodies on the line to save trees, some move strategically in political circles. They came from all over the United States and Canada.

There followed a lengthy discussion on the difficulties involved in defining a Pagan 'code of behaviour'.

"Paganism is a continuum," said someone, "and there are a lot of places along the way where you can fit in". "We don't seem to have a common ethical system," commented someone else, 'Do as you will except that you harm no one', the old Gardnerian creed, is the ethical system of adolescents. "It only works while you are fighting your parents. Now is the time to build something, and that means rules of some kind. We don't need ten commandments carved in stone but there is, nonetheless, a craving for boundaries."

"The crux is," said a priestess from the mid-west, "in Paganism, we're supposed to make our own boundaries but many of the young people who are attracted to Paganism come from dysfunctional families and don't have the tools to do it themselves. They are often negative. They understand freedom to mean *not* having to do something, rather than the freedom to *accomplish* something. There are a lot of people who are acting out and working through personal problems. Partly because this is such an open and accepting culture, it is very easy to do that to excess."

"It's inevitable that we're going to attract people who have been very hurt in their lives and haven't healed," said Pete Pathfinder, "because, as a movement we're accessible, welcoming. A lot of them are immature and rebellious – mistrustful of any kind of authority – yet needy as hell. In my experience they either self-destruct or move on somewhere else."

An old woman dressed in a hessian sack belted round the middle with a length of rope spoke up, "A community shouldn't define itself by who it excludes but by embracing diversity. 'Perfect love and perfect trust' is a journey and not a destination. If you are in a position of leadership you must open yourself to serve. You have to be vulnerable and take risks. We have a responsibility to take care of this world and that means those on the margins as well."

The discussion continued well past the allotted time and focused primarily on ways in which Paganism could become a viable, vital force in the twenty-first century – with organic rather than authoritarian structures. What I saw was a very supportive, tolerant group of people struggling to define their commonalties in a community where diversity is so fiercely trumpeted.

The meeting was followed by Jacque's workshop on Advanced Wicca which turned out to be essentially 'less is more' and came across like any sound practice which takes care of itself once you shut up and stop proselytising and act from your loving heart.

"This is not a spectator sport – some kind of 'Dungeons 'n' Dragons – it's a religion," concluded Jacque who, in addition to being an ordained minister in the Aquarian Tabernacle Church, also used to be a flight instructor and has a degree in Systems Management. "We need to create a vortex of magic, to weave ourselves together reaching for that higher space. The world is full of people who want to dominate other people. Wicca offers a better way to live than that. A lot of it is about reverence and gratitude, about defending the Earth. The emphasis is on how to do magic to make the world a better place and ourselves better individuals. *Focus* is magic. *Intention* is magic. Stretch yourself and help others to stretch. Make environmentally responsible choices. It's not to do with initiation or dressing up. We're looking for that moment of clarity – of epiphany. Gradually you begin to change the way you see things, the way you act. As you change you also start to make personally responsible choices about taking care of yourself better. I say to people, 'Don't come in my circle with drugs in your body. Don't come in my circle with alcohol in your body – even caffeine. Chemicals ain't what we're trying to do."

Alas, our culture's relationship to the living Earth has lost the quality of balance and reciprocity that, say, the Aborigines and other indigenous peoples had. I thought about the time I spent with the Aborigines of the Western Desert in Australia while working on my book, *Older Than Time*. In none of the many Aboriginal languages is there a word for ownership. They had evolved a way of life that was richly spiritual and connected to the natural world in which relationship was everything. Relationships with each other and with the land. Their beautiful Dreamtime creation myths portrayed the physical world as a language to be learned – part of the education of every child. Reading the seasons, talking to trees, listening to the emanations of plants, feeling the energy of rocks, being in communication with the elements and with the spirits. Ritual and religious knowledge involved patient learning throughout a lifetime. The Aborigines had much to teach Westerners which, if we hadn't been so busy destroying their culture, we might have had ears to hear. They lived in harmony with their environment because they had developed a capacity to integrate their inner and outer worlds, their waking and dreaming states, their conscious and unconscious minds. They had a sense of common consciousness, of the interrelatedness of all things very difficult for a patriarchal mindset to understand.

And now it is only by valuing again the 'feminine', by restoring a love affair with the living land that we have a chance to pull back from the brink of madness and extinction. I long to believe that it isn't too late. As the forests disappear and disease, depression and social chaos become more widespread we are brought face to face with the folly of 'dominion over'. It is time for an animistic perspective – for the 'God/dess in everything' to come again. We chanted, "We are the old people, we are the new people, we are the same people wiser than before."

I thought of a line from Rilke, "*Go to the limits of your longing. Embody me.*"

The workshop was followed by the Lesser Mysteries – The first part of a dramatic presentation of the myth of Demeter and Persephone in which we all participate. The basic story is as follows. In the perpetual spring of the world, the Goddess Demeter was the giver of the fruits of the earth. Beautiful and golden, she was the personification of the gentle mother, accompanied everywhere by her beloved daughter, the fair Persephone (also known as Kore, the maiden). One day while Persephone was out picking flowers with her friends she heard the terrible thunder of hooves underground and out of the bowels of the earth burst Hades, the Dark Lord of Death, in his chariot drawn by six black horses, who snatched her up and carried her, screaming in vain for her mother, to his realm in the Nether Regions where he ravished her and pronounced her his bride – Queen of the Underworld.

For nine days, grieving inconsolably, Demeter wanders the earth looking for her daughter in vain. Neither Gods nor men dare tell her of Persephone's fate. Finally, Apollo, the sun god, who sees all on his daily journey across the sky, tells her it was Zeus, himself, who had plotted with his brother, Hades, to let the Dark Lord marry the maiden.

Wasting with grief for her beloved daughter, Demeter sends a terrible drought upon the earth which threatens to destroy the human race. No seed grows, no flower blooms, no stalk of grain ripens, no trees bear fruit. She spurns all messengers from Zeus and refuses to set foot on Olympus or let anything grow on earth until she sees her daughter again…

In part two we all wore masks we had made earlier, having written inside them words that described what we perceived as our own particular strengths. The purpose of the mask is not to protect you from the Underworld but to help you know yourself. I had started out making mine rather irreverently, sticking on lots of feathers and a long, dangly rubber snake but then I really got into it and wanted to make it beautiful. My strengths I inscribed inside as: 'a capacity for joy' and 'a genuine love of diversity'.

Finally, persuaded by Zeus, who sends Hermes as a messenger, Hades agrees to let Persephone come back to see her mother but not before tricking her into eating three pomegranate seeds thereby breaking her fast.

We processed through the woods wearing our masks, crossing the frontier between the worlds, until we reached the gates of Hades' realm, (a wonderful disused power station with a labyrinth of underground chambers which had been decorated valiantly with drapes and candles, mirrors and tableaux vivant). There we had to take off our masks and leave them outside before entering, symbolically naked – stripped of our earthly power and strength, into the Underworld where a mirror was held up as we passed through the gates. "Know thyself", someone whispered. See that the Goddess is an aspect of oneself. Be responsible. Own your power.

By eating the pomegranate seeds, Persephone is compelled to return to spend a third of the year as Queen of the Underworld but then for the rest of the year she may live with her mother and the other immortals. Death and resurrection 2,000 years before Christ. Mother and daughter are joyously reunited at Demeter's temple at Eleusis. After the barren winter, the springtime comes back. Beneath their feet, the earth grows warm, life stirs and blooms again with fruit and corn.

I am deeply touched by the myth of Demeter and Persephone. In addition to the aspect of renewal of the Earth's fertility, of a celebration of the corn that dies in winter and revives in the spring, of the buried seed springing from the earth and its comparison with human destiny, it illuminates timeless themes of the mother–daughter relationship. It touches upon all the fears and terrors you confront as your precious child separates from you and goes off into whatever her own version of Hades' realm might be.

Demeter is a very real woman to me and I identify with her uncannily. She reminds me that I cannot protect my daughters from whatever fate has in store for them, that possessiveness serves no one, that I can only enjoy them moment by moment and give them warmly to the world with love. She tells me of the need to let go. She speaks to me of a way to grow through loss and suffering, that after the barren winter, spring will come again. Hers is the eternal story.

Pondering on the meaning of the myth for me I come face to face with my fear of losing my own daughter, my lastborn – my precious Francesca – in the light of the discovery of a lump in her breast. With irony and poignancy I dwell every minute on the beauty and power of my love for her. When I conjure the image of her lovely face, pain and panic brews within me and I fight to contain it. It is every mother's worst nightmare that her children will be taken from her. Demeter is the embodiment of the inevitability of loss and the inescapable nature of human suffering.

I have long been aware of the dangers of the empty nest syndrome to a woman like me for whom motherhood has been such an important part of my life and tried to prepare in plenty of time for the inevitable day when I would be left standing on the doormat waving goodbye to my last child. But I never expected this. Perhaps we can never truly be ready, because we never know in what guise the 'abduction' will come; what underworld experience, what chaos lies in wait for them. In the agony of my failure to be able to protect my daughter, to make the pain go away, to kiss it better, I can only be aware that someday, somewhere, further along the road maybe a greater wisdom and spiritual understanding will be possible. Demeter's story is a rite of passage, a story of loss, desolation and recovery.

I was later to discover much about not-knowing and the cracking open of the heart. Life presents us with opportunities for this which cannot be rushed. We are constantly being asked to choose passionate engagement over denial, to choose between succumbing to despair and embracing life, to let go of that over which we have no control and to love beyond the bounds of time and place. Death and rebirth have their own rhythm. Each woman will have to go through the rage and terror and agony of separation. For Persephone it is a truly transformational process. She must die to her previous self and be reborn and in so doing, finds who she is as a woman.

Somewhere in the deepest recesses of my being I have always known how much of motherhood is loss – and long before the news of my daughter's cancer, have always anticipated the separation that tears Demeter and Persephone apart. In the myth, Demeter is initiated into an understanding of death by the loss of her daughter. As I write, my daughter is not lost but the knowledge of her illness and the fear of her 'abduction' to a place where I cannot follow her is very present in my heart. Demeter and Persephone portray the timelessness of the mother/daughter bond and the famine of human grief. The eternal winter that Demeter brings upon the Earth is a moving representation of her response to her pain and suffering.

The underworld can also represent a place into which I am plunged at those times of deep reflection on my own life. I am abducted, along with Persephone, into a place of not-knowing where there is no choice but to confront the darkness. The myth also teaches me about letting go of my own youthfulness, my own maidenly aspect. Persephone represents not only my daughter but the young, innocent, carefree me to whom I still cling and whom I must leave to take on the challenges of the second half of life. It is about acceptance of the irretrievable losses and limitations of ageing; about acceptance of the inevitability of suffering and its transformative potential. The Mysteries are designed to teach a different understanding of loss and death – to prepare one, perhaps, for the shock of repeated and unpredictable losses in middle and later life. It brings me face to face with the impossible wishes of childhood and the adult recognition that individuals are finite and vulnerable and that life is transient. The price we must be willing to pay for tremendous love is tremendous grief. The price we must be willing to pay for life is death. This is due to the poignant fate of being human. Separation must be accepted. Death rises up and takes away our belief in everlasting spring.

Everybody worked very hard to present The Mysteries in a dramatic way and it was lovely to be with a group of people who have a goddess and her earth mysteries at the centre of their spiritual life. We have become so accustomed in our Judeo-Christian, Western culture to think of everything Divine as masculine and 'up there' that we have almost forgotten what it is to regard the earth we walk upon as sacred, as truly our mother – the source of life and the dwelling place of gods and goddesses.

We cannot survive on this finite planet unless we can forge sane relationships with our environment. Pagans are reclaiming something akin to the perennial shamanistic practices of all indigenous peoples – the oldest form of body/mind/spirit healing known to humankind. Pagans believe that a good life is a balanced relationship with all living things and that we all have to do our bit to keep the earth alive. You tend the gods and goddesses who reign in the natural world and they, in turn, empower you and give you good health and energy.

The Mysteries ended with the words, "Blessed are they among mortals who have witnessed these things. Those who are initiated into the mysteries know bliss and do not fear death."

The real sanctuary of Demeter at Eleusis in Greece, where her Mysteries were celebrated, was in active use for over 2,000 years. It was destroyed in AD 396 by Alaric the Goth. Scholars believe that the spirit of the mysteries did not disappear entirely and that the Troubadours' courtly worship of 'the lady' drew upon the remnants of Eleusinian worship that survived among the country peoples (*pagan* being derived from *paesan* or *peasant*) of Europe.

Jennifer and Roger Woolger in their book *The Goddess Within* speculate that Eleusis was not about simply the renewal of agricultural fertility but about the greater mystery of life itself – the transformation of the feminine. Each woman whether she bears children or not must honour the monthly death and renewal that takes place in her body, a never-ending cycle of death and potential fruitfulness.

> *'You know that the seed is inside the horse-chestnut*
> *tree and inside the seed there are the blossoms of the*
> *tree, and the chestnuts, and the shade.*
> *So inside the human body there is the seed*
> *and inside the seed there is the human body again.'*

> KABIR

Our sense of powerlessness as women is beginning to evaporate as we come together to conjure energy and power and to direct this force towards global healing. The old shrine of Demeter's temple in a subterranean chamber in Eleusis is now a rather tacky tourist site surrounded by an industrial seaport with oil refineries but against all the odds the Great Cosmic Mother is making an eleventh-hour comeback. The river of life flows on in a story told in order to be retold. The ancient voices still speak and they speak a warning. Should the Goddess be betrayed or forgotten, eternal winter will prevail on earth.

On Easter Sunday the day dawned foggy. Silent and white it blanketed the entire peninsula but lifted miraculously in time for the closing circle, the warm early April sun plucking the last shards of mist into the air and evaporating them. The wild deer, their huge ears like finely-tuned satellite dishes, stood still as statues staring at me then melted into the woodland cover. All over the campsite, not a single piece of litter could be seen. The pagans walk lightly upon the earth.

The closing circle was held in perfect bright sunlight. The Gods were thanked. We bade them 'hail and farewell!' We sang; 'the circle is open, yet unbroken. May the peace of the Goddess be forever in your heart. Merry meet and merry part and merry meet again!' The mood was playful yet serious. Complete strangers came up to me and said how much they appreciated my coming to join their celebrations. Maybe people would stop judging them until they were a bit better informed. One woman said, "I see myself as a peaceful warrior for the earth. I just want to understand her ways and work in harmony with her." Her partner, an adorable young father (a sailor in the merchant navy) carried their two babies around tied to his body – one front and one back – practically the entire weekend. I was so taken with the quality of the relationships between the men and women that I saw there. They were humorous and respectful. Women did practically all the ritual work but it never felt abusive to the men. They played their part and had their own rites – finding new ways to be real men in a world where the old ways are no longer appropriate. In addition to their personal relevance to me, I found the re-enactment of the Eleusinian Mysteries a moving testimony to the hopes for creating a post-patriarchal world in which concern for the earth might again become a central value. And even though the Mysteries centred around the mother/daughter bond there was also a universal principle being enacted where both men and women could identify with the feminine, with the figure of Demeter and with the possibility of moving beyond grief and despair to renewal.

People piled back into the assortment of vehicles in the carpark and began to pull out, returning to their everyday lives. I gave a lift to the ferry to Melanie, a Wiccan minister from Wisconsin. "People are starving for spirituality," she said. "Many have been suffering for years trying to make sense of the lifelong mystical experiences they have had since childhood that just didn't fit into mainstream religion. My work as a priestess is really about healing – healing the human spirit, the human body, healing the body and spirit of the Earth, teaching respect for the ancient ways, learning how to live in harmony with the land."

I understand that longing, that desire to restore a sense of the sacred to the everyday things of my life – to the movement of the stars and the moon, the tides and the seasons, to the miracle of the whales migrating in the bay, to the birth of my newest granddaughter, Freya, tiny Goddess of love and light, who arrived on the Spring Equinox.

Crossing to Whidbey Island on the ferry, a layer of fog came down again and lay like a cashmere blanket between the sea and the mountains. Dozens of low flying cormorants led our boat on like mythical watersprites. Occasional walls of mist into which we drifted lent a dreamlike, ethereal quality to the passage, as if from one world to another, the foghorn booming in the nothingness.

Chief Seattle, for whom the state capital is named, is buried on the Olympic Peninsula overlooking the Puget Sound. He is famous for one of the most moving and powerful speeches ever given, on surrendering tribal lands in 1855.

> *"...Every part of this soil is sacred in the estimation of my people. Every hillside, every valley, every plain and grove has been hallowed by some sad or happy event in the days long vanished. Even the rocks which seem to be dumb and dead as they swelter in the sun along the silent shore, thrill with memories of stirring events connected with the lives of my people ... When the last Red Man has vanished and his wilderness and his memory is only the shadow of a cloud moving across the prairie, will these shores and forests still be here? Will there be any of the spirit left? ..."*

I could feel the presence of the great man's ghost still restless in an uncertain world.

Chapter 2

❖ ❖ ❖ ❖ ❖

'Whatever you can do or dream you can,
begin it! Genius has boldness, power and magic in it.'
GOETHE

When I was a child I lived in America. Sharon and I were best friends in primary school. We came from different worlds. My family were Bohemian Jewish immigrants from Europe while she had been born into a conventional middle-class American family in Tulare, a small agricultural town in the central valley of California. My dad was a rabbi, hers was an airline pilot. My mum was a chicken farmer, hers was a housewife, but we recognised each other as kindred spirits.

Pranks and gangs, secret codes and dares consumed our puppydog days. She showed me how to make an owl hooter out of a blade of grass. I nicked a book on how babies were born because she refused to believe I wasn't making it up. We climbed trees, rode on the farmer's donkey and hid in the sweet-smelling long summer grass of childhood trying out rude words and laughing till we ached.

At a Saturday matinee we saw a Western about comradeship where the two Red Indians cut their wrists with a tomahawk blade and mingled their blood in an awesome ritual. So we scratched ours with a pin, wincing at the pain, and swore to be 'blood brothers' for life. Sexist role models hadn't occurred to anyone in those days. We certainly didn't wish to identify ourselves with 'drippy' girls. We *were* Tom Sawyer and Huckleberry Finn, Cochise and Sitting Bull, Frank and Jesse James. When I recall that incident from an adult perspective I feel a great sadness that there were no strong heroines for us to emulate. In the movies women screamed a lot; they were carried off by King Kong; they were tied to the railway tracks and rescued by men. We were searching for a meaningful initiation rite but only a male one was available.

Gradually the pigtails changed to perms, the lollipops to lipsticks and the dares to dates. We sprouted into awkward adolescents and both got 'the curse' at 13. There was no rite of passage to help us. No family of women to welcome us – only ill-informed peer-group lore. With what disrespect and carelessness did our culture treat the feminine – and still does. And what a contrast to the rich and beautiful Apache Sunrise Dance Ceremony I was privileged to attend in Arizona some years ago.

In Apache tradition, when a girl begins her menstruation, her parents select a godmother – specially chosen as the older woman of ideal character whom they most want their daughter to emulate – to stand by her side as a guide and mentor throughout the four-day ritual. The ceremony, also called 'The Gift of Changing Woman', is the single most important event in an Apache girl's life.

Changing Woman was the first woman on Earth (created before man). She made love with the sun and gave birth to twins. The twins grew up to clear the world of evil and make it good for humankind. During the Changing Woman ceremony, the young girl, dressed in exquisite beaded buckskin clothes, will become the embodiment of the deity's spirit and be prepared for her role as an Apache mother and life-giver. The ceremony also ensures that she will have strength, an even temperament, prosperity and longevity – all qualities associated with Changing Women. In preparation, the men of the tribe spend the whole of the night before the ceremony in the men's sweat lodge chanting, praying and purifying themselves. There is feasting, dancing, and elaborate gift exchanging. It is a re-enactment of the creation of the world and the coming of the Apache people. It is a celebration of life.

I asked the young girl, Reynelda, how it felt to be the centre of all the attention. She grinned and said it was both wonderful and embarrassing, 'Like, everyone knows you've just got your period – but you feel so proud to be a woman.' This was the first time I had ever been in a culture where it actually felt more important to be a woman, where the whole tribe celebrated the onset of the life-giving menstrual blood – an occasion for joy, not a 'curse'. I took away with me an indelible vision of renewal – of older women handing on their wisdom and experience to the next generation.

Well, none of that happened to Sharon and me and I grieve for the missed opportunity. Shortly after, my family moved abroad. Sharon and I didn't see each other again for 30 years.

Twelve years ago when I went to the US for the first time since I'd left, I looked her up with some trepidation. Would we have anything to say to each other? Would we have anything in common? Would I even recognise her after all that time? I didn't feel any different inside. Would she have changed? Within five minutes we both knew that those essential qualities we'd loved about each other at seven years old were the very things that hadn't changed. We spent four days together on holiday in the glorious Olympic Rain Forest of the northwest coast of America. We talked all night and laughed all day just like we always had. It was reassuring to know that one's childish instincts could have been so sound all those years ago.

We said goodbye and I went back to England. Life had been kinder to me than it had to her. I thought of her often and wished things didn't have to be so hard for her, wished that she could find expression for all the rare things in her nature that have sustained the spark of spirituality through all the wilderness years. Then an extraordinary sequence of events happened and what could have been a gruesome tragedy pointed the way to a new and hopeful future. There was a horrible accident at the mill where Sharon worked and her right hand was nearly severed by a circular saw which cut right through the bone. Only intricate painstaking surgery managed to save the use of her hand. There was no way she could work at the saw-mill ever again but the injury compensation and disability pension gave her the financial security to take up a new challenge. Sharon enrolled at her local college and took a degree in Social Psychology. She now has an interesting, worthwhile job in rehabilitation, using her own experience to help others and has found contentment and happiness with a woman partner. She is the first to say that although she would never have consciously harmed herself maybe a wiser part of herself knew that only drastic measures would stop her in her tracks and force her to make changes.

Now Sharon was coming to meet me on Whidbey island so we could spend a few precious days catching up on each others' life stories. We've been friends for 50 years and I could hardly wait to see her again. She'd rummaged through boxes of old photos and found a few of us when we were 13 taken just before my family left California for Brazil – our Persephone days. My heart went out to those two touching, clueless new little women with no idea what difficult journeys lay ahead and no rites of passage to prepare them.

Sharon suggested that, as part of my search for spiritual women, I should visit Gwynne Warner, a member of the community at Breitenbush Hot Springs. Over the years, Sharon and her partner Darlene have been many times to the retreat centre there for solace and spiritual refreshment. So, when I left them I headed off into the Cascade mountains of Oregon in another borrowed car.

Gwynne lives in a yurt which sounds rough but was actually a little piece of paradise. She and her husband Eric have fixed it up to perfection with an old porcelain bath sunken into the floor, an old-fashioned cast iron stove, richly coloured hangings, a real bed covered with oriental cushions, an altar for her sacred objects, lots of books, a music centre and a glass section set into the middle of the ceiling through which to gaze at the trees and the stars. It suddenly made city living seem terribly deprived.

Gwynne is a lovely woman of 32, the same age as my daughter Francesca, – intelligent, committed, loving and true – a delightful example of the new breed of young people, like my own grown-up children, who are trying to live authentically. She has lived here for four years doing reiki and dance, gardening and teaching, healing and serving. There is an ecstatic, mystical quality about her that I imagine St Claire had, or perhaps Theresa of Avila or Julian of Norwich. She loves the Divine and seeks to find it in herself, to commune with others and with God, and yet she's not at all remote or unworldly.

I asked Gwynne what it was that attracted her to life in a community. "The word that moves me is communion", she said. "The longing in me is to be a mystic as best I can. I don't necessarily have the mind for it but I know I have unlimited capacity in my heart. It's a longing and a yearning for God and it's beautiful to do it in community. I am quite content to sit in silence with people. We dance, we chant, we have a communal chalice and we say prayers and drink the water. I adore that feeling. I *adore* with my friends. We do ceremonies together. It's communion. Communion with the Divine beckons me on and although it's possible to do it alone, there are so many opportunities when you have 40 something brothers and sisters. All of us have made a commitment to process our 'stuff' – our rubbish – and the *land* requires it because of all the geysers. The hot springs are alive. There's a lot of transformational energy ... WHOOSH!", she mimes a jetting water spout. "It is a brilliant opportunity to walk my talk. It's one thing to get up in the morning and read an inspirational quote by the Dalai Lama where he talks about praying for the Chinese who are perpetrating hideous crimes on his countrymen, but can I sustain that when I run into someone who challenges my compassion? It's easy to do it here. When I was at drama school my purpose began to clarify. I wanted to return to the ritual and holiness of sacred theatre work – bringing theatre back to that place of wonder and mystery and communion that happen through laughter and tears.

"If I want to work with the energy of Kwan Yin, for example, I evoke her to *come into my body*. A lot of my spiritual work is about *embodying* because unless it's in here (she places her hands over her solar plexus), it's only in the head and that really doesn't work for me. The feminine face of the Divine is what changed me. The first face that came to me in my longing for the Beloved was that of Kwan Yin. She's been with me a lot and recently the Shekinah has come and Mother Mary and Kali. I don't know how to describe these encounters. Perhaps recognitions would be a better word. They appear and they comfort me and it's like a quiet cry. I cry a lot but my tears are no longer of sorrow and grief but of joy and wonder that taps into a very very deep faith in Divinity. God is in us and all around us. The Mother is *here!*"

In the late afternoon Gwynne had work to do so I joined a yoga class in the Forest Sanctuary. The teacher, Sarahjoy's words perfectly captured the spirit of this gentle community: "Breathe!" she exhorted us. "Feel life energy supporting us. We can surrender, let go, be received, and be receptive. Our quest is opening to life, opening to this day, to this moment, to this breath. Opening hearts, bodies, minds. Opening to the source that animates my life energy, your life energy, our life energy, life energy of trees, plants, rivers. The need for distinction and names lifts – return to Oneness. Reunion. This is the heart of Yoga for me, and the passion for sharing yoga is about sharing this celebration of life: a celebration of our humanity, our uniqueness, our ancientness, our transcendence, our rootedness, our interbeingness with all life. We breathe and sing, opening lungs, resonating voice and sound. We stretch, softening muscles and form.

"In the posture of Yoga, can we experience our posture to life? Is it possible to approach myself with reverence and acceptance? With a sense of appreciation about the mystery of who I seem to be? Is it possible for me to be softer with myself, with my fears and judgements? Can I bring receptivity and surrender into my life? Can we take a posture of prostration before ourselves, before our brothers, sisters, teachers, experiences? Can I prostrate deeply in my heart to the great Mystery, to the God/Goddess presence and all that is offered? Can I see it as *prasad*, a gift, an opening, a moment for awareness, an expression of love, as a doorway home? Can I embrace this body, this life, this sorrow, this joy, as prasad? Can I live a life through compassionate service? The path of Yoga is about union, reunion; an expression of our transcendent union with life all around and within us. Yoga for me is an offering. You are welcome. Beyond all else you are welcome to come as you are, to receive here as you need to, and to share what you receive. I hope sharing yoga with you offers you an opportunity for greater well-being and ease with your body and your life, that you cultivate loving-kindness for yourself and others. And ultimately may we all be teachers by witnessing the mystery of this life, opening to serve, to love, to remember."

The class was brilliant and quite challenging. Yoga is one of the options on offer to weekend guests. The community support themselves by the services they offer – primarily a healing retreat and conference centre promoting holistic health, spiritual growth, personal accountability and environmental responsibility. It is idyllic. Their land borders on territory belonging to the Warm Springs Indians – very sacred ground that was decreed always to be a weapons-free zone. Anyone who came had to leave their bows and arrows or guns in the meadow. The whites violated it of course – one of many terrible betrayals which blight the history of this country – but the Breitenbush Community with their tender sensitivity to the spirit of the land are doing much to heal the wounds of the past, performing their tasks with devotional intensity and open-hearted simplicity. It is a thriving business with up to 300 people converging for the Summer solstice. Gwynne and the others take their turn with the cooking and gardening, cleaning and maintenance as well as offering workshops and individual sessions of massage, reiki, shiatsu and other complementary therapies.

The area is famous for its outdoor natural hot tubs which are truly wonderful. I went in at night under the moon and the scudding clouds in the freezing nocturnal air. Clothes are optional but nobody wore any – pale, naked bodies wreathed in steam flitting between the very hot water in the big round stone tubs and the icy-cold plunge tank. Later Gwynne led a session of ecstatic dance by candlelight and a remarkable man called Dannie, with no body, who lives twisted up in a wheel chair, drummed and told stories to the children. It was impossible to think of him as anything other than completely whole.

In the morning as I looked out of the door of my little log cabin, snow was gently falling and it was as if winter had returned. I put on my hiking boots and set off along the Spotted Owl Trail into the great silent cathedral of ancient forest all around – the old grandmother trees standing there so old and wise – hemlock, yew and the enormous Western Cedars hanging with moss. The loudest sound was my own heartbeat and high above, at the top of the forest canopy, the thin, clear songs of little birds trilling in the air. I walked for hours and then came back to a soak in the meadow pool – the best place of all. A stone lined pool which has been fashioned over a natural hot water geyser positioned high on a gently sloping meadow above the rushing river. Wild deer and bobcats and other forest creatures venture out of the tree cover in the magical silence to share the view. Tiny flakes of early spring snow landed softly on my hair and skin while my body was gently caressed by the hot mineral-rich waters. For many centuries, before their property was seized and they were pushed off into smaller and smaller areas, the Indians would have used these sacred springs for healing and for ceremonies. I felt so happy that the land has been returned to its original purpose.

Gwynne trained as an actress before she came to live at Breitenbush and as an actress, her gift for empathy is a plus. As a healer it can feel like being skinned alive, she says. "I know I get too involved in the suffering. I'm constantly battling with how to keep my heart open and not be sucked out, not be such a sponge. Sometimes I feel I don't have anything left to give. It's no use at all to fall into a great caved-in black hole of grief. How can I be *present*, authentic, open but not destroyed? I struggle with, 'If there is the Divine, then how can Bosnia happen or Rwanda?' I know I'm of service here but what I wrestle with is, am I really making a difference? Most of the guests who come here are middle-class, well-off. It's not the same as going where I'm really needed. Sometimes I feel like a sham."

I disagreed because I think that, for any of us, the best work we do is whatever is at hand. Providing a peaceful healing space for tired city folks is real and important too. Being mindful, recognising the sacredness and the interconnectedness of all things, being the very best that you can be wherever you find yourself is a choice we can all make. Anyhow, nothing is disconnected from anything else. Living holistically is knowing that the air we breathe and the water we drink are primordial. They've been here from the beginning. My body has been plants and animals. It's been blood and rain and waterfalls and snow and juice and sap. There's no distinction. We're all part of this Mother Earth. Everything in the world is magical. An acorn becomes an oak. Your whole life is an offering.

"You're right," said Gwynne. "I worry should I come off the mountain and go out into the 'real world' but I know the real world is everywhere. One of my resolutions last year was to be more *involved* – to attempt a marriage between politics and the path of the heart. I don't want there to be a separation between my spiritual work and my everyday work. I don't want my work to be happening in a vacuum but to have *intention*. That means making sure I'm registered to vote, writing letters for Amnesty, signing petitions, being more active, more vocal, more conscious. Do I buy a dress from China when I know what they're doing in Tibet? It's too easy for me to be on retreat all the time – isolated, cut off. I'm glad there are people doing that – cloistered, sequestered, holding the silence – but I don't think all of us can do that so I'm sort of half-way. The act of silence and devotions before the altar of my heart with my eyes closed is very important for me. It is glorious to know that I can be anywhere – even in prison – and no one can take it from me.

"I didn't ask Kwan Yin to come into me, or Mother Mary, or Kali, the terrifying Dark Mother, for that matter. I danced her, I sang her and deep down in my cells she left me her gifts. She cut away all my fears, all my rubbish. It was so important for me to find and befriend one of the Dark Mothers. I used to be scared of her wrathful image, but not any more. She's terrible and awful but there's also so much love in her. Death and destruction are part of the complexity. She's the rotting down and the compost out of which comes new life. Why are we so afraid of the dark? The New Age is constantly preoccupied with Light all the time but the nourishing darkness is where things grow."

These are the very words Anna used in her teachings about magic. Sometimes it is hard to hold the paradox, the very one embodied in the Demeter/Persephone myth – that death, destruction and darkness are essential to a deep experience of the feminine. As death can't exist without life, so life can't exist without death. Everything rises out of Kali and melts away into her. She is the primal Deep.

Inanna in Sumeria, Babylonian Ishtar, Astarte, Isis in Egypt, Cybele in Rome, Demeter/Persephone in Greece, Kali. These are the different names of the Goddess who takes us into the heart of darkness, into the heart of the mystery, who teaches us that out of shit comes fertilizer.

Embodiment of the dark side was Gwynne's point, facing it, taking it into yourself, but she also echoed something else which is important to me and involves another understanding of the concept of *em-body-ment*. It is to do with the recognition of the sacredness of every moment of ordinary life, including our sexuality, as being the feminine way. My holiest, most deeply spiritual experiences have been not so much transcendent as earth bound – pregnancy and birth, breast feeding and love-making, gardening and dancing. Learning to love and celebrate the body – rescuing it from the fear and loathing in which it has languished during the centuries of patriarchy – to me, this is the beginning of honouring *all* life. The revolution of the sacred feminine can only happen if we trust and empower ourselves – approaching the Divine by whatever way feels right to us. There is no one right way. Each person will find their own unique path – by prayer, meditation and service. "Saying the name of God in your heart", as Gwynne said. "Sweating your prayers in dance. Finding simple, tender forms of meditation which open the heart and allow the Divine to come in. Respecting every living thing as a Divine event, as a droplet of Divinity. Acknowledging the Divine in each other."

I also share Gwynne's views about personal responsibility. Much as I respect anyone's path in following a guru, I have always felt a niggling uneasiness about projecting onto any human being Divine status. Surely claiming and celebrating the divine within oneself would seem to be the ultimate goal. So many gurus, churches, religions and spiritual leaders have shown themselves to be corrupt and bankrupt – filling their own pockets while the world suffers and their followers remain blind. A mystic is what Gwynne would like to be (is) – someone who has a naked, direct relationship with the Divine Presence. You see it as she dances, whirling like a dervish, pounding and prancing like an Apache, shining with devotion in meditation. As she knows in her heart of hearts, there can be no transformation in the name of the sacred feminine without a passionate, deep commitment to the turning of ourselves towards the service of other beings, to saving the environment, to challenging the abuse of power in all its forms.

Gwynne lamented how few committed relationships there seem to be these days – how few models of long-lasting, happy marriage. Together with her husband Eric representing the Divine Masculine they are sincerely trying to heal the split between Men and Women that has blighted our species. This is something that interests me very much as the veteran of a 40-year-marriage – relationship as a spiritual path. The path of love where the partnership is the vessel, the cauldron of changes in which transformation and growth can take place. Ever since I can remember I have had a vision of marriage that I carry with me in my mind's eye. It is given form in the shape of a large Nepalese wooden carving of Shiva and Parvati that stands in the library of my home in London. The God and Goddess stand side by side, a complement to each other, their multiple outstretched arms offering gifts and blessings. They each appear complete in themselves and yet together they make more than the sum of their parts. They are equal, they stand their ground, they smile serenely at the vicissitudes of life. They are the Divine Marriage. They are that to which I aspire.

If it could be possible to combine the wisdom and connectedness of pre-Christian matriarchal cultures with the intellectual advances of the patriarchy as a blueprint for a new marriage of the feminine and the masculine we humans would be well on the way to healing some of the mess we have made. Nothing in life could be more rewarding than the joy of union on all those levels – physical, emotional, spiritual, karmic – and nothing can be more miserable when it goes sour. Eric and Gwynne had a beautiful wedding ceremony in the water here at Breitenbush surrounded by their elected family. They believe passionately in the possibility of wholeness. May they continue to see the Divine in each other in this beautiful place, where it is still possible to hear the sacred ancestral voices of the indigenous peoples who were once the guardians and caretakers of Mother Earth. I remembered a saying of the native elders of the Onondaga nation: 'Mother Earth is where you are. She hasn't gone anywhere.' I drove back to Portland feeling inspired and renewed. I was so lost in my little glimpse of perfect understanding of the oneness of all things that I drifted across a busy intersection having failed to notice a red light and mashed up not only my borrowed car but someone else's shiny new Mazda. Luckily no one was hurt but it did bring me back to earth with a bump. Kali whispering from the wings.

The following morning, browsing through the free Oregon publication called '*Reflections*', I saw this advertisement:

> *Spiritual Directions with Nelly Kaufer. MA LPC*
> *Searching for your truth?*
> *Spiritual Direction focuses on developing a personalised spiritual orientation which provides meaning and connection. Spiritual Direction provides support to take the risk to deepen your spiritual journey. I'm a spiritual guide and licensed counsellor with a Master's Degree in Transpersonal psychology. I have 20 years experience providing spiritual direction and 14 years teaching meditation. In my own life I integrate Buddhist meditation with Jewish mysticism with a love for nature and the feminine divine. My gentle approach honours your natural process and guides you towards deeper truth.*

I was curious to know what you would get for your money as an ordinary punter so I called up for an appointment.

Nelly, a pleasant, humorous Jewish woman of my own age, had been a hippie tearaway in her youth and had a terrible experience on LSD with apocalyptic visions of the end of the world. Bad as it was, it was the crisis that proved a turning point in her life. She calls it her 'wake-up call'. "It got me on the path," she says, "I couldn't stay asleep any longer." She believes the wounding of women has been very profound and much of her work is about helping women to speak out about this unfathomable sadness and find ways to express and celebrate their spirituality. I asked her how a novice seeker could ever navigate a way through all the spiritual paths on offer and wasn't there a danger in running from one to the other – a bit of Sufism here, a bit of Zen there?

"I absolutely believe it's legitimate to create your own hotch potch," she answered. "It can also be problematical just like everything else. The danger is in sacrificing depth in favour of a bit of supermarket shopping – picking the most attractive bits off the shelf, getting as many outfits as you can and not making a real spiritual connection. However it's also important to throw out systems that haven't worked for you and to re-integrate whatever is good."

I observed that it is also possible to piss about for your whole life and kid yourself that you are being spiritual. "That's true", Nelly answered, laughing. "Certainly the huge amount of freedom we've had in the West has given us the scope to make a lot of mistakes. Maybe we've slept around a little too much or taken too many drugs but, in the end, because of that freedom of the individual we have the opportunity to learn and to grow. Gradually, eventually, you set for yourself a path that doesn't need anyone else to tell you what to do. You will know when it resonates with your own inner truth. There is a Buddhist teaching story which says that the ultimate truth is the top of the mountain but people are approaching via very different paths through different terrains. If your path runs through a desert, a spiritual truth for you would be, 'Thou must carry water'. For the person coming up river it would be, 'Thou must carry a paddle'. Both are true although not necessarily useful to everyone. That's what I love about the new spirituality. If I'd lived a hundred years ago I wouldn't have been exposed to Buddhist teachings. It just wouldn't have been an option. Now I have access to thousands of books on different approaches to spirituality from all round the world which I have the unique opportunity to pick from. I'm in love with it! I feel enormously grateful for the opportunities I've been given. Of course it demands a lot of integrity as a person not to be just messing about with drums and flutes pretending to be an American Indian or mouthing platitudes in church."

We talked about the difference between good teaching and dogma. "How do you tell them apart?" I asked her. Good teaching, she said, empowers a person. It gives them courage and inspiration and options whereas dogma tells them what to believe and how to act. Nelly herself has a spiritual teacher, but believes in the advantage of multiple mentors over one guru. "In fact my own clients are often my best teachers. They bring me my own issues, pushing me to work deeper." And that deep level, for her, is reached through regular meditation practice. "Meditation", she says, "opens you to the 'ground of being'. It has been incredibly beneficial to me for so many years – eighteen or more – both at a physical level and a spiritual level. I couldn't have done it without. Even 20 minutes a day and my life changes substantially. It is a place of replenishment."

Worried that our conversation was not furnishing me with the spiritual signposts that I'd paid for, Nelly asked me how she could help me on my path. So I asked her for guidance with my meditation. For me this has been an area singularly lacking in success. I'm alright when I'm walking or cooking or doing Tai Chi – in other words, something active, but as soon as I sit down I get fidgety. My friend Levana went to a three week Zen meditation retreat where they sat for eight hours a day with short breaks to eat a small bowl of boiled rice and vegetables. I don't think I could have done it. I have been to Transcendental Meditation classes. I have plugged myself into soothing tapes. I have sat with my back to trees. I have perched on mountain tops and sacred stones. I have joined with other Crusties (as one friend calls them: cranky upwardly spiritual tryers) in group endeavours. I have never been able rest in an altered state of bliss for longer than about four seconds before my mind begins its subversive machinations – turning somersaults, bombarding me with trivia, rudely butting into the spacious void. I become conscious of every toilet flush or dog's bark for miles around instead of being able to shut them out. So Nelly taught me the Hearing Meditation. The great thing about this method is that you accept what *is* rather than trying to ignore it. "Sound just keeps happening so make it your anchor point," said Nelly. "If you choose this technique it's actually helpful to think of each sound as an opportunity to focus still deeper. Put your awareness at the ear where the sound comes in. It will teach you about surrender. You're not *supposed* to shut anything off. This is conscious awareness in a body sensation way. Sit straight. Feet flat. Eyes shut. Be present. Be aware. Think: 'I feel my tongue on the roof of my mouth', rather than having a pre-conceived idea about what a meditation should look like or fretting 'why aren't I having a WOW experience?' Cut through the expectant mind and just live in your body a bit more. If you're hearing the clanging of the fire-engines or the roaring of the planes let's make *that* be spirit because it is." I tried it right there in her office as she talked me through it and it worked brilliantly. I like it because it embraces what I am rather than trying to be someone different.

I asked Nelly how she feels that we, as women, can best do the work of spiritual renewal and reclamation. "Through re-affirming our spiritual identity," she answered. "Even if we are not teachers in the professional sense, we can be guides and role models for our family, colleagues and friends. By *knowing* I'm divine, knowing you're divine and giving you that acknowledgement and affirmation – both in my words and in my heart. I think it is the greatest gift we can give another human being. We need that re-enforced all the time, particularly women for whom the bottom line is often, ' but I'm not spiritual' – well I know that's not true. What we have learned in patriarchal society is not to value ourselves as spiritual beings. Women have experienced a terrible collective wounding and marginalization from mainstream spirituality as if they just didn't count. As if The Father and The Son and The Holy Ghost just didn't include the feminine. I'm continually astonished by the creative ways women have found to express their spirituality. It's thrilling. But now, this is about owning it publicly – about feeling free and celebrating it in our own way."

As I left, Nelly gave me a big hug, a copy of her recent co-authored book, *A Woman's Guide to Spiritual Renewal* and her blessing. "I want to honour the work that you're doing," she said. "I appreciate your getting out there and hitting the road! Good luck." $60 well spent.

In San Francisco I stayed with Cecilia Hurwich my astounding 78 year old friend who received her doctorate at the age of 70 and now triumphantly drives a bright red sports car with the number plate: CEC PhD. Cec wrote her thesis on Creative Ageing and she walks her talk.

I had come to San Francisco because so many people on the cutting edge of the new women's spirituality movement live here, but by the middle of the second week I was getting lots of doors slammed in my face. Joanna Macey regretted she was on a writing retreat and couldn't give time for interviews; Joan Halifax was too busy; Angeles Arien was out of town; Vicky Noble wanted $100 an hour, Rowena Kryder was in Europe. Several others didn't return my phone calls. Of course they must get approached all the time but it's hard to take when it's *me* they don't have time for!

After about my tenth rejection I sat slumped at a cafe table wondering whether I would ever manage to see anyone, doubting that I could write at all, that I could possibly have anything of value to add to the gross tonnage of blah blah blah choking the bookshops. In the face of all the setbacks I caught myself feeling like a motherless child a long way from home. Perhaps an aspect of Persephone is always with us.

Maybe I should just *go* home, pay back my publisher's advance and do what I do best, holding the container, being there for clients and family, sharing my quiet, simple knowings, putting them into action. Inside me I know that the answers are so simple they can be taught in five minutes: be kind, be fair, be honest, be non-judgmental, give time, be open and willing to learn, be respectful of all other beings. That's it. How do all these workshop people manage to spin it out into a lifetime's way to earn a living?

Much as I love the New-World energy and yea-saying, a sort of Old World weariness overtakes me from time to time, especially in California. Everybody is so full-on. Everyone is OUT THERE – IN YOUR FACE – yet the more famous they become as spiritual teachers or healers or therapists, the harder it is to gain access and to have any kind of human relationship with them. Of necessity they have to find ways to protect themselves from the endless neediness of others. Obviously the seekers can't all be attended to personally and this isn't a criticism of anyone or their need for privacy – it's just a general lament that life has become like this. The very books and workshops and teachings that you want to sell become the things that eventually separate you from ordinary life. You become a guru. An unfortunate side-effect, perhaps, of the general climate of frantic spiritual materialism:

"Come to me", for Shamanic Journeying, Soul Retrieval, even Masturbation Lessons! ('The Art of Self-Pleasuring For Women' – Kundalini yoga exercises and hands-on self exploration.') A quick glance through the weekly free contacts newspaper gives an idea what's on offer:

> *"Teachings of the Extraterrestrial"*
> *"Doorways to Soulwork"*
> *"It's never too late to get rich"*
> *"Re-inventing yourself for the 21st century"*
> *"Sex Charm: 'Within 10-15 minutes I've got guys coming on to me.'* (Nancy 52, legal secretary)
> *"Turn your idea into a Hollywood Blockbuster"*
> *"Conquering procrastination"* (I liked the sound of this one but I kept putting it off!)
> *"White Buffalo Medicine"*
> *"Lightbody Integration"* by a lady called Amara: *"I channel celestial and intergalactic energies to assist you in raising the frequency of your physical body."* She claims to, *"erase lifetimes of karma, overlay your cells with a celestial blueprint, remove dark crystals and de-code pre-encoded info in your DNA to awaken you to who you really are and why you are here."*

Awash in a sea of assertive personal development marketing coupled with my complete failure to gain access to any of the stars of the circuit I pondered a bit on rejection being part of the journey. You don't always get what you want, you get what you need. I'm always having to re-learn this lesson.

Then, finally, a chink of light. Patricia Sun is a well-respected spiritual teacher. She was on the guru circuit for a long time but the stress of it made her ill. She had a heart attack and now looks kind of careworn. I had a personal introduction to her from my friend Lucy and got a lift up to Wildcat Canyon to visit her in her home .

Spirituality is a practical path, she maintains, a matter of developing a whole way. "Whole comes from holy and sane comes from healthy and healthy comes from whole," she reminds me, her love of words and their derivations teasing out meanings and connections that have often become lost in our sloppy usage. ("Even the word virgin really means whole which, to my mind, is a much better way of looking at it", she throws in as an aside). "And although there may be a lot of books on female spirituality already, they really don't address the wholeness and the living realities." The crux of the matter is the 'immature mind' versus the 'mature mind'. "We are all adult children of adult children – nobody's been raised by a grown-up yet!" she says.

We were sitting in her cosy sitting-room drinking tea, looking out on the budding trees and the coming Spring. "The human race has yet to grow up. All the systems are in dire straits because you can't rely on rules anymore to control people. We need to be mature to be self-governing and, to me, that's the essence of spirituality. When you listen to your inner Geiger-counter (that used to be called conscience) – when your heart and your guts are aligned, the body is wholesome. And when you use each day, each incident to assess which choice you will make, *that's* being a spiritual person."

I asked her if being grown-up meant owning our own Divinity and got a gentle slap on the wrist. "So much of the language turns into psychobabble and jargon," she answered with a frisson of impatience, "and the meanings remain unclear. I try to choose words carefully, even a little eccentrically, so as not to get caught in the jargon trap. What is important is to 'tune in' to people, to listen very carefully to what they really mean. Something I say in every workshop, which empowers people to this evolutionary leap is: 'Begin to consider, from this day forward, that everyone you meet can read your mind'. It would alter how your brain works. Most of us only keep track of what we say so we can't get caught out – so we can't be wrong or get blamed. This is thinking like a child. But reality is bigger than right or wrong – it is to do with goodness. It is more powerful to be good than right. There is a sanctimoniousness about being right which limits whatever knowledge you have, whereas with goodness you allow yourself to feel spirit. You make yourself receptive in your deepest being and ask, 'what is good to do? What is wholesome?' That, I believe, is the only solution to our maturity and our spirituality – not to mention our political, environmental and social problems and the destruction of the family and women and men not loving each other and people not loving their own bodies. *That* is owning our divinity." She grinned.

I made the observation that this is perhaps the first era where responsibility for everything that happens in our lives has got to be taken on board. "Absolutely!" she agreed. "And the way we take on responsibility is not through blaming or judging ourselves because then it's too unbearable and we can't face anything, but by being *response-able*, in other words, able to respond. For me, an adult isn't someone who knows the right answers. That's a childish perception which traps us into having to bluff instead of grow up. Either we pretend we know everything or we go into denial so intensely we become fanatical. Trying to control everyone else we limit our own growth. Thomas Edison once said, 'A man who has made a hundred mistakes is a hundred times ahead of one who has made none', because he knows a hundred things that don't work. Also in the mis–take, through trying, you have learned a million other things which will help you be creative and have insight."

So why are we so afraid of personal responsibility? Why the huge expansion of religious fundamentalism?

"Fear is the immature, linear right brain needing to be right. We have a terror of being wrong, as though we almost don't deserve to live." She continued, "I grew up in New Jersey during the McCarthy era, amongst finger-pointy, pursed–lip, squinty-eyed people demanding to know, 'Are you a communist? Do you believe in God?' Their certainties combined with their meanness always puzzled me. I'd think; 'God gave us the intelligence to doubt so he surely can't mind. Do we worry if ants believe in us?' Then I suddenly realised it was they who didn't really know God. That's what made them critical, rigid, blaming. Meanness is none other than self-hatred projected outwards. Immature thinking demands certainties. You're either right or wrong. Your self-hatred is because you know you don't know and it's terrifying and unbearable to admit so you join a club which says 'this is the right way and everybody else is wrong.' Your security comes from finding a traditional role to follow. I call it the Sieg Heil factor. WE GIVE AWAY OUR POWER. The irony is, Jesus said (practically using the word fundamental); 'I give you but one commandment and that is that you love one another even as I have loved you' and that is so seldom the tenet of people who profess to being Christians. So often Christianity is about ostracism, meanness and lack of kindness not to mention love. On the fundamentalist issue, (and I hesitate to use the word because it is so highly charged), fundamental means 'to the root', the foundation. Most fundamentalism is nothing of the sort. It is conservative judgmentalism. It would be fine if you just did fundamentally what Jesus taught or Buddha or Mohammed . We'd be in great shape! The fundamental tenet of Islam is 'God is love'. What a wondrous principle to live by. That allows, as they say in Sufism, for the God in me to salute the God in you. It puts a reverence to life and to how we see each other. It allows us to pause and to think and to be respectful. Those are the qualities that are grown–up, spiritual and whole-making."

What then is the spiritual teacher's task, I wondered. Is it to hand that responsibility to their students rather to become a guru for them to follow?

"Of course. The whole point is to find the Christ within. The longing to sit at the feet of someone who has all the answers is the longing to remain a child and let someone else do it for you. Alas, many gurus encourage this kind of dependency, whereas being a grown–up is to accept the moment and to do the best you can in that moment to perceive what is good."

Did she share my view that maybe we have to go back to parenting as the source of all this? And that people who seek a guru and who have not had good parenting will still be in the mode where they need someone to tell them what to do?

"That is my belief", she answered "Humans have an intense, complicated imprinting period, like ducks, during which they absorb their surroundings. It's hard to make changes once this imprinting is completed. One of the weaknesses of our culture is that we give people power by title instead of by their actions. A responsible teacher does what a responsible parent or responsible adult does – they speak with respect. They model, or rather *vivify*, what they teach. They are willing to learn from their students. There would be no abuse if people respected children. Never in human history have children on such a massive scale been murdering other children, committing suicide, dropping babies out of windows. This is beyond not facing. We can no longer deny it. This is directly related to being disrespected and abandoned in early life. It is related to being left for hours on end to watch television where they can see murders and abusive behaviours during their imprinting years. They are brutalised because of the lack of tenderness and connectedness. A lot of the trouble we are in is caused by women's dissatisfaction with and lack of honouring themselves for the job of mothering. A terrific amount of women's suffering is caused by their own judgmentalness. If they truly loved themselves better and loved their children better and enjoyed having them more we would have huge changes. But instead we lie to each other, fear one another and are not fundamentally respectful because of the conditioning we've inherited and because of our own painful experiences and imprintings. One in five children in major US cities is born addicted to a drug. And so it goes on. To heal what we've been conditioned with means we have to face our grief. It means a willingness to be vulnerable. I don't believe anything can change until we stop being judgmental. You create war by hating war, you create peace by loving peace."

Patricia talked about what she calls 'the law of matching energy'.

"Whatever you are feeling, you are sending", she says, and went on to explain; "I may say the correct words but if I'm feeling insult or condescension that is what the person will receive. Conversely even if what I'm saying isn't too well thought out or articulate but my heart is full and my love is genuine and my acceptance is real then that is what you will feel. I have dedicated the past 30 years to facilitating this. If you send it, people feel it. You just have to live it. It's your choice. The power that Jesus taught about turning the other cheek isn't about becoming a doormat or a victim it's about refusing to match energy. If someone ridicules you, don't match with them. Send them love. If you send love consistently enough what will happen is you won't have an enemy any more."

Patricia is a wonderful talker. In her lectures she uses no notes and her words flow out as if from a deep well. She teaches from her intuition and her dream is to be able one day to reach even more people through the medium of television. "We've all been conditioned with garbage. We are all hurting, all wounded. What I want to see happen is for the mass media to allow there to be *vision*. Jesus said, 'Without vision the people will perish.' I teach what I have discovered myself," she says. "I believe you have to *be* it in order to communicate it. I try to live religion, in the sense of *re-tying* the link to that which is greater, every day of my life."

But for the past couple of years she has been healing a broken heart. "I got burnt out", she says simply. I became physically exhausted from being on the road for 20 years and I hated the whole commercialisation aspect – the terrifying and terrible marketing that goes on. Unfortunately, in this culture, selling yourself is the game and the 'get noticed team' gets noticed. Everyone is greedy for attention and focused on making money. Also, people are not very supportive. They beat you up for being vulnerable. They want you to be a perfect mommy and if you don't do that they get mad at you. The person with the notoriety, with the fame, with the infamy gets all the attention. Murderers get fan mail and marriage proposals, for goodness sake! It is a madness. I don't fit in here. It's very painful."

As a tender, gentle, mystical person, Patricia has been buffeted around a lot in her life, refusing to compromise, and paying the price. "You know, what has given me my strength and spiritual power is that I didn't give away my reality in order to *belong* but it is a lonely road. Even my youngest son once said to me, 'Mom, aren't you lonely? You're so patient. How can you keep doing it over and over?' I answered, 'Because it's who I am. There's no choice. Each person has to take on what is here and work with it.' I used to be filled with such enthusiasm for the possibilities that I gave myself whole-heartedly. I spent my life with no regrets. I spent it with joy. I spent it", she flings her arms open wide, "*well*. But now I can't take it anymore. I am thinking of selling up and going to Ireland. I love the place, the culture, the psychic sensitivity, the pace of life. The Irish have the great courage to be *real*. I'll walk from village to village doing what I do best which is to tell my stories, to be receptive to people, to listen to them carefully and respond to their need."

Patricia tells the story of her recent attempt at meditating on what direction her life should now take. "'What am I supposed to do?' I asked, and in that deep reverential stillness the words rolled up in my mind – 'Your purpose is to end wars'. 'Give me a break! I can hardly live. How can I end wars? What does that mean?' I went back into the deep meditative state and saw a beautiful vision of the Earth like the photo from space – blue and green and lovely. My heart throbbed as I looked at it, so alive in the darkness and I was overwhelmed. I saw cylinders of light coming down and I realised that each one was a person who had learned to love themselves completely well and with compassion. As I watched, each one turned to someone in the shadows with such love and understanding that they, too, became illuminated and so it went. A critical mass was reached and then there was a quantum leap and the whole world was lit. This is something that we as a species could do. You can't teach it by scripture and dogma. You teach it by *being* it.

Jesus said, 'Be like a light. Don't hide it under a bushel'. When you are that light, people will see it, want it. When you make your home a centre of light people will come because it feels wonderful. It's catching. It's transformative. That is the mechanism by which we will make this evolutionary leap. This is spiritual truth. It's that simple but also difficult because each human being is confronted with the pain of the world and has to choose to 'match' that energy by sending love. And I don't mean make-nice, new-agey, Pollyanna-ish love because that's fake and we're too appearances oriented as it is. The U.S. has gone mad over appearances. 'Doesn't matter if it's true – market it!' I'm talking about the real thing. I'm not a Christian but I see the beauty in Christianity and it's awesome. I have no problem resonating with that in my heart. So long as I stay in that frequency I'm OK. That's what spirit is – *knowing* that God is real."

We poured some more tea and the old cat climbed up onto the sofa with us. The low afternoon sun shone mellow on the steep sides of the canyon. Patricia's vision of a world peopled by beings of light seemed very attractive and not impossible but in the meantime we are dangerous, angry babies busting the place up in our immaturity. How do we start?

"You start by aligning your real feelings with what you say. That, in turn, leads to being more genuine, more intimate, more *present* with people. It's what we are all hungering for – real communication between mother and child, man and woman, employer and employee. We will not need power *over* people, we will not be wanting to fool people or to hurt them. Anyone who gains some maturity has to be patient, consistent and constant. Above all we need to have children only when we are ready and when we will love them. We need to support each other and help the whole thing to grow in this calm way, not losing track of what needs to be done."

And what needs to be done? "Disconnection is the big problem. Whether we're talking about wars, the environment, overpopulation, factory farming, poverty, addictions, care of the elderly – in all these aspects of our lives, the cause is disconnected from the effect. We currently have 48 nuclear reactors sitting on the bottom of the sea! Everything is insane, out of sync with the natural wholesome order of things, disrespectful to life. God gave us this perfect planet where everything is well-balanced. Now, either we crash and burn or we make that leap to becoming grown-up and taking responsibility. I can't stop because I'm built to do this. I came to do this. I can't not pay attention. I have to stay until it's done."

As I was getting ready to drive back down Wildcat Canyon Patricia reminded me of a wonderful Sufi teaching story. Six blind men encounter an elephant. The first gets hold of its tail and says, 'It's a rope'. The second strokes the length of its rough side and declares, 'It's a wall'. The third feels one of the massive legs and says, 'You're both wrong. It's a tree. The fourth touches the elephant's trunk and is convinced it's a snake. The fifth, grasping a tusk, is sure it's a spear while the sixth, fingering one of the massive ears says, 'You are all mistaken, it's a fan.' They're all right yet they're all wrong because they haven't enough information to take in the whole picture.

Patricia laughed. "Every experience you've ever had in your life is right except that it's all wrong because there is so much missing. If you can accept the power of embracing that which you know and being open to that which you do not know you're a grown up!"

Chapter 3

*'The temple bell stops but the sound
keeps coming out of the flowers'*
BASHO

Looking out of the window into my friend Lucy's little garden, still overgrown with last season's neglect, I watched a tiny green hummingbird drink the drops of rain from the needles of a small evergreen fir tree. Its wings a blur, it stood still on the air, an iridescent promise of Summer. It was such a perfect encapsulation of 'being in the moment'. This is it, I thought, the moment is all we have and it is *huge*! It exists outside of linear reckoning. It contains everything that ever was or ever will be. In that microcosm of time, we live. How to convey something so plain yet so startling is the dilemma. At times I feel quite overwhelmed with feelings of inadequacy.

To keep on spinning out words seems only to add to the confusion. No wonder people retreat to monasteries, mountain hideaways and desert vastnesses – trying to escape the constant pulls and shoves to make a name, make a noise, make a living, market that little bit of whatever you've found out or discovered that others might conceivably want. Knowing that nothing is permanent is simultaneously a great liberation and a bottomless pit of existential loneliness – those two strange paradoxical bedfellows which dwell inside of me and tell me that my journey through time is a solitary one and that spirituality is the only thing which can assuage my longing for belonging and give me a sense of being connected to all living creatures and to the Earth and the cosmos. Separate though we are, we are cells of one body. Really making that leap of understanding and not just paying lip service to its enlightenment. Can it really be that simple?

Like everybody else, my desire is for wholeness, to gather up the scattered fragments and climb, step by step, that ladder to the moon where the light glows softly. Sometimes that feels like a place to pull the duvet over my head and sleep, like a child, peacefully in the arms of the universe and sometimes it feels like a place of enlightenment where I can be fully awake. I want both and hope they aren't mutually exclusive. The good news is, as many spiritual teachers would have me know, that in spite of all the mistakes, the confusion, the wrong turnings, that which I call 'I' can never be harmed. It is eternal. I am a spiritual being having a human existence. I am already divine. I am one with all life. Everything I need comes to me. I am protected, loved, guided. All is well. But I keep losing sight of all that. The challenge of this quest is to be *real*. To admit that I don't know anything and yet ... just knowing that much is knowing a lot. I acknowledge my frailty, my failure, my frustration, my disappointment. Like the condor in my dream, I want to come home.

After my mortifying car crash in Portland it took me a while to muster the courage to drive across the Golden Gate bridge into downtown San Francisco, up and down all those precipitous streets where movie car chases happen. I had heard of an event taking place in the labyrinth at Grace Cathedral and I wanted to join in, but I got all the way there to find the event had been cancelled and the cathedral was locked up. There must be a lesson in all this short circuiting, I told myself. Maybe it is that the so called 'spiritual' is not only to be found when you expect it or in the obvious places and amongst the celebrated teachers but in the everyday things which we overlook: in the walk that Lucy and I took in the Tennessee Valley through poppy-strewn meadows and green hills with giant turkey vultures riding the thermals overhead; in the sea and the waving grasses and the hissing surf; in the baby reaching out her little hands to stroke a puppy; in the young couple walking with their arms around each other; in the tiny green hummingbird. Yes.

The everyday sacred was beginning to emerge as a theme. The small sacramental moments that come to me through being a human, especially through being a woman. Relationships as a spiritual path; parenting as a sacred way; cooking as a meditation; making rituals – holiday feasts, ceremonies, celebrations, festivities – as a divine offering; honouring those natural feminine, womanly, motherly things for what they truly are – acts of love and devotion. Those little things, the quiet things, the random acts of kindness are, perhaps, the truest manifestation of spirituality.

A more successful adventure was finding my way to the Spirit Rock Meditation Centre in Woodacre for Sylvia Boorstein's Wednesday morning meditation and Dharma teaching. I loved it. And I loved her – an adorable elfin grandmother, a Jewish bubba cum bodhisattva with a laughing face and a brilliant way of making bittersweet stories of ordinary everyday life into teaching parables. She gave a brief instruction: meditation is to rest in the spacious mind. All we have to do is to focus on the breath coming and going as a metaphor for everything else in life that comes and goes. We sat in silence – about 100 of us – in a lovely atmosphere of peace and tranquillity, followed by a ten-minute 'metta' practice where you send loving thoughts to your family and friends (this is what my mum did every night of her life only she called it saying her prayers).

Then Sylvia talked about the ten–day silent retreat she had just led in the desert. The purpose of a silent retreat is to do the minimum, to rest, to be quiet, to be still, to pare down the structure of the day. "We take life down to its most simple form and just watch how the mind operates", she said. "By putting in less stimuli, the mind returns to its natural state. Even without instruction, the structure, by itself, works. You don't *do* anything. You just hang out, smell the flowers, sit, walk, eat, sleep, just by being there the mind settles down." The truth is that we surround ourselves with so much busy-ness and so many distractions and worries that we hardly ever give ourselves that precious time just to observe how our minds work, how mind–states arise out of nowhere and consume us. "Retreat practice is the opposite of punitive. It is alive and exciting. You begin to perceive on a directly intuitive level what the Buddha taught," said Sylvia.

A participant who had been on the retreat told of meeting her own foot-prints in the desert where she had been walking around. The experience had filled her with immense compassion for this earnest, plodding seeker who was herself. Another woman told how she had been struggling for the first few days of the retreat, preoccupied with a recent personal tragedy but suddenly, one mealtime, she'd heard a "symphony of sound" – the dishes, the cutlery, the people making quiet grazing and munching noises – and in that moment, a new awareness was born. She really understood the First Noble Truth of Buddhism that 'pain is inevitable but suffering is optional'. "What a sensuous experience it is," said Sylvia, excited by yet another person who had 'got it'. "In spite of the ascetic appearance of the retreat it is really a passionate experience. It's like an initiation with the purpose of passing on the secret adult wisdom of the tribe to new seekers." She talked about the next of the Four Noble Truths – that clinging is suffering. It is a simple truth but one that is very hard to keep in focus. Even when you know it you don't always heed it. And when some well-meaning know-it-all tells you to "just let go" it's a terrible spiritual put-down like the infuriating "just say no" to a drug taker (for a start it carries the subtle implication that you could but they can't). Of course we don't always get it right but the practice of mindfulness (which is the whole purpose of meditation and retreat) helps us to recognise the clinging. If we are *conscious* we can make more skilful choices. We can make a paradigm shift from "Life is happening to *me*" to "life is happening". Waking up is possible.

The Third Noble Truth is about just this – that there is a way to unhook attachments. It is possible to cultivate a mind so spacious that it can be passionate and awake and responsive and involved and yet not struggle. The Fourth Noble Truth tells you how to do it – by following the eight-fold path: the right ways of understanding, thought, speech, action, livelihood, effort, mindfulness and concentration. Easier said than done, of course. The pleasures of gossip and shopping go out the window for a start.

After the Dharma I went for a walk in the splendid surrounding 412-acre site. It was bought in 1988 from the Nature Conservancy for $1 million with generous gifts of money from anonymous donors. It is a wonderful piece of land, now safeguarded in perpetuity, in a storybook happy valley location surrounded by child's drawings of green hills, smelling divinely of wet flowers after rain. I walked through the garden and the symphony of birdsong trying to imagine what total oneness would feel like. Like a hawk on a current of air perhaps. No place where one ended and the other began.

More than 2,000 people visit Spirit Rock each week to enjoy its unspoilt perfection and to take part in the Buddhist teachings. Most of those who come are adherents of other religions – Jews, in particular (Bu-Jews!) – as is Sylvia herself, who see no contradiction. The Buddhist teachings are an enhancement to their spiritual lives not a replacement. Somebody mentioned this and Sylvia quipped, "Sometimes when I'm teaching at a seminar or retreat, I look down the list of teachers and we look like a Jewish law firm – Boorstein, Kornfield, Goldman and so on." It's certainly a striking fact that within the American Buddhist community there are many Jews. Maybe, like me, they are attracted to teachings that don't require you to take on a whole package of beliefs. I have no desire to renounce my Jewishness but I have never felt welcome, as a woman, in a synagogue. Patriarchal Judaism doesn't reflect my own understanding of what it means to be spiritual. The Buddha said that spirituality should be one's own direct, personal experience. My personal experience is that the universe is a web of interconnecting energy patterns and that everything we do effects everything else so to practice kindness and compassion towards each other and towards all living things, including the Earth itself would seem to be a good idea. Better than 'dominion over', that's for sure.

There had been lots of questions and comments in the session. Someone asked, "What I've always worried about Buddhism is – isn't it all a bit passive? I mean all this letting go and non-attachment?" Sylvia answered, "The Buddha taught that in all circumstances we should cultivate a heart of benevolence toward all beings, including ourselves, no matter what. That does *not* mean allowing people to do evil things; it means stopping them. But it means doing it without ill will. It is not teaching passive acceptance; you can be a tremendous social activist." The answer pleased me as I have often felt uneasy about what I feared could amount to a rather laissez-faire, emotionless, detached response to life. But it isn't and we don't have to be powerless or passionless. What this tells me is that uncertainty is the only thing we can be certain about, but we have the power to make a distinction between the things we can change in life (our response to it, basically) and the things we can't (death, loss, disappointment). We can never get it right but we can cheerfully keep on trying.

The other Buddhist teaching I really like is the mindfulness one. Sylvia calls it "the aware, balanced acceptance of present experience", but qualifies that by repeating that acceptance does not mean passivity but rather "passionate accommodation". Passion is important to her. She writes in her book, *It's Easier Than You Think*; "Calmness and tranquillity are lovely states of mind; balancing vigour, interest and rapture so that clear-seeing can emerge. But calmness and tranquillity aren't the goal of practice, at least not for me. I want to be able to get excited ... Here I am in life. I want to *remember* that it's only a movie, and I want to *live* it as if it's real." She says she has become more passionate, not less. So, yes, it is possible to be peaceful and passionate.

There is a capacity for the heart and mind to expand in a way that can hold those life experiences we would not have wished for but are none-the-less there. It doesn't mean we feel the pain any less intensely but it is a way to accept the as-it-is-ness of life and death without getting caught in an endless cycle of misery. We all have the capacity to transform our own suffering into compassion towards the suffering of others. Making the world a better place by first and foremost transforming ourselves. These are the teachings I have tried to respond to in the knowledge of my daughter's cancer and they have helped me more than I can say in those moments when a wave of anguish seems to be sweeping me away. Open the heart. Stay with the feelings. Deepen. Breathe.

Sylvia is a natural born storyteller and she teaches with funny, accessible, Jewish grandmother-type anecdotes. As somebody said, "she lowers the threshold to enlightenment" and Stephen Levine, one of my great heroes, called her teaching, "Grandma Dharma – a soft persevering of the heart toward the place we each took birth to discover." She has been married for 40 years to the same psychiatrist husband, has degrees in maths and chemistry and has brought up four children. She speaks the truth clearly and humorously, cleverly building a bridge between ancient wisdom and everyday life. She tells a great story about the Buddha but it could just as well be about herself: The Buddha is stopped by somebody who asks if he is divine or is some kind of holy man. And the Buddha says, "No". "Then what are you?" asks the man. And the Buddha says, "I am awake."

I wanted to buy a copy of Sylvia's book, *It's Easier Than You Think*, but didn't have enough cash. "Take it," said the woman in the office, "and send the money when you get home." I did. It was so lovely to be trusted by a complete stranger.

The next day Lucy had fixed for me to meet a woman named Suzanne Segal who had kindly made time for an appointment in her busy schedule. Suzanne had the disconcerting experience 14 years ago of a 'spontaneous awakening' while standing at a bus stop in Paris. The 'I' that was her disappeared. A time of fear and confusion followed when she thought she was mad, but she eventually came to see that she had stumbled on The Truth, the unnameable infinite mystery that there is no separation. Everything that *is*, is itself and nothing more or less and it is all one. A holographic model of existence, she says, best illustrates the concept that each minute particle is also the whole. Now Suzanne's life's work is dedicated to describing the experience which she calls 'encounters with the vastness' or 'collisions with emptiness'. It is difficult for the mind to grasp because, of course, it is ungraspable but somehow I felt that if I only could, I would posses the secret of liberation. Suzanne, an attractive slim young woman in blue jeans with an animated face and friendly manner is a PhD, therapist and psychologist. She now helps people wrestle with the vastness idea. Whatever her clients present with the answer is always the same; once you can see that things are what they are and that's it, you can stop worrying. Like a dream that slips out of reach on waking, just as I thought I'd got it, it evaporated.

Lucy and I went to hear her public presentation later in the week to try and get more clarity but it was pretty much word for word the same spiel I recorded at our meeting. I found being told that things 'are as they are' disturbingly Alice in Wonderland and not particularly helpful. "The infinite isn't perceived through the circuitry of the body. It actually perceives itself out of itself," said Suzanne. "The mind constructs a reference point but that construct is what it is – a construct." When someone in the audience asked about what type of spiritual practice she would recommend, she answered, "There's no *one* who's a doer. There's no *I* that needs to do something in order for the infinite to be seen. People want practices in order for them to get something which will enable them to get someplace that they feel they're not! That insinuates that there is an *I* who has to do something. The only practice I'd come close to suggesting is a non-practice. The eyes of the vastness are always seeing everything, seeing things to be what they are. The vastness, which is what you are, is always perceiving itself. It's about bringing the eyes of the vastness into the foreground to see mind being mind. Everything is arising in the ocean of yourself."

"I wish I'd gotten stoned this morning so I could understand what you're saying," said someone. "You don't have to get it, it gets itself," was the enigmatic reply. "A particular circuitry moves into consciously participating in the sense organ." Pardon? The 'I' that was Suzanne never returned. It was a sudden and irrevocable shift of consciousness but as the Western mind does not respond well to the ungraspable experience of the infinite she went to a psychotherapist feeling it needed fixing. "De-personalization disorder" was the diagnosis. She went to another and another. They all wanted to cure her of the vastness. She started talking to some spiritual teachers. "People spend their lives in caves trying to have this experience," said one. "You're lucky, this is it!" said another. But it was not the total bliss we are led to believe and Suzanne struggled for 10 years with the conflict of choices and possibilities, all the while trying to bring up a child and lead a 'normal' life where "walking, talking, sleeping was happening but there was no *one* it was happening to. The personal reference point for everything was gone." Well now she lives constantly in this boundless state and seems to be doomed forever to have to describe it. "The vastness is the sense organ of the infinite," she went on, "experiencing itself, perceiving itself, because that's what we all are – a seamless intimacy." Both Lucy and I fell asleep and I felt sorry for Suzanne trapped in the endless cycle of explanation.

I think most of us probably glimpse this state of oneness with the infinite from time to time but it's not permanent, for very good reasons, and we can get on with the business of being normal individuated droplets the rest of the time. My mind kept formulating the questions, "So what?" and, "How does this help me live in the world?"

"How do you know you are right?" I asked Suzanne when I swam back into consciousness again. "It's not a question of right or wrong. I'm only describing the way the vastness is showing itself," she replied. "It is an ever-present reality. If the infinite waited for the mind to grasp it we wouldn't have clouds or trees, animals, growth." Fair enough. She left me with a quote from Rumi:

> *Out beyond right doing and wrong doing,*
> *There lies a field. I'll meet you there.*
> *When the soul lies down in the grass,*
> *Even the word 'other' doesn't exist.*

I came out into the fresh air with my brain aching a bit, but guessing that there is probably not a lot of difference between what Suzanne is saying and the concept of the spacious mind and oneness with the void that Buddhist teachings try to illuminate. Lucy and I, feeling a bit like naughty schoolgirls, had dinner at a surprisingly great little restaurant set in a dreary, non-descript shopping plaza. We were all fired up to go dancing afterwards, having sat on our bottoms for too long, but we ran out of steam and came home to have a cup of tea and an early night instead. I read the newspapers in bed. There were two appalling lead stories: Some Muslim extremists burst into a hotel lobby in Cairo shouting "God is Great!" and massacred 18 Greek tourists; Israeli war planes bombing the Lebanon killed 90 civilians. I also read a heart-breaking piece about Bosnia in Vanity Fair (sandwiched between an article on Sharon Stone, movie phenomenon, and a Versace fashion spread). It was asking the perennial question 'Why?' in regard to the basest, cruellest, most sadistic acts that humans seem so easily and so regularly to commit – the unspeakable tortures and acts of random brutality. The article ended with a quotation from Rebecca West's "thunderous masterpiece" of Balkan history. *Black Lamb, Grey Falcon* written in 1941. Since she wrote this passage, more than half a century ago, a genocide has been carried out against Europe's Jews, not to mention the horrors in Cambodia, East Timor, Rwanda, Nicaragua, Chile, Tibet, Sri Lanka ... and now Bosnia:

> *"Only part of us is sane. Only part of us loves the longer day of happiness, wants to live to our nineties, and die in peace in a house we have built that shall shelter those who come after us. The other half is mad. It prefers the disagreeable to the agreeable, loves pain and its darker night, despair, and wants to die in a catastrophe that will set back life to its beginnings."*

The feeling of helplessness is so overwhelming in the face of this dreadful human tendency towards destruction that the only course of action left is either to put one's head in a gas oven or to dedicate one's life to small acts of beauty and kindness. I heard an apocryphal story which could well be true. I hope it is: 'Someone drives up to the toll booth on the Golden Gate Bridge ready to hand over their $3. "It's O.K. sir, the car in front just paid that for you." What if that suddenly happened all over the world? Well, there's nothing wrong with having the vision.

The next day was a Sunday and I wanted to attend the early morning service at the famous Glide Memorial Methodist Church in the poor, Tenderloin district of San Francisco. The Reverend Cecil Williams is renowned far and wide for his inspirational sermons and the church choir, the Glide Ensemble, has an international reputation. In contrast to declining attendances in British churches, the service has become so popular that they now have two sittings on a Sunday morning. The place was packed – at least 500 people – and Lucy and I could hardly squeeze in the door. There were, encouragingly, as many whites as blacks, in every type of dress imaginable from track-suits to purple satin and pearls. Dead on 9am the rock band exploded into a gutsy, hard-driving gospel number and the 50-strong choir, all wearing African caftans, came on from the wings. The sound was thrilling and the atmosphere electric. Within seconds the whole congregation was on its feet clapping and dancing. Then, the Rev. Cecil, arms raised, eyes closed, got us all to hold hands. He entreated us, beseeched, implored us; "I want you to **hold on** to your neighbour, **hold on** to your brothers and sisters. I want you to **hold on** this morning." All the while, huge photographs of people comforting each other were projected onto a giant screen above the stage in the place where the Cross used to hang. Cecil took down the Cross years ago "so we'd stop focusing on death and put our energies into life."

The Rev. himself has a beatific face, white woolly hair, white woolly beard and kind eyes. He is everything you would want a pastor to be. His sermon was short and sweet – hardly mentioning God or Jesus at all – emphasising justice, community, action, love, neighbourliness. It was everything I always wanted a church service to be. Everything I imagine Jesus would have wanted a church service in his name to be. "The Dream Lives On", is the Rev. Cecil's slogan and Martin Luther King his inspiration. The church feeds a million people a year and runs a spectacularly successful 'crack' addiction recovery programme. They campaign against homophobia, poverty, domestic violence and low self-esteem offering support, welcome and real help to those in need. Cecil Williams' own son was once a crack addict.

The Reverend Cecil's voice rose to the rafters in a great crescendo, "In our community we take *seriously* the poor, the ostracised, those on the periphery.

We embrace everyone. Homophobia is swept out the door. It is *spirit* you hear here!" (Cries of 'Amen'! and 'Hallelujah!'). "In our community we risk everything, everyone matters, we celebrate and affirm unconditional love and unconditional acceptance. The spirit leads us on. It moves us to open up. Hallelujah! Shalom! Salaam!" ('Yes!' 'Tell it like it is, brother!') "In our community we *empower* each other. There's nothing we can't face if we're working together. There's nothing we can't face if we're working towards empowerment. Doesn't mean we're gonna *make* it, only *face* it. I'm not gonna lay a positive trip on you. Life is painful. It's painful to give up old habits. It's painful to feel helpless. We're afraid to trust, afraid to forgive, afraid to let go of old stuff. Have courage, whatever you're facing! Say to someone today, 'I love you but I don't know how to say it'. Say to your children, 'I'm not gonna put you down today, I'm gonna lift you *up.*' Say to yourself, 'I'm now courageous enough to move on in *spite* of my fear that I may not be able.' People, we will not see our poverty-stricken brothers and sisters go down. We will come together. We will walk hand in hand. The dream lives on. My God! The desert is going to blossom. Waters shall break forth in the wilderness. I say to you, RISE AND WALK AND COME HOME!"

People were nearly fainting with the ecstasy of it all. The message was simple and beautiful – we can all be effective in making our communities loving places, making ourselves into real families, standing up against the casual cruelties and the hardships of modern life. There was no proselytising, no ranting, no bullshit, only inspirational encouragement to be human. And every five minutes there was another gospel number (with brilliant soloists as good as any top recording artist). All the while a gorgeous young man in orange shorts stood at the side of the stage interpreting for the deaf. He was a delight to watch as he mimed and signed the songs in perfect rhythm. I loved the whole ecstatic experience and felt very moved and tearful at the vision of such a world of loving kindness in action. It was a good release from the feelings of sorrow and helplessness I had after reading the Bosnia article. It is possible. It must be possible.

A woman got up on the stage and said, "I'm a proud black lesbian and a proud recovering alcoholic. I'm here to ask for your generosity to help send inner-city children to camp to experience this beautiful earth and some fresh air. We also arrange free mammograms for women with no medical insurance. People, we have to take care of our health!" Everyone dug deep into their pockets to support the huge outreach project. Reverend Cecil stood by the door as we left, greeting and embracing everyone – a gentle and gracious man who seemed completely unaffected by his superstar status. He is leading a life of service. A real hero.

> Martin Luther King once said:
> *"Everybody can be great ... because anybody can serve.*
> *You don't need a college degree to serve,*

you only need a heart full of grace
and a soul generated by love."

Lucy and I had breakfast in a colourful outdoor Cuban café before going on to a very different experience in a quiet residential suburb to bask in the presence of Gangaji who was giving *satsang* in the Hindu tradition in a vast auditorium in the Dominican College.

"Women Who Run With the Cushions" we coined, to describe the ardent acolytes hurrying from the carpark to sit at her feet. A long queue to get in stretched round the block and the auditorium was overflowing. Volunteer helpers held up signs requesting everyone to maintain a respectful silence. So we did. We sat like excited children, massed together on the floor before the throne/sofa where the enlightened one would appear. Other spokespersons told us how to behave if we were lucky enough to get selected by Gangaji to ask her a question. Then, at last, 45 minutes late, she entered, dressed in flowing celestial blue robes with a flowing crimson scarf, a cloud of ash-blonde hair, expensive teeth. She sat cross-legged on the throne and closed her eyes. She said nothing. No welcome, no acknowledgement. Nothing. We all sat in silent meditation for maybe half an hour. Then, the eagerly awaited question and answer session which was recorded and videoed. Lots of hands waved in the air and the chosen few were handed the microphone.

One woman said, "I feel as if the divine is taking me over. It's like a powerful force thundering in my head. It's like being overcharged all the time. Can you shed some light?" Gangaji laughed a tinkly laugh like the good fairy in Pinocchio. "Just relax! First of all and last of all. If there's shaking, there's shaking. Let the divine eat you however it chooses – fast or slowly. Once a really big elephant walks into a tent, the tent is never the same. Don't try to contain it. Look deeper than your nervous system. Things will stabilise."

I felt very bolshie and out of place in the prevailing guru-worshipping ambience. The questions were all sincere and the answers all sensible – no quarrel with that. Her message was essentially: "Recognise yourself as needing nothing to hold it up, no body, no structure, no belief system ... it is time to be an adult, time to hear the truth, time to discover yourself," but it was like everyone was clamouring for the attention of a lovely, wise mummy and Gangaji was playing up to it or at least doing nothing to counter the projection. There was a gap between what was being said and what was being acted out. She said, "The best way is no way at all. Just be absolutely here with a still mind." She said, "You are pure awareness resting in the bliss of yourself." There was nothing to disagree with but it was all kind of abstract and I found myself much more drawn to the Glide school of joyful action.

The next day I braved the drive into San Francisco again. It's not actually that bad when you get over being scared of 12-lane highways and suspension bridges in an earthquake zone and your brakes failing on a 90° hill. All was well and I felt quite chuffed with myself. I even found a parking space and arrived exactly on time for my appointment with Blanche Hartman, the Abbess of the San Francisco Zen Centre. I thought she was a terrific woman – kind and humble – 70 years old and really living her practice. Alas, she spoke so quietly and the interview I recorded came out so faint I could hardly hear it. I remember what she said but I wanted to be able to quote her accurately and I cursed myself that after waiting so long and coming so far I went and cocked up the technical bit. Crappy old tape recorder! Why didn't I get a new one? The experience prompted some philosophical musings, though. Somehow in my meetings with spiritual women I must be brave enough to come out from behind the tape recorder and live *my* way along this path that winds far off into the distance. Perhaps the failure of the Blanche recording was a lesson to help me. Other people's exact words aren't it. It's all within etc.

Blanche Hartman, a tall slim woman with close-cropped grey hair dressed in austere black Japanese robes, described herself as a tomboy from Alabama. She followed in her father's footsteps and became a mathematician. She had felt passionately moved, as a teenager, by issues of civil rights and justice and became a committed political activist in the sixties. My friend Cec knew her at Berkeley where their children were friends. That was another surprising thing about her. Somehow you don't expect a Zen Abbess to be a married political activist with four children. Her husband is also a monk and lives at the Center.

Blanche told me the story of her own moment of awakening. During the sixties, politics had begun to get more and more confrontational and the paradox of fighting for peace had not escaped her sense of irony. She had been wondering why pacifism always seemed to be so violent. Then one day during a student strike she came face-to-face with a fully armed riot policeman on campus in a highly charged atmosphere of tension and found herself looking right into his eyes. "I suppose up until that moment I had thought of a riot squad policeman as the epitome of everything that was not me", she said. "I was extremely self-righteous and confrontative but suddenly, in that instant, all differences between 'me' and 'not me' disappeared. I knew I would have to change everything about the way I perceived life; things like 'I'm right and you're not'; things like 'peace is something to go to war about'. I saw that 'self' and 'not self' were not different. Once that boundary dissolved, all boundaries dissolved. The world was not as I thought it to be and I had no idea how to live in it. I knew I'd have to change myself. The reality was so much more total than all the concepts and arguments and my political life ended at that moment. It was not open to discussion, it was, 'how do I understand it?'" Looking for someone who would understand what she was talking about, she heard of Suzuki Roshi the great Japanese Zen master.

Suzuki Roshi originally came over from Japan for a short visit in 1958 but he was so moved by the passionate sincerity of Westerners who really wanted the Dharma teachings and were prepared to sit *zazen* (silent meditation) in a way that only monks, not lay people, do in the East that he stayed and stayed and when his wife arrived from Japan to fetch him home, she stayed too and they made their home in San Francisco. The Zen Centre came into being under his abbotship and he founded the first Zen training monastery outside Asia.

When Suzuki Roshi looked at Blanche she saw pure love, she saw someone who was capable of unconditional love and wanted to be like him and so she became his student. Sitting *zazen* was his way of quieting the mind in order to notice what it does, how it works, a way of seeing how we create the illusion of separateness and how much suffering that causes. It isn't the only way, as she says, there are many ways to approach spiritual practice (There's a Zen koan, or saying, which goes: 'There are 8,450 doors to enlightenment. Can't you find another?'), but it suited her. It took her three years before she could sit still so she teaches a more forgiving practice for beginners. When you are ready, she says, you will be able to sit without moving. You will be able to observe each thought as it comes up and ask, 'do I want to hang on to this?' "Our minds are very restless," she continued, "obscuring the very part of ourselves that we find most difficult to accept, the very part of ourselves that we've rejected or that perhaps was rejected by our parents. That is the part where our own suffering is but it is also the gateway to compassion – the door through which you can understand the suffering of the world. For me it was about softening the macho approach to life. The part of me I rejected was being female. At an early age I abandoned being a girl and became my father's longed-for son. I studied in his field. I became a mathematician because he was. I was ambitious and successful but a lot of my womanliness got lost in the process. I had to reclaim the part of me that was abandoned.

"One of the most influential teachers in my life was a Japanese woman who came over here to teach us how to sew the traditional vestments, the robes. I was so excited and wanted to hang out with a Buddhist *woman* teacher. But I had a surprise in store. She was a very traditional person from a very traditional culture. She taught traditional women's things. I had never done traditional women's things since I was five years old. She put all her devotion into her work. Sewing Buddha's robe was *completely* an act of piety. In my Junior High School, the teacher had suggested I would be better occupied servicing the sewing machines than trying to sew. So I did! I was the first girl in my school to do the machine shop class. It's one of those ironic karmic twists that I later became a sewing teacher. As I sat and sewed, the male/female polarity didn't seem to be such an important issue. I saw that if you do what you do with complete attention and devotion and it doesn't really matter what it is. Our suffering is in wanting things to be otherwise. As a child I had wanted to be a boy. Part of my compassion for myself was to own and integrate the feminine."

I asked her what spirituality meant to her. "I don't use the word spirituality" she answered "We talk about 'being awake'. There's a lot of emphasis in the practice of appreciating everything just as it is." "So", I asked, "the as-it-is-ness of life is the concept we have to try and grasp?" "Well," she answered, "You've just brought up two words I would never use, 'concept' and 'grasp'." She was right. As soon as they left my lips they sounded cheap and media trendy. "It is about *experiencing* the fullness and the wonder of everything just as it is, nothing added," she said. "But isn't there a danger," I asked, "once the wonder is experienced, of just sitting there glowing instead of getting on with the business of being compassionate towards others?" "I don't think so," she answered. "When you are truly awake, if someone is in pain you are in pain and you need to respond. When the attention is focused the non-separation is there. As Suzuki Roshi said, 'The waterfall does not realise it is part of the river. Whether it is separated into drops or not, water is water.'"

Blanche Hartman is the first American abbess trained in a monastery in the United States. There are women abbesses in the East but only as heads of women's monasteries. Blanche's ordination was a very happy occasion for women. "I was astonished at the joy," she remembers. "there was such a wonderful feeling of celebration. Some people felt I should use the title 'abbot' but I'm perfectly happy with abbess. I see it as a feminine form, not a diminutive. The great thing is that the ancient lineage of patriarchs now includes women."

Buddhism in America has undergone some invigorations, changes and modernisations every bit as profound as when it first migrated from India to China, Tibet and Japan. It has taken root here in its own form with, for a start, monasteries for men and women together like this one. Buddhism's 2,500 year old message of wisdom and happiness and an end to suffering is attractive to Westerners because it is so simple. It is possible to hear the teachings and immediately understand them. It is a beautiful philosophy and although not overtly feminist it seems to leave room for women as equals. I was happy to learn that Avalokiteshvara, the Bodhisattva of Compassion whose living incarnation is the Dalai Lama, is none other than Kwan Yin, the Goddess of mercy in her female form.

Blanche Hartman says her life's work is to 'be available' to anyone she can help, to "take this transmission which I regard as a great gift and pass it on", to dedicate any merit she might accumulate to the ending of suffering. I asked about how to bring the teachings into everyday life. "By living them," she replied simply. "By making them everything you do. There is no preparation for something else. It's everywhere – in the kitchen, in the hallway, in the bathroom."

> Someone once said:
> *Learning is finding out what you already know.*
> *Doing is demonstrating that you know it.*
> *Teaching is reminding others that they know it just as well as you.*
> *We are all learners, doers and teachers.*

Blanche showed me round the monastery – the shrine to Suzuki Roshi, who died in 1971, with its simple vase of his favourite dogwood blossoms; the meditation room, the garden, the lovely ceremony room. She gave me a gift of Suzuki Roshi's book, *Zen Mind, Beginners Mind* and hugged me warmly. She personally saw me to the door and stood waving until I was out of sight. A lovely and spiritual person (sorry – *awake!*). As I drove back to Mill Valley I reflected that the hardest thing to keep in balance seems to be the paradox of living life with passionate appreciation *and* non-attachment. *And* not letting non-attachment become indifference. Loving anything makes you vulnerable to loss, but the passion makes the pain worth it.

At regular intervals in my life I have tried to meditate but until Nelly Kaufer's illuminating 'Hearing Meditation', no one ever really told me what to expect so I never knew if I was doing it right. Mostly I fell asleep or sat straining like a dodo trying to get off the ground, flapping my metaphorical wings. Just wanting that lift-off, mind-expanding, flying feeling was making me frustrated. So I quit. Wanting equals Suffering. Better, perhaps, to say, as Sylvia Boorstein said in her talk, "Well this isn't what I want but it's what I got, so okay." On the journey to happiness you start anywhere. Wherever you are is an entrance to the Dharma. Be Here Now equals Happiness.

One of the five great hindrances to clear-seeing in traditional Buddhist teachings is Doubt (the others being Lust, Aversion, Torpor, and Restlessness). It keeps sneaking up on me. Some mornings I wake up just wanting to howl from the pit of emptiness into which I seem to have fallen. That mortifying place where I feel utterly without talent, without words, without ideas. Wanting to be a writer! What a nerve. Running around asking everyone what does spirituality mean? Reading books by people who put it all into flowing felicitous language. I ask myself, 'How does it all connect to what I know?' For a start I know I couldn't sit zazen for hours, days at a time. I'm a fraud. I'm a grasshopper. But then … the disturbance passes like an electrical thunderstorm and I expand into the spaciousness that Buddhists talk about. A friend reminded me of Tennyson's words:

> *"There lives more faith in honest doubt,*
> *Believe me, than in half the creeds."*

When I'm not fretting about not being good enough, I'm actually quite content. Even the loneliness, the fearful negative feelings, the impatience become part of the whole and I know that they, too, will pass. The 'ground of my being' is happiness. I guess it was no accident that I was named Allegra.

Blanche Hartman spoke about the solemn responsibility of giving someone a Dharma name. You look at them and ask yourself, 'What is the colour of this particular jewel?' When she herself was given her own Dharma name, which translated means 'Inconceivable Joy', she didn't think it fitted her but now she understands that, by choosing it, Suzuki Roshi had planted the seed of possibility of that which she could become. "What did he see in me that he gave me such a name?" she marvelled. "It was something to grow into." What did my parents see in me that Allegra was something I'd grow into?

I was a bossy, angry child a lot of the time. 'Fierce' probably describes me best. Fiercely passionate, fiercely loyal, fiercely adventurous but not very happy. There's still a restlessness in me, born of my scattered roots, but bit-by-bit I have been gathering those roots into this ground of my being, learning to respect and care for the straggly bits of me, bringing it all home to the oneness. I'm slowly but surely growing into my name. As Blanche said, "The awareness that you are *here right now*, is the ultimate fact." As the longed-for eldest child of two orphans I was the focus of a lot of love but it was hard to even imagine what 'here and now' might mean as we never stayed anywhere long enough for it to feel safe or solid. Our chaotic, peripatetic family life made 'home' a moveable feast. Maybe that was an advantage in the long run. One less thing to hold on to, one less attachment to suffer over. Even in my happiest moments, in my adoration of my children and grandchildren, part of me is preparing all the time to let them go. I rehearse in my mind, frequently, the news that they are dead not because I think it would make it any less devastating to lose them but because I want at least to try out the idea of 'who am I without them?' Is there a place where I and they and the whole of creation are so in and of each other that both having and not having are both illusions of separateness?

Sylvia Boorstein said, "Mindfulness is the aware, balanced acceptance of present experience." It isn't more complicated than that. It is opening to the present moment, pleasant or unpleasant, just as it is, without either clinging to it or rejecting it. Mindfulness brings clarity and clarity is freedom, moment by moment. Now is the only time we have. She told a little story about a monk who was being chased by a tiger. The tiger runs him right off a precipice and the only thing that stops him plummeting to his death is a little vine that he manages to grab hold of. Then along comes a mouse and starts nibbling the vine. In front of the monk, growing out of the cliff edge is a beautiful strawberry plant with one luscious ripe, red fruit. The monk metaphorically shrugs his shoulders and eats the strawberry. Now is the only time we have so make the most of it.

I remember many years ago, when I was studying part-time for a degree in education, screaming at my children, "For God's sake shut up and leave me alone, I'm trying to write an essay on child development!" That was a sharp lesson for me in being here now. Neglecting my children so I could become a good teacher! Even I could see the humour of it and made a resolution never to have anything be more important than them.

The next morning, photos of my new granddaughter, Freya, arrived with a beautiful letter from my son. The baby is divine. I wept with happiness for the hope that is reborn, for the spring, for renewal, for love. My heart was full with the magic of it all. I had stayed up half the night trying to map out a few questions for my appointment with the Rev. Dr. Lauren Artress, Canon of Grace Cathedral. It was hard to do since I knew so little about her. I didn't even know that Grace Cathedral is Episcopalian (or even what Episcopalian means. I looked it up. It means governed by bishops and is like the Anglican Church in Britain) and I didn't want to waste her time by asking fatuous questions. What I did know is that hers was the initiative to construct the Labyrinth that I had failed to get to see earlier in the week.

Her assistant came out to greet me when I arrived, offering coffee. Then a tall, rangy woman with short grey hair and a young, humorous face came bounding down the stairs. "Are you looking for Lauren Artress?" she asked. "Well, that's me!" Energetic, friendly and forthright she made me feel as if she was answering my questions for the first time although she must have given thousands of interviews. The first thing she said was, "Let the Labyrinth soak into your bones", and she took me high up into the organ loft to look down on the Labyrinth from above. The ancient sacred geometrical pattern – based on the one at Chartres – is woven into a vast carpet that covers the narthex, of the cathedral. It is a walking meditation, an ancient archetype, a metaphor for the spiritual journey – a journey to the centre, to the feminine, to the heart of the matter.

A truly wonderful person, clear and direct, knowing her strengths and her purpose, Lauren Artress' full-time work is now the Labyrinth Project – taking a portable replica into prisons, talking about walking the Sacred Path, getting other churches to consider constructing one. On the anniversary of the terrible Oklahoma City bombing she set up a labyrinth for people to walk in remembrance.

Lauren was ordained in 1975. I asked her if she had had a hard time rising to a high position in the church. "The women who went before me definitely had a fight," she answered. "The first ordination of a woman was in 1974. As a woman in the church I've had quite an easy time of it although I'm a fighter, that's for sure! And a leader, that's for sure! I'm a bridge person as well and a synthesiser. As Brooke Medicine Eagle has put it: 'One of my challenges is to bring us gracefully over the rainbow bridge into a new age ... A harmonious transition into a time of peace, manifesting the golden dream that each of us holds in our heart.'

"Somehow I've been able to work in the church – challenging where I need to challenge and making my own path," she continued. "I was already practising as a psychotherapist and did not intend to work for the church full-time, but I became very interested in the *transcendent* which seemed to be the missing ingredient in psychotherapy. It took me a while to get in touch with that but as it grew within my own being, I knew ordination was right. I can't say that I've had a hard time as a woman but I can say that what I learned as a therapist I've applied very well as a priest – to know where you can name the resistance and approach it with humour. To know when something is so resistant you shouldn't touch it! Also to understand that, really, institutions are like human psyches so you know when to press a point and when not to."

I wanted to know why she had hung on in there when so many women have abandoned the church because of its perceived misogyny. "I think being able to see the bigger picture helped me," she answered. I can see the misogyny and hatred as not *personal*. It's part of the collective pain we suffer, part of the misogyny that's on this planet. Women's groups and deep friendships with women have been very important and sustaining for me. It is enough to be fed outside the church so as to be able to keep surviving within it. That doesn't sound very kindly but it's true. I think the Church, which is literally man-made, is the best attempt at describing the invisible world. And when you can keep in mind that although it's not very good, this is what we're working with, it helps. When I was invited to come to Grace Cathedral by the Dean, I came feeling that I was supposed to be here and that there was something very special that was supposed to happen. I also came here holding the thought that this was boot camp for me. I needed to learn so many skills – how to administer a staff, set up a programme, preach to over 500 people at a time, be totally comfortable in front of groups and so on. Once that feeling started to lift I was able to start designing my own work a little more uniquely."

Lauren got some grant money and launched 'Quest', a spiritual centre to reach out to the community and build a bridge between the people outside the church and those inside. "There's much more spiritual growth and challenge, I think, outside the church than in," she said. The all-night 'Women's Dream Quest' was one such initiative which has been hugely successful. She explained how it works. "Twice a year for the past eight years 80 women have come with their sleeping bags, their journals, their sitting pillows and warm clothes. We do an opening ritual, warm-up and greeting. It is non-sectarian. We honour the four directions. We mention and include all the spiritual traditions because no one should feel excluded. We have live music. The Labyrinth is the focus but we form ourselves into groups of six, sharing thoughts on what we are seeking on our journey. People can choose bodywork, movement, dance, chanting, journaling or just sitting and watching. Then we sleep in different areas around the cathedral. Women's Dream Quest was popular right from the start because it identifies a place where the *hunger* is. My main reason for being on the planet right now is to help address the spiritual hunger of our times which is *vivid*. What I offer is integration of psyche and spirit and the Labyrinth is so perfect for that. Since it opened, literally thousands of people from all spiritual persuasions have come to walk it. It transforms lives."

As a woman in a very patriarchally dominated religion, was the feminine face of the divine important to her? I asked. "Oh yes, very important," she answered, "But not publicly. I'm the only priest who has ever done a blessing in the name of the Father/Mother God at the end of the service. People sort of held their breath! The Labyrinth is a way of introducing the feminine into the church without needing to talk about it because as you move into the Labyrinth and as you are walking the path you open to your experience in an entirely different way than the force, push, shove, quick pace of everyday life. You are opening and you are receptive. You are in touch with your body and your breathing. It is a feminine experience." My heart quickened as Lauren said that, just as it had during my conversations with Gwynne. 'A feminine experience'. And I thought again about how often I have lamented the terrible denial of the body by the patriarchal religions – the body regarded as something to be risen above; as nothing but a disgusting conjunction of functions and fluids to be tamed and tortured into submission; the body as sinful; the body as shameful; the body of a woman as merely an instrument of unholy temptation. And yet so many of my own most holy and sacramental moments have been experiences that were in the body and of the body – my female body. Experiences of celebration, of making love, making life, and nurturing. Until we can honour the body as sacred temple, how will we honour Gaia, the Earth itself? How will we care for our Mother?

The church, agreed Lauren, has always emphasised God The Father, Out There, Up In The Sky, "but that idea is breaking down and it is why the church itself is breaking down. The church does not seem aware that God the Father blocks the way of many people attempting to relate to the Christian path. People don't know what to do. They don't understand what's next. Well, it's obvious what's next. It's not obvious to everybody but that's okay – it takes time. This is why the Labyrinth is such a wonderful tool because it brings the *feminine* in. It recaptures the feminine sense of Source. It utilises the imagination and offers a whole new way of seeing. It brings in a different kind of prayer: 'What do I truly need for the journey?'; 'Where is the spirit in me?'; 'Where is my strength coming from?'; 'How can I take the next step?' We have forgotten how to pray other than to read it out of a book; ('Dear God, da da da da da and please may I have ...'.). We need to welcome the feminine back into our male-dominated world so integration can occur between all those polar opposites – receptive and assertive, imagination and reason. The Labyrinth restores the feminine which was banished from the patriarchal church.

"The church is in a terrible place right now. The mainline doesn't know its message. It doesn't understand many of the factors that are fuelling the spiritual revolution so the clergy tend to focus on the dangers – condemning cults, charismatic leaders, 'happy clappy Evangelism', 'New Age woolliness' and so on. They fail to recognise that people everywhere are looking for guidance. They are seeking what they think the church no longer provides. It seems so sad."

I put forward my view that the rapid growth of religious fundamentalism, whether Christian, Jewish or Islamic, seemed to be one of the most frightening manifestations of that need in the world today. Lauren agreed. "The fundamentalists have retreated back to rigid, literalistic dogma – killing off the imaginative

and the creative. Fundamentalism born of fear breeds small-mindedness and mean-spiritedness. The tyranny of the letter of the law, reflected in the Religious Right, is overshadowing the spirit of love that was intended by the law of the Divine. The church needs to forge a new identity, one that provides spiritual guidance and nurtures creativity. So I'm working with the edge of that in people's minds. Again, this is where the Labyrinth is such a wonderful tool on so many levels. So perfect for our times."

Lauren explained about the two ways in the Christian tradition of describing the path to the Sacred. "The first is called the Apopathic path, or the path of silence and meditation. The second is the Kathopathic path, or the path of images, memory and creative imagination." The Labyrinth is a metaphor for both ways; quieting the mind to discover a place of inner concentration and spaciousness and bringing the imagination out of exile. "When I am teaching it and using it as a tool, I'm supporting something in our culture that's diminishing and becoming more and more suppressed in certain areas. It lifts people into the mystical realms. It feeds the soul. Aristotle said, 'the soul thinks in images' but people's imaginations are starved. We live in a spiritually unimaginative world. It is the experience of the soul we hunger for. Dreams, stories and myths have been relegated to make-believe. They are not honoured for their healing and prophetic qualities that have guided human beings through the ages.

"These are things that a woman can bring to high office in the Church. Also being able to be much more flexible with leadership; moving away from a hierarchical mode of operation, from Jacob's Ladder to a circle. For instance, with the Women's Dream Quest, my role is to be the interface between the women who would otherwise never have set foot in the cathedral, and the patriarchy who they don't understand and who don't understand them. Not only providing this interface but being willing to take the heat for it! And it can be a bumpy road. I can provide the sacred space and the permission. The structure is decided by the women themselves. There are a lot of other issues too: how to be resilient; how to take criticism, how not to be crushed by the patriarchy, or crushed by someone's opinion, or crushed because you made a mistake; how to develop the strength to keep going. The labyrinth is a major breakthrough. It's so gentle, so allowing. People just walk their own path, and as we are all doing that anyway, the literal and the figurative come together. That's the beauty and simplicity of it."

I talked about my thoughts on the sacred in everyday life and how my spiritual moments usually come in completely unexpected settings. "Me too!" she agreed vigorously. "The spiritual in everyday life is a mind-set, an open mind to the synchronicity and to the totally crazy creative that can happen in a moment, a sense of flow where we're not cut off. I don't think that happens for a lot of people during church services. They might hear something unique and meaningful in the gospel but the ritual has become so familiar and predictable that they can just 'zone out' and be on automatic pilot."

I asked Lauren about the wedding ceremony she famously performed for the writer Andrew Harvey and his partner Eryck. Had it been a battle to extend the marriage sacrament to gay couples? "Oh very much so," she answered. "I am very sympathetic and will do whatever I can but it's a huge battle right now. You can do it like we did in their living room but not in the Cathedral (*Common Boundary* magazine reported that it was at Grace, but it wasn't). The Episcopal church is in the middle of a heresy trial about ordaining a gay priest – another example of how the church doesn't know its own message. The message is love. It should be affirming. It should include everybody of *course*. I mean, come *on*!"

I told Lauren the story of my friend John, an Irish Catholic priest. A gentle and compassionate man, he served for many years in an overseas mission in Africa. When he discovered he had contracted HIV, he decided he had no option but to tell his superiors. But instead of being able to use his pain and suffering as he would have liked, continuing to serve as an even better priest in a country where AIDS is a galloping epidemic, he was thrown out of the church. Quite apart from anxieties about his own health, his sorrow and frustration at being cut of from his vocation are very hard for him to bear.

"That is blind! That is so dumb!" said Lauren in disgust. "That is why people are leaving the church in droves. People *know*. They sniff out the hypocrisy. There's a bumper sticker which reads: 'If the leaders followed the people they'd know what to do'. It's sad. It's sad. The church is meant to nourish the soul but it is not meeting the spiritual needs of our times."

I recalled an English Bishop who recently announced that he was going to give up reading the Bible for Lent and use the time to study the Qur'an – the better to foster cross-cultural understanding. It seemed an excellent initiative to me but he was vilified by traditionalists who denounced his decision as 'crass and bizarre'. "Unfortunately," thundered one vicar, "we are living in a generation in which church leaders are giving the impression that all religions lead to God." Where does he think they lead, for goodness sake? I asked Lauren what she felt about the notion that we are all fellow travellers rather than rivals on the journey. If we could only see that, wouldn't we stop slaughtering each other in the name of the true faith? Isn't the truth contained in each religion? Aren't they all facets of the same sparkling diamond?

"One of the new exciting things that's happening is the de-regulation of religion," said Lauren, "but even in an open-minded cathedral to go and say, 'Christ is not the only one', you'd really offend people. It would be insensitive to approach it that way. We're approaching it through the labyrinth. I went on television and said that a Jew, a Buddhist, a Muslim could all walk the labyrinth and find a metaphor for their own path". (She was attacked by fundamentalist Christians for inviting 'heathens' to share in the Christian symbology!) Lauren's hope is that by taking the labyrinth to the anniversary of the Oklahoma City bombing it would reach out to the Muslim community as well as those who lost loved ones. "The Muslim community were much maligned – extremists were blamed for the atrocity before there was any evidence one way or the other. Also in communities like Northern Ireland where there has been so much conflict and tragedy we can offer the labyrinth as a living prayer. Over the years I have moved from curiosity to scepticism to profound respect for the uncanny gifts of insight, wisdom and peace the labyrinth offers. It connects us to the depth of our souls so we can remember who we are. My work with the labyrinth aims to integrate people's psyche and soul. I am not a historian; I am a priest and a psychotherapist. My fundamental question has always been: How do I help people, including myself to change?"

I asked Lauren what she would say to those people who would rather leave the church than accept a woman priest. "I'd say 'Grow up!'", she came back, quick as a flash. "I'd say, 'start extending your vision about what the Christian faith could be'. Those people are in a fossilised, atrophying religion and they're being confronted. A woman at the altar is no small statement because all of a sudden God's not male! They need to adopt a new mind. We have confused religion with spirituality, the container with the process. To be spiritually mature is to grow in an ever deepening sense of compassion, lessening our fear of change and of the differences between us."

Hasn't the Christian church always been bedevilled by narrow, literalist interpretations of the Scriptures instead of delighting in the beauty of the metaphors? I asked. "Yes," she answered, "and the spiritual life lies in the metaphor. Again that's what the Labyrinth teaches us. It is a way of feeding our soul. The soul that thinks in images. People have described it as an invisible thread to the God within, a touchstone, a mirror, an opening door, a beating heart. There are layers and layers of meaning in the labyrinth. It invites us to step out of the linear mind and allow the intuitive, pattern-seeking, symbolic mind to come forth. A lot of the wonderful imagery in the Bible is coming alive with the Labyrinth."

So how did the labyrinth come into being? In 1991 Lauren needed a break, took a sabbatical and went to a retreat with visionary teacher Jean Houston who taped a labyrinth, a little-known medieval pattern, to the floor explaining that its purpose was to take you to the centre of yourself. "It was an informal one – not sacred geometry or anything – but when I walked it, it was a very powerful and unsettling experience for me," said Lauren. "I came back later that night and walked the labyrinth three more times alone with mounting excitement. Some part of me seemed to know that in this ancient and mysterious archetype I was encountering something that would change the course of my life." Lauren had a series of disturbing dreams and found herself pacing the floor, walking in circles back home with a strong feeling of having been seized by an idea but not knowing what it was. "Finally I heard the answer: 'Put the labyrinth in the cathedral!' I have not borne children this time around but it was like a pregnancy! I went through nine months of gestating and birthing this idea."

First she paid a visit to Chartres Cathedral to experience the ancient authenticity of the surviving medieval labyrinth which had long fallen into disuse. Even though she had to move 256 chairs to walk the labyrinth and felt uneasy about not having obtained official permission, everyone in her group felt an awesome and mysterious sense of grounding and empowerment. The cathedral seemed to come alive with excitement. "I feel we had touched the Holy Spirit," she said. "I received the embrace of Mary that day. I had ventured into her glorious web." Money came from different groups, friends came to help design it, dowsers helped with the sacred geometry. "It was amazing, exciting! All the synchronicities fell into place." On the day Lauren presented the first canvas prototype to the public at Grace there was a six hour-long queue of people waiting to take their turn.

Labyrinths are usually in the form of a circle with a meandering but purposeful path, from the edge to the centre and back out again the same way. The one at Grace is a classic eleven-circuit labyrinth based on a thirteen-pointed star. It is not a maze. There is only one way in and one way out. Once the choice is made to enter it, the path becomes a metaphor for our path through life.

After my meeting with Lauren, I did the walk myself with workmen hammering and drilling all round the cathedral. It was a good exercise in staying present and acknowledging that the path is not always serene, that there are often distractions and difficulties. I thought of Nelly Kaufer's hearing meditation again and made the as-it-is-ness part of the experience. One foot in front of the other and straight away I came face to face with metaphors of my own – how I hate to be lost and long for certainties, for invariables. The wilderness is a terrifying place for me. I need to know where I am. So I am glad this is not a maze. I can leave my problem-solving mind at the door and just walk deeper into the arms of the mystery though, perhaps, losing my way is also part of the spiritual path. Mistakes are part of the journey. It's part of being human. This mysterious archetype moves me. I feel a curious sense of unfolding.

Someone once said, "Unless we carry within our hearts the God whom we are seeking, we will never find God". That phrase comes into my mind as I walk the labyrinth. I carry a simple image of Divine Grace in my heart. It is the great oak tree in my garden – a miracle of life, shade, shelter, growth, beauty, strength and patience. It is constancy in the face of change. It is forgiveness and inspiration, the mystery of creation, death and rebirth. It unites heaven and earth. Its branches full of squirrels and little birds, it stands on the turning world and reaches for the dancing stars. It asks nothing and gives everything. As soon as I think this thought I realise that, for me, the labyrinth leads to the tree. There it sits in the middle, waiting for me. Lauren had said that most of the experiences that occur in the labyrinth are unexpected – guided by a sacred wisdom, a creative intelligence that knows more about what we need than do our conscious selves.

The good women I have met are like trees. They are around me but they are also in my own heart. I have to travel to find them but they are also at home in my own garden. Perhaps my search is for a network of trees, a global forest … I am loving this walk to the centre. I don't have to be logical and rational. My mind is free to create. I am in the invisible realm of symbols and forms, of seven-league boots and animals that speak. The connection between my inner and outer worlds seems enabled and enhanced. When I reach the heart of the labyrinth, I sit down under the tree. An inner resonance hums me. A column of breath like the music in a flute vibrates my hollow bones. I am in tune, mind, body and spirit. I am home. A couple of other people come into the cathedral and begin walking the labyrinth … They pass each other on the path – now turning away, now coming towards each other again. It is another poignant metaphor. We are all on this journey together, all part of the great dance of life, unfolding moment by moment, accepting not judging, allowing not forcing.

One of the most interesting things Lauren said was that we experience *another way* of seeing things when we walk into the non-linear path. "We experience 'God-in-process', that *we* are part of the divine order." For too long we have "limited ourselves to only one understanding of God. We need to discover that the Holy dwells within and around us." In her lovely and important book, *Walking A Sacred Path* she quotes Karen Armstrong, a former nun, writing of her struggle to find God: "I wish they would have warned me not to expect to experience God as an objective fact that could be discovered by the ordinary processes of rational thought. They would have told me that in an important sense *God was a product of the creative imagination* [my italics]." Lauren goes on to say, "The product of our creative imagination is found inside ourselves not 'out there' or above us. This is what people are discovering in the labyrinth."

As I walked out of the labyrinth I carried a lighted candle back along the winding path to the outside world thinking with great clarity, 'I don't want to be a tourist. I want to be a pilgrim.' It throbbed in my head and I suddenly understood this to be the single common denominator in all my books. The shift, in Lauren's words, from "the interested eye to the searching heart". Perhaps because I never had a stable home during my childhood, the longing to belong everywhere, anywhere, is so important to me. Thank goodness for women like Lauren, bearing all the slings and arrows, bringing her interfaith commitment right into the heart of the established church, integrating and honouring the feminine, creating a safe place for weary souls to find peace and a vision of wholeness.

Before I left San Francisco I came back two more times to walk the labyrinth. And now I'm all fired up to set in motion the possibility of constructing one back home. Just think, in every town a spiritual tool to awaken us to the light that calls from within. A simple tool that would not require great concentration or effort. A sacred place that could give us first hand experiences of the Divine. A little winding path to healing and wholeness.

Chapter 4

❖ ❖ ❖ ❖ ❖

'... with an eye made quiet by
the power of harmony, and the deep
power of joy,
We see into the life of things.'
WORDSWORTH

"**M**y body knows it has been here before, has walked silently in deer-skin moccasins, has breathed the scent of brown-crumbled forest floor, has bathed naked in the clear streams. Thousands of years pass in a moment and my spirit flies to places half-remembered or perhaps not yet found. Some kind of Arcadia." I scribbled this in my little notebook sitting on a fallen log in one of the most beautiful, heartbreaking places on Earth – the forest of giant redwood trees known as Muir Woods. As soon as I took my first steps along the trail tears came to my eyes. The tears that come when there is no way to contain the hugeness of the experience.

The whole world was once unspoiled like this and I was caught by a wave of sorrow at the havoc our species has wreaked upon the body of the Mother. The enormous trees, some of them over two thousand years old, just stand there, enduring, witnessing, waiting. They were here at the time of the Crucifixion, they saw the destruction of the Native American tribes, the last of the buffalo, the testing of the atom bomb. And they are still here, with their patient, forgiving arms outstretched, welcoming all into this holy place. I laid my cheek against warm, soft bark, I leaned my back against dear old trunks, I stroked and adored to my heart's content. I confess to being an unashamed tree hugger. The only way I know to express my love and gratitude.

The woods are a peerless glory – long recognised, thank goodness, as precious and being in need of protection. As long ago as 1905 they were purchased and given to us in perpetuity to save them from developers – unlike many thousands of others which continue to fall before the axe and the saw. An inspiring place of silence and timelessness, Muir Woods were chosen as the setting for the post-Second World War U.N. Peace Conference in 1945 and again on the 50th

Anniversary of the armistice last year. A little plaque commemorates the spot where the delegates assembled amongst the great trees – a mighty grove of giants known as the Cathedral Grove.

> *'Persons who love nature find a common basis for*
> *understanding people of other countries since the love of*
> *nature is universal among men of all nations'*
> Dag Hammarskjöld

It's a nice sentiment but I couldn't help thinking it was the *men* of all nations who had got us into this mess in the first place and perhaps if the feminine principle had been more equally integrated into the fabric of our society, right down to the re-wording of his speech in which women are so glaringly omitted, it might have been a different story.

Like all famous beauty spots, the place can get horribly crowded at peak times but I was lucky to have it pretty much to myself in the early hours of a cold, Spring morning. It was a gift of a day that will stay in my heart forever – perfect rays of slanty sunlight filtering through the pine-scented air down to the mossy forest floor – the only sounds, the rushing stream, the soughing wind and the birdsong. I walked and I sat and I wrote in my journal. I prayed that my grandchildren and great-grandchildren be able to sit here one day in a peaceful world. I thought big thoughts about the future of life on Earth and how it really depends upon the restoration of those things we have nearly lost in the great scramble for personal fulfilment. Things like the ancient order of family, community, creativity, contentment, service. Things we have come to despise, as women, in the drive towards equal opportunities. There is a crying need in the world for acknowledging the 'yin' qualities of feeling and gentling, for valuing the work of the parent (usually the mother) who makes community happen – raising the kids, having friends round to dinner, holding the space, containing the love, providing sanctuary.

Not long before, I had read an article in *Harper's Magazine* saying that no matter what their income, a depressing number of Americans believe that if only they had twice as much they would inherit the state of happiness promised them in the Declaration of Independence. "A man who receives $15,000 a year is sure he could relieve his sorrow if only he had $30,000. The man with $1 million knows all would be well if he had $2 million. Nobody ever has enough." People get into debt to get more 'stuff' but rather than make them happy it makes them paranoid and they have to surround their homes with alarm systems and guard their possessions with guns. Well, it isn't just America. It's a worldwide epidemic. The truth is, consumption is incapable of providing the fulfilment we all long for. It remains forever just out of reach.

I tut-tutted of course but it was with a blush of recognition. I have not yet managed to develop an immunity to the disease of consumerism. I'm so easily seduced by another pair of earrings or the purchase of yet another book, whereas the things of real value – loving relationships, satisfying work, time for friendships, time to develop whatever talents I may have, a pace of life slow enough to let me sit on a fallen log in the redwood forest or watch the changing patterns of the clouds – none of these require great wealth. Perhaps the secret of the future of life on Earth lies with something so simple as learning to enjoy sufficiency rather than excess. Part of my spiritual journey is about *really* learning this in my bones. "Eyes unclouded by longing", in the beautiful words of the Tao Te Ching. In other words, spiritual joy and wisdom do not come through possession but in the capacity to be open, to love more fully and to be free. I know that, really. The trick is to live it.

Next morning I flew down to Los Angeles and 70° of Southern California sunshine where a friend had invited me to give a series of workshops in the nearby university town of Claremont. Warm at last! L.A. is where I lived between the ages of six and thirteen when Sharon and I were friends and, although practically unrecognisable all these years later, there is something about the smell in the air, the lemon trees loaded with fruit, the abundance of fresh mint, that transported me instantly back to my childhood in the time it took to breathe in.

I was conveyed to the place where I had my seventh birthday. Back to our small chicken farm in Van Nuys. Wild mint grew all around the back door and in amongst the grove of lemon trees. My family had arrived in California from blitz-shattered England, from rationing, air-raids and firebombs. It was the fulfilment of a dream for my father. He was a gentle, impractical, scholarly man who loved nothing more than to immerse himself in a pile of books while the world turned. A Jewish refugee from Poland who had lost all his family, he longed to provide for his children a different, safer, more abundant life than his had been. Oranges, palm trees, and a place for us to play pre-occupied his thoughts and eventually he came up with a scheme, a plan to bring us to the New World. We fetched up on the West Coast after a year or so of meandering and he rented this small-holding in the San Fernando Valley. In those days it was still Steinbeck country, rickety Model T Fords and walking barefoot to school. We were in paradise and tasted our first corn-on-the-cob, our first peaches, our first bananas.

Unfortunately, being the egg-head dreamer that he was, he didn't know the first thing about chicken farming so my mother, ever the sensible sleeve roller-upper was stuck with it. She shovelled chicken shit, raised the tiny, yellow, fluffy, peeping balls in an incubator and wrung the necks of the old hens when they stopped laying. She sold eggs out the back of our jalopy to the movie stars' homes in Beverly Hills.

Ma came from an impoverished aristocratic English/Irish family who had a great deal of style but no money. They had the built-in confidence of their class even though their particular branch had got shunted up a derelict siding for a couple of generations. One of her dictums was that a *real* lady should be able to turn her hand to anything if the occasion demanded – from scrubbing toilets to dining with the Queen (I remember plenty of the former, none of the latter). The 19th century women explorers and the suffragettes were forged out of such indomitable stuff. I see her still in her Grapes of Wrath dungarees, red hair flying, my baby brother in a wheelbarrow at her side while she tried to flesh out dad's fantasies with reality.

That chicken farm dream, one of the happiest times of my childhood, only lasted just under two years. The price of animal feed went up, the price of eggs went down and then one night a gang of delinquent dogs dug under the wire of the chicken enclosure. Ashen faced, my sister and I surveyed the scene next morning. The slaughter and devastation were truly shocking. Limbless, headless birds lay scattered across the ground, a froth of feathers congealing in the bloody earth. I remember my mother's face as she stood there looking at all her hand-reared biddies murdered in cold blood. She wasn't one to cry or carry on in a crisis, but I can still see her white knuckles gripping the fence post to steady herself as the smell of mint and lemon blossom mingled with the hot, sickening odour of spilled entrails. The farming venture ended soon after and we moved away to another part of town.

I made a pilgrimage to another of my homes from those days – the last place we lived before my family left the U.S. for good, en route to Brazil and a whole new adventure – 23rd Street, Santa Monica. Many of the little fifties bungalows are still there but my house was gone – in its place a block of flats. The land must be pretty valuable now and one by one the bijou haciendas are being replaced by apartment buildings. I walked down to where my old Junior High School still stands but it wasn't like it looked in my head. I talked to some 7th grade kids hanging around outside. They seemed so little and I had felt so grown up at eleven. I told them I had gone to their school over 40 years ago and they said 'Wow!' with round-eyed disbelief.

An ice-cream van used to park outside Lincoln Junior High each day after school. There was a particular type of lurid purple, grape-flavoured popsicle that I adored and I would save my dinner money to buy one on the way home. That's the good part of the memory – dawdling along the hot pavements with molecules of synthetic sweetness melting on my taste buds. Everything else about those days and that school is quite painful to recall. I was an overweight and spotty eleven-year-old and my hair never looked right. Until that year I had had beautiful thick, long, honey-coloured Rapunzel plaits but I hated them and thought they made me look babyish so I begged my mum to let me have short hair. It was a long battle which I eventually won but instead of taking me to a proper hairdresser, she braided it tightly – vengefully – like a horse's tail and hacked it off with a pair of nail scissors saying I'd be glad later to have such a wonderful switch of real hair to pin on as a chignon for a change of style. Chignon! Of course I never did. Chignons went out with long cigarette holders and that bloody plait of hair stayed wrapped in a box for thirty years until the moths got it in the end. I was left with an appalling thatch sticking out in all directions which, combined with my funny-sounding foreign name, ensured even more emphatically that I would never be one of the 'in' crowd. My parents were not sympathetic to my adolescent angst and extolled the virtues of individualism and originality when all I wanted was to change my name to Katherine Jones and look exactly like those sleek, smug girls who wore long, tight skirts, matching twin-sets, bobby-sox and a particular kind of brown and white shoes called saddle-oxfords.

They were cruel, those girls. They had perfected the subtle art of the turned shoulder, the whispered giggle that went dead quiet when I walked past, the special way of holding their books just so that no matter how much I practised I never got right and dropped mine all over the place. I was the kid who got picked last on every sports team. I was crap at games and hated them anyway – couldn't see the point of chasing a ball around – and had zero co-ordination. I wasn't popular with the boys either until much later when my tits sprouted and my hair grew again. The fact that I was top in spelling and story writing did nothing for my status. It only confirmed that I was a 'spaz' and a teacher's pet. Endurance is the word that best encapsulates that time – just getting through each day, day-dreaming out of the window and creating fantasy worlds of noble, beautiful, kind people in my stories.

Looking back, I can see how so much of the pain of not belonging can be directly linked to a complete lack of any kind of meaningful ritual for adolescent girls in our culture. There wasn't a good model of 'womanhood' for us to aspire to only a cliquey secret society of popular girls which I could never hope to be part of.

Luckily, home life was tolerable. My parents loved me and loved each other in a tempestuous sort of way. But we were an eccentric family and they were a source of continual embarrassment. My father was an old-fashioned gent with exquisite Continental manners. Women adored him. Stone-faced matrons and flinty bus conductresses went weak at the knees as he paid them flowery compliments and raised their hands to his lips.

My mother was beautiful and stormy. Her famous Irish temper and flaming red hair carried her through life like a capricious goddess; a ship's figurehead. Lilith was my dad's nick-name for her and it was only half in jest. She loved and made enemies with equal ferocity and protected her family with warrior-like loyalty. She would brook no argument on any subject and always knew best. I was never really able to stand up to her. If I had known then what I know now I would have been more subtle, more diplomatic, but looking down the years I see that how I dealt with her was often by deceit.

It wasn't really safe to be me. I did a lot of pretending. I remember coming home one day and telling her I was so proud because I'd been voted the most popular girl in the class. Nothing, of course, could have been further from the truth and I only avoided the horror of actually being bullied because I looked fierce. I told the kids at school that I'd been torpedoed by a German submarine while travelling by ship across the Atlantic during the war. That I'd been in the water for two days and been picked up by a fishing boat. I don't know if they believed me or not. They thought I was weird and left me pretty much alone. It was the most lonely time of my life and the age I'd least like to revisit.

And here I was revisiting it, gathering it up, making my peace with it, laying it to rest. I went down to the sea front, driving past all those evocative street names; Wilsher, Sepulveda, Santa Monica, Sunset Boulevard. It's ritzier now and an enormous, deluxe Sheraton dominates the esplanade but the old pier is still there. I stood watching the sun sink into the Pacific and knew a healing had taken place. 'Belonging' is a funny old business. Perhaps another way of looking at the spiritual journey is to see it as a way of coming home to your true self. A contentment spread through me mirroring the technicolor sunset performing its everyday miracle. I felt huge compassion for the spotty, fat kid with the terrible hair cut and the longing to belong. She belongs to me.

Now let me try to describe Nuala Ryan, a music therapist at Lanterman Hospital – a residential facility for people with learning difficulties. Nuala is a Catholic nun – a white-haired, soft-faced woman with a beautiful Irish voice, a straight back and a purposeful stride. She passionately cares about the mentally handicapped people at Lanterman whom she regards as her teachers and healers. "Organised religion has failed", she said when I talked to her about the subject of this book. "It is locked up and suffocated by its own dogma." And yet she has remained a nun. Why? "Why should I leave?" she asks. "The sisters are my family, my community. We care for one another. I have changed from within. I am strong now. My advanced years have brought a stubbornness. I know who I am and I can stand tall. I'm not going anywhere."

Nuala has been suggested for the post of Chaplain at Lanterman (which is a secular institution) and she would love to be appointed. The residents know her and know she loves them. However, other Catholics there are fretting about a woman giving the Sacrament and would rather bring in a priest from outside – a visiting peripatetic who knows nothing of the residents – many of whom have been there for 30 or 40 years.

Nuala has been wanting to introduce spiritual healing to her staff of excellent music therapists and recreational therapists, so she invited me to facilitate a workshop. We spent a lovely time together learning and applying simple healing techniques, using touch, massage, visualisation and relaxation, opening the door to a more honest acceptance of the fact that we all need each other to give a hand through the hard times and the sorrows. So many of the answers to life's dilemmas lie in living truthfully and in being able to ask for support when you need it.

I loved Nuala's feisty spirit, her belief in miracles, her warmth and humility. She questioned the whole idea of the 'healer' as somehow different from the patient – each was being healed by the other, each helping the other see themselves in a new light. We sat in the shade of a lemon tree in the California dusk and talked on into the night. "One might say, in the light of all the experiences I've had since," said Nuala, "that the vows I made when I became a nun are no longer valid but, as I see it now, what I had then was sufficient knowledge to make a commitment to this 'journey' though I had no idea what form it would take. With each challenge has come an invitation to renew and deepen that commitment. It has been like a rock and I am sitting on that rock which has sustained me in times of crisis even when my faith was so tiny it was like a spy hole in the front door but it was enough."

Nuala was born in Ireland. Her father was an alcoholic who died when she was just 15 and she threw herself into music at which she excelled. "Music became my companion, it soothed my soul, it gave me a sense of worth, it was an affirmation that I was OK. I had thoughts of becoming a concert pianist but the strongest pull was wanting to be nun. At the time I said it was because my father was a binge drinker and I needed to make reparation for his sins, but really God had always been like a magnet in my life. I was tremendously lonely and wanted to belong somewhere. I loved the convent life, it fed into my obsessive perfectionism. I had a very narrow understanding of perfection. It was a series of rules and laws, credit and debit. You keep the commandments and go to mass otherwise you build up this mountain of mortal sins. It was like a bargaining unit. The convent was to a be a place where I could be pure. So the emotional deprivation of my childhood was compounded by the denials of religious life."

It wasn't until years later, while working as choral director in a Catholic Girls High School, when she had a complete mental breakdown that Nuala was able to speak about some of the bottled up darkness at the heart of her being – in particular the sexual abuse she had suffered at the hands of two priests. "I blamed myself" she said, "and felt I belonged as a prostitute, that I was tainted and worthless. For years I couldn't see the hypocrisy and abuse that had taken place. But it all finally came out when I had this mid–life transition breakdown. I remembered from my childhood in Ireland, menopausal women (which is what I was), being put in the lunatic asylum which was right behind my house. I grew up with all these secrets and lies, all these myths in the closet and it is very important for me now to be able to tell the truth, to be able to say 'I've had a nervous breakdown' and not to be shattered by it. How lucky I was to find the space to break down and to speak about the old buried shame. How fortunate to find the grace to be healed. That magnetism toward God is what kept me going and it still is. It's so vibrant now. So intimate.

"What sustains me is truth. I can *be* in my own truth. Pretence and cover-ups drive me crazy. I can *see* that the church is in a mess. Why pretend it isn't?

We're a messy, motley bunch, like the people who gathered around Jesus – a motley bunch but a beautiful bunch. I am letting go of the perfectionism, letting go into the beauty of life which is chaotic. Out of the chaos comes creativity. I have an image of myself as a shattered vase and I'm now gathering up the fragments – putting those pieces back together."

There is something about the beauty of broken things that resonates deep within all of us. I know of a potter who deliberately breaks his most perfect pots then carefully sticks them together again, and I also heard about a museum in Korea where the broken pots have been painstakingly mended with lines of silver – valuing that which has been broken and made whole. Nuala's beloved music – particularly Haydn's 'Creation' – was the lifeline from breakdown to breakthrough, the line of silver with which she mended herself. "Music gave me an insight into what spirituality really means. I asked my Mother Superior for permission to see a psychiatrist. It was much frowned on but I knew it was time to take my life in my hands and do something about it. It was the first time of embracing myself and I decided to be responsible for me. I told each sister individually and asked for their support.

"For a long time I wasn't well. I was very brittle, very vulnerable but I think it has given me great insight into how long it takes anyone to recuperate from a major crisis. To some extent we never get over these things and thank God we don't because it's the *wound* we carry that makes us able to heal. It is my wounding that has opened my eyes to the humanity of my residents. The first day I met them I said to myself, 'I'm home' because I was experiencing my own handicap."

Nuala has been a Music Therapist at Lanterman for twelve years. "It is a difficult, wonderful job. And now that the chaplaincy post has come up, I'm ready. It's time to take a spiritual leadership role. And I know I'm going to come back to Catholicism in a very different way. I had to leave the structures of Catholicism and say to the pointing fingers, '*I* am the people of God. The Divine is within me. I carry it. So off you go! Be about your business of loving. I don't need all of your dogma, all of that crap. I go to confession when I need it and it's very real to me. I love my sacraments.'"

Nuala told me the poignant story of her precious friendship with Lee, a brilliant young pianist whom she has known since he was a student. Lee is dying of AIDS. "It was my first real understanding of unconditional love," she said. "I realised how much I cared for him, revered him, believed in his talent. Whether he was gay or not had nothing to do with it. He had left Catholicism and hated it because of its treatment of and attitude to homosexuality. He challenged me on issues and made me think. Then I had a lesbian experience with an older nun – a not uncommon happening. Boarding schools were rampant with those type of crushes – compounded in religious life by what they called 'particular friendships' which you weren't allowed to have. Of course they were talking about homosexuality but they never mentioned the word. It was just so weird! Total denial.

"Lee and I have both been healers for each other. I empowered him to be his beautiful self. It was the first time he had got to tell his story to someone who was never shocked. And he, because of his utter truth, empowered me to tell mine. Here I was, afraid of men, loving them, attracted to them but having had this thing with another woman. I had to look at all of that and to see my story with the same compassion as I could see his – as the on-going Bible of life. What a journey, what a gift, what a friendship! All nurtured and cradled in music. He gave me the courage to be myself – to acknowledge my woundedness and my intense, artistic psyche that had been buried for years. There's a much greater balance now – just me and God. No interference. I find myself talking to God all the time. The first bottle of wine I opened for myself, I poured a second glass and drank to God! And now Lee is dying which gives me great pain but it is also the greatest gift and grace and privilege to be with him. I have come to regard the gay and lesbian movement as a prophetic movement. AIDS is prophetic, homelessness is prophetic, gangs are prophetic. Why? Because they make me uncomfortable. They make me face my own sexuality, my own sense of homelessness, my own death, my own need to belong. Each part of my journey is coming home, home, home, deep within my own being."

There is a wonderful honesty and clarity about the way Nuala is living her life – strong and free and unafraid to stand alone. "The fact that I have challenged the church by my identification with the gay and lesbian movement means I'm suspect," she says, "but I don't care. If somebody thinks I'm a lesbian, great! If they think I'm straight, at this stage of my life – 64 – it doesn't make any difference to me. I know the beauty of Nuala. For me the feminine face of God isn't as important as claiming myself as feminine and myself as masculine. In the balance there's a gentleness, an integration. I threw a birthday party for myself at 60. Unheard of! None of the nuns had ever done that. And now every day is my birthday – a celebration. Allegra, I was so aware of how *whole* I was becoming at 60. I wanted to gather around me all the people who were contributing to this wholeness. It was so wonderful. I felt I was at my own wedding. The love! The energy! It was pulsing.

"For a birthday present, someone gave me a music box of Our Lady that plays Ave Maria and Mary has become a very vibrant companion to me. I have become aware, in this period of Lee's dying, that I need to learn her *waiting*. She was a wonderful woman. Always waiting, waiting, waiting at the foot of the cross, pondering. She was always there – so patient. To wait with no words, wait with, wait on, wait in, waitressing. That word began to float all around. The world now needs the power of the Mother. Women must be the saviours of the world. My dream is to break down the walls of our community and embrace the wider community – to join hands with all women. If each one of us could walk with a person who has AIDS we would be transformed, or walk with the homeless, or walk with a gang member. For me it is a wonderful thing to be able to say, 'Lee, I love you'. It has freed me. As for the chaplaincy? I'm right for the job because I love the residents, I love being an elder and a crone, there's an openness about me, I'm a woman, a worker, a servant, a *waiter*. Lanterman needs me because I'm a healer."

I only hope the administrators have enough sense to agree.[1]

That was my last day in California and I was away to Albuquerque, New Mexico where I picked up my Rent-A-Wreck from the airport and checked into the Monterey Motel. A strange melancholy settled over me like cling film. I could see through it but it wrapped itself tightly around my head. As the lights of the city came on and all the unknown lives were lived – making love, bathing children, eating supper, going about their night-time business – I felt my aloneness and homesickness like a dull ache in my bones. It's a particularly acute loneliness to be a nobody in a new place. I thought about how hard it must be to be a refugee or an illegal immigrant – slipping across a border, fearful of being caught, homeless, penniless, jobless, far from loved ones, unwelcome in a hostile, indifferent world.

I felt overcome by a wave of sadness and compassion. I thought of Thich Nhat Hahn's beautiful poem, 'Call Me By My True Name':

> *Do not say that I'll depart tomorrow*
> *because even today I still arrive.*
>
> *Look deeply: I arrive in every second*
> *to be a bud on a spring branch,*
> *to be a tiny bird with wings still fragile,*
> *   learning to sing in my new nest,*
> *to be a caterpillar in the heart of a flower,*
> *to be a jewel hiding itself in a stone.*
>
> *I still arrive, in order to laugh and to cry,*
> *   in order to fear and to hope,*
> *the rhythm of my heart is the birth and*
> *death of all that are alive …*
>
> *Please call me by my true names,*
> *so I can hear all my cries and my laughs*
> *   at once,*
> *so I can see that my joy and pain are one.*
>
> *Please call me by my true names,*
> *   so I can wake up,*
> *and so the door of my heart can be left open,*
> *the door of compassion.*

1 A year later I heard that Nuala has, indeed, become a chaplain.

On the aeroplane that morning I had sat next to a business executive with whom I made the mistake of sharing some of my thoughts on the rising tide of spiritual materialism and the way aggressive marketing strategies are increasingly deployed to tempt the punters. He laughed, "Business is war, honey." And when I looked aghast he went on, "Look, being realistic, the marketplace today is unforgiving and there's no room for fat. Success is the ability to get along with some people and get ahead of others." Bad karma, boyo! Thank God for people like Nuala Ryan.

In the morning the sun was shining but I couldn't shake my melancholy mood. I had a couple of hours to wait before my appointment, so I paid a visit to the museum to see a historical exhibit about the town of Albuquerque. Then something extraordinary happened ... .

I went into the lovely old mission church, still much used – used continually since the 16th century – by the Hispanic community. An old woman on her knees alone was the only person in there, muttering to herself, telling her rosary, interceding for her family, comforting her soul. I sat down at the back, moved by the peacefulness and the old woman's humble piety but she turned and beckoned me to sit near her. A bunch of flowers wrapped in newspaper lay on the pew beside her. She took one and gave it to me saying, "May the blessing of Our Lady of Guadalupe be on you." Then she fished in her pocket and produced a little card with the saint's picture on it and pressed that into my hand as well. A radiant, toothless smile cracked her leathery old face and she gathered her things and left. It was as if she had been waiting for me. I sat there for a minute, rather stunned, pondering on the strangeness of the event then I realised I hadn't even thanked her. I also thought I would like to talk to her more about her faith and her spirituality so I rushed after her but she had vanished. I looked up and down the nearby streets but there was no sign of her. If I hadn't been left holding the flower and the picture I would have thought I had imagined the whole thing.

Who was Our Lady of Guadalupe? She features in sacred art all over Mexico and the South West. I looked her up and found out that she was a manifestation of the Virgin who had miraculously appeared to an Aztec Indian, one Juan Diego, in 1531. This was at a time when the Spanish conquest had decimated the Aztec people, destroyed their temples and broken their spirit. 'Nothing but flowers and songs of sorrow are left', wrote an Aztec poet.

One morning, Juan Diego heard music in the air. He looked to the east and saw a Lady, 'clothed in the radiance of the sun'. She spoke to him saying; 'I am the Mother of God, the Mother of the Giver of Life, the Mother of the Creator, the Mother of the One who is near.' She told Juan Diego to build her a temple where she could bestow her strength and compassion to all who came to her. Most importantly, she asked for it to be built on the site of the ancient shrine to Tonantzin – one of the major Earth Mother deities of the Aztec people.

Three times Juan Diego went to the Bishop. He was humiliated, ridiculed and sent packing. So he asked the Lady for a sign and she sent him back one more time with an armful of un-seasonal roses and her likeness, on a dark blue

background covered with stars, imprinted on his cape. The bishop fell to his knees repenting and the temple was built.

The interesting thing is that the vision was the moment of fusion where the two very different strains – Spanish-Catholic and pre-Conquest Indian traditions – came together. To the Mexican Indians she was the Aztec goddess of childbirth, Tonantzin, dark-skinned like themselves. Now she became Our Lady of Guadalupe, the feminine, compassionate face of the new religion. They celebrated her with pagan dances but within the framework of Roman Catholic worship. I was so happy that the old Aztec Goddess had been petitioned to bless me. I hoped she was listening.

By now it was time for my visit to Meinrad Craighead, an artist who lives in Albuquerque. This was an encounter I had looked forward to for a long time – ever since a mutual friend in London had talked about her. She is the reason I came to New Mexico. I had already bought a copy of her beautiful book, *The Mother's Songs – Images of God the Mother.* In it she had written; "My personal vision of God the Mother, incarnated in my mother and her mother, gave me from childhood, the clearest certainty of woman as the truer image of Divine Spirit. Because she was a force living within me, she was more real, more powerful than the remote Fathergod I was educated to have faith in. I believed in her because I experienced her ... Each painting I make begins from some deep source where my mother and my grandmother, and all my fore-mothers still live. Sometimes I feel like a cauldron of ripening images where memories turn into faces and emerge from my vessel."

"How can I serve you?" she asked when I arrived at her little house – the last one down a dirt road on the edge of town by the Rio Grande. She has a lovely, cool, shady yard and a grove of cottonwood trees. Singing birds and whirling, wheeling flights of crows visit her driftwood bird hotel. Two huge brown German pointers gallop around and sit on the porch furniture like pussycats. Her studio is wonderful; built, literally, with her own hands. On each wall she has constructed an altar – all lovingly tended – to a goddess from a different tradition: Kwan Yin, Crow Mother, Shakti, Artemis and the Egyptian canine spirit, Anubis. The whole place is redolent with spirits and everywhere, stacked against all available surfaces, are her remarkable paintings. I love them. Images of birth and life, pomegranates and bleeding wombs, animal companions, moons and trees and eggs. They speak to me at a very profound level, weaving webs that mesh with my own knowing. When I try to imagine the Goddess, I see an oak tree, a field of poppies, old standing stones. I hear bird-song and ocean waves, I feel a baby's breath on my cheek, a lover inside my body. It is women's sacred art and that is what Meinrad teaches – running four-day creative retreats here on her own land for small groups of women to come together and explore their archetypal images in art.

"How can I serve you?" What an amazing thing to say and how it warmed my heart. I just wanted to immerse myself in the ambience of devotion and creativity and to talk with her for a while. I had come armed with a list of questions and, to be honest, some trepidation as I had heard that Meinrad does not suffer fools gladly. I hoped she wouldn't think I was one. As it turned out, nothing about her was intimidating and she had kindly made space for me in her very private life. She brewed a pot of proper English tea and shared her home-made biscuits with me and we sat with the dogs on the sofa on the veranda looking out on the cottonwood trees and the bright desert light.

I knew Meinrad had been a nun in a Benedictine monastery for many years and that now her work as a creative visionary includes shamanic and mythological imagery and the Divine Feminine. I wanted to ask her about the apparent contradictions so she told me about an experience of great significance she had as a child. "It was a hot, lazy Arkansas afternoon and I was lying under a hydrangea bush at my grandma's house with my dog. I heard rushing water inside my body. It didn't alarm me at all. With it came the immediate understanding that this was God inside me, and furthermore that God was Mother – this water inside me was Mother. I never talked about it but I was as deeply grounded, until today, in that experience from childhood as I was in the Catholic church. I went through a Catholic education and was in a monastery in England for 14 years, but with that understanding of God as Mother I felt no anxiety, no feeling of any threat. For me, the mother image was there as a balance all of my life. As I matured I saw it everywhere – a personal understanding that my spirit was inside me; that my life belonged to the spirit."

When Meinrad eventually decided to leave Stanbrook Abbey where she had lived as a nun for 14 years she wrote, "It was impossible, disintegrating to support a liturgy that exalted a masculine God image and encouraged women to lead limited, subordinated, clerically-defined lives". So she left.

"I just began to feel oppressed at Stanbrook", she told me. "The amount of scripture you read in a monastery is tons more than you get on Sunday at mass 52 times a year – our daily diet was the Bible and the complete Hebrew scriptures and after 14 years I had to acknowledge, 'this stuff is horrific and I no longer want to subscribe to it.' The reason it took so long was because, of course, there is so much in both the Old and New Testaments that is fabulously beautiful so it's easy to shut your eyes to that other stuff and let it wash over you. My deep inner understanding of God as my Mother kept it at bay. Nothing had suppressed Her in my heart.

"My life before the monastery, my years in the monastery and my life now are virtually the same. I lead a life of solitude which doesn't mean I don't have very close friends and don't spend time with people but I am wholly focused on my work as an artist." After *The Mother's Songs* was published in 1986 there was a rash of invitations to speak and give workshops which Meinrad accepted as a means of earning a living. But as time went by she found it increasingly frustrating not being able to work in depth with women hence the four-day Creative Retreats which she loves doing. "It's not easy to make a living as an artist," she says. "I'm not interested in making money, I'm interested in making a living without having to think about money! That's true liberation!"

I had heard Meinrad described as a 'cosmic midwife' and I asked her what she thought that meant. What is it that we are we trying to give birth to? "Truth," she answered. "I think I see it as the inner experiential truth of the spirit that lives in us and that needs to be able to work through us for the moment-by-moment transformation of society. We can't look for agents of change from within the system. It's about people listening for their own interior truth and working out of that truth – not worrying about who's going to publish it or buy it or rave about it – but being really willing to stay inside the perfect beauty of being unknown and anonymous. At the deepest level, it's only people who are in touch with their spirit who have the task and the grace to do this cosmic midwifing. And I think it's happening. There are more and more of us."

So how do we recognise each other, I asked – knowing the answer already because I think it had just happened. We both knew, instinctively that we were in the presence of a like-minded soul. "It takes very little insight," she said, "to absolutely *know*, within a few minutes, the people who are really *there*, the people you can give yourself to and know they will take it and keep distributing it. The secret is to be able to hold onto the deepest intuitions you had as a child, to keep centred in those gifts you had in the beginning. Then your life will unfold as it was meant to and you will get the support you need. All of us are only vessels for this divine energy. It doesn't belong to us – it is to share and to pass on. I have the greatest faith that what will be has already begun, and it fills me with joy even if I'm not going to be here to see it flower generations after I've gone."

I wondered what she meant by spirit and asked her if she could explain. "Spirit," she answered, "is the energy manifesting in me from the creative source. I believe we come from that source, we continue to live by virtue of the energy from that source and we return to that source. I believe in a cyclic regeneration. I don't believe we die and disappear, nor that we die and go to heaven or these other symbolic places. I think that we return and energy shifts, energy changes. That's what energy is. There are times when it is manifest and times when it is hidden. My mother has been dead for over 20 years but she's as real to me in my dream life and the life of my imagination – which is 'life' after all – as she ever was when she was alive." Meinrad grew up poor with no toys but in an exceptionally loving environment. Her relationship with her mother, her grandmother and other wise women in her life have given her that core certainty that it is safe to dwell in her interior landscape and give expression to it through her art.

Another question I wanted to ask her was about 'walking the talk' as the Native Americans call it. Given the environmental crisis we're in, do we perhaps need to redefine the connection between spirituality and politics? Is it enough just to recognise each other and meet in our little groups or do we need to be more active? More 'out there' in the world?

"You can only know that in your own heart," she answered. "I have the greatest respect for people who march and protest and man the barricades but I don't think it's my way. I really believe that the most violent political statement is art. There are days when I'd much rather go out and help my neighbour Marie, a Franciscan nun, work on the compost heap of her biodynamic farming collective but for me that would be, not just a distraction, but the wrong thing to do. My job is to stay at my drawing, at my painting, at my typewriter, keeping faith with what I know how to do. If you know you are standing at your centre, making something that has never existed before for the honour and glory of the spirit you can't *not* do it. I know when I'm at my centre – I've known it since I was a child. It's not exactly a fun life but to do otherwise would be an un-truth. My work is right here."

So much of Meinrad's life has been intimately bound up with the Divine Mother – the Goddess – who has been worshipped in various forms down the ages since the dawn of human history. How, I asked, can those of us who have lost her find her again? "I'm not sure you find her," she replied. "I think she finds you. To be found also implies you've been looking. I've always thought, for example, that creative inspiration happens not when you're aimlessly looking at the clouds but when you are actively engaged in working. It's the same thing. You move forward to meet the Divine Mother. Jung says that whatever it is that fascinates you means that your soul is picking up signals – a sort of vibration or resonance – about the next step to take you on your journey. I am always alert to what fascinates me. I pay attention and the clues present themselves. On this journey we are certainly fed along the way. That's the promise and I think we can take it for granted that if we lead a life of the spirit we're going to be taken care of. That has nothing to do with comfort or longevity or lots of good friends and chances to travel. It just means we'll be kept safe in terms of the spirit working in us. Look around you at the poison that comes to us from society, at the brutality everywhere. We are discourteous to each other and corroded by fear. Most people are destroyed by it. How come I'm not like that woman at the check-out counter who's smacking her child for saying 'Mommy I want a lollipop'? If you are doing the work of the spirit I think that somehow you're kept clean of that poison."

I told Meinrad about the little rat-race advice I'd had on the aircraft, "... Success is getting along with some people and getting ahead of the rest." "Horrific!" she exclaimed. "What a motto for life! No wonder cancer is raging. Our souls are dying before our bodies. If this is what we have done to our souls how can our bodies not respond? Just look at what people watch on television." She shook her head. "There's so much fear."

On the question of fear, our conversation ranged onto the topic of religious fundamentalism and why some people would rather choose rigid dogma over the freedom to make their own discoveries.

"There seem to be people who need to walk along fences to know exactly where they are," said Meinrad. "The fence turns, so do they, but in my view our journeys, at whatever age we begin them, are not linear but cyclical. As they go round and round you begin to see what themes emerge; what kinds of person you're drawn to again and again. However, to live cyclically, in a desert where there are no paths, no fences, no boundaries, with only the sun and the moon and the stars for orientation, to live where there is just flux and no signposts – most people cannot do that. In societies which are filled with fear and dread, they turn to others, they want to have eternal verities blabbed at them, they want to know that if you obey the rules you will get the rewards. People want answers and certainties, but I am of the opinion that there are no answers. There are only ways to keep asking the same questions, in different ways, based on your own experiences."

I told Meinrad that my own religious tendency was rather eclectic. What I'm searching for is a celebratory, ecologically sound religion that will appease my hunger for beauty and myth. Sometimes I think I have grasped it then I worry that perhaps I am too much of a bumblebee buzzing from one flower to the next, attracted to bits I like from all over the place, trying to create my own spiritual authority. Is that arrogant? Am I in danger of kidding myself? Ought I to have a 'discipline' and try to stick to it? Meinrad smiled. She had no trouble with the eclectic approach at all, she said. Her Catholic heritage and God the Mother are not and have never been in conflict. Her love of Catholic ritual remains as strong as ever. It is just another strand in the web. "All these things", she said, "water different levels of my soul. I think that eclecticism is a natural outcome of what you see and perceive and experience on the journey. If you have your eyes open, how could all the parts not add to the whole?"

But maybe I should be sitting zazen for six hours? "Hmmmm!" she answered with a comical look, "well that certainly is far removed from my way. I don't have any discipline like that. I have *my* discipline and much of it revolves around the dogs and getting to the river every morning for half an hour. I guess the Buddhists would call it a walking meditation! I feel that I am side by side with all those people who have a very structured spirituality but I have a very unstructured one. As a creative woman, I don't see how it could be otherwise. Your creativity takes you off in every direction, veering this way and that but all the time you're praying. When I'm working, that's an act of prayer. Right now I'm drawing sacred animals and I spend the whole time praying and talking to them. They teach me and inspire me. It sounds simple but it has been very profound. I ask them: who are you? where are you coming from? where are you going? what are you trying to say to me? They come in my dreams and they meet me on my travels. I went to Egypt specifically to worship Anubis, the great canine spirit who has been one of my most important archetypes since I was a child."

I was so glad and cheered to hear her say all this, nodding my head wildly in agreement as she went on, "... and caring for things too – a child, a cat, your half-acre of land, your friends – these are prayerful, sacred acts. I don't know how else to say it. The heart of prayer is being totally in the moment as we are, as we speak, as we draw or cook or care for an animal. That's all we've got. And if you cannot be wholly in the moment with whatever you are doing, in a state of gratitude and joy, I don't know what life is except that."

It's true what she says. When I am preparing a meal and cooking something special for friends it can take all day. I am completely absorbed – thinking about them, anticipating their pleasure in the food, enjoying the acts of chopping, peeling, stirring. It is a meditation and an act of love. If that is the heart of prayer then I'm doing it! This brought us onto ritual and its importance in our lives. I make up my own because I don't know what else to do. I invent rituals to bless babies, to cleanse houses, to heal grief, to mark transitions. Most of us are starving for meaningful rituals. How can we, I asked, re-member and re-invent appropriate ones for our time?

"What you just described, preparing food, is an elaborate, lengthy ritual. What else do you need? People think it has to be done in some special prescribed way by someone 'higher' than them whereas ritual comes out of the joy of everyday life. I begin each day with a ritual. I go to the sink, I fill a glass with water, I take it outside anytime of the year, I pour half into the ground and drink the other half. The taking in of that universal element is my morning prayer. To thank water is to thank the essence of life. To give it to the Earth and to drink it connects me to the Earth. In the winter I have another ritual. I light a sacred fire at dawn in my studio so that when the sun comes over the mountains there's a little fire burning here to greet it. At this time of year I use the little stufa in the garden – just a few twigs, a symbolic fire. I say my prayer there at the little altar which I built on my 50th birthday over the body of the crow which I found shortly after I bought this property. And that's another story ... As soon as I found that crow I knew it was a central experience and it has influenced my whole life since then.

"By burying that crow I called the Great Spirit Crow Mother into my life. I've come to understand that Crow Mother, revered by the Hopi and Zuni and considered the mother of all Kachinas (rain spirits), is also a manifestation of the Black Madonna. And because she has a black, enigmatic face – a face you can lose yourself in – she is also the abyss. Since then my imagery, my life, *everything* seems to have revolved around Crow Mother and the presence of crows. In the winter there are thousands of them in the cottonwoods and the Rio Grande valley. In January and February, pre-dawn, they start screaming and flocking and the trees are black with them. They flock to the east, screaming, then they wheel around and come back to settle in the trees. It's quite remarkable – as if their energy was pulling the sun over the mountains.

"Many birds are important to me but the two animal spirits which I can truly say guide my life and to whom my life is committed are the canine spirit and the crow spirit. And this is basically the subject matter of all my paintings. To really desire to pray in a ritual way you have to commit yourself to be aware of the mysteries in your life, the very small mysteries and even your own habitual routines. Any ordinary human act can take on a ritual aspect when you can feel the wholeness of it – the simplicity of it coming forth and flying away as prayer."

I felt so happy and excited to hear all my thoughts on the everyday nature of the sacred being echoed and validated. I suppose it's pathetic to need to have people you admire agree with you but it does feel good and I thank my guiding spirits that I have been led to encounters with such wonderful women. I wondered if Meinrad thought that we all have the potential for creative image making. "Oh sure!" she answered emphatically. "We do it every night when we dream. We may never put fingers in clay or learn to paint but the potential is always there, the creative imagination fed by the great, great mystery of memory. Everything we experience falls into some kind of centrifugal force which is always moving in us. We remember things which have stuck to the wall and rise up at will when we're writing or painting or dreaming. The rest is forced to the bottom but that doesn't mean it is lost. Its energy acts like a composting material, a deep inner fertilisation. It's all inside us waiting for space and silence, waiting for solitude and encouragement – things that women often lack – in order to emerge."

So this is where Meinrad's creative retreats come in – women coming together in this blessed place, telling each other stories, walking by the river, immersing themselves in the magic of the desert, touching areas of their own spirit more deeply than ever before, finding ways to bring new depth and intimacy into their everyday lives. I can't think of a better person to be their mentor.

Meinrad once wrote, "The purest acts of worship acknowledging Her presence within us are the simple, significant gestures toward the natural objects outside us – touching a stone or a tree, drinking water and milk, being with fire or standing in the wind or listening to birds." She gave me, as a parting gift, three shards of very ancient Indian pottery which she had found on her land. Pottery, in the South West was always made by women, anonymous women whose creative imaginations turned utilitarian, everyday objects into works of art. As I held the precious fragment in my hands I closed my eyes. I could hear the cawing of the crows and the warm wind in the cottonwoods. Between my fingers I rubbed the little pieces of baked clay painted in the dusky earth colours of this parched land, beautiful broken things which had once stored grain and water. I felt I was reaching back down the years to touch the women who made them – an unbroken female lineage. Yes, the sacred is not in some other realm. The heart of prayer is being totally in the moment as we are, painting, writing, making pots. In my body there was a vibration, a hum, connecting me to all women, all beings, to the Mother.

We said good-bye and I walked through the Bosque, a wild, wooded area, to the fabled Rio Grande of a hundred cowboy movies and songs. I stood there for a while thinking about how important it is for us to value and reclaim our feminine nature while the river flowed on by, wide and sparkling between its sandy banks. Then I drove Northeast through a shimmer of sun-baked air feeling absurdly buoyant. The raw, bare, seductive beauty gets under your skin. People fall in love with New Mexico and I felt that spell come over me as I drove on through the golden desert landscape arriving at dusk in Santa Fé.

D.H. Lawrence once wrote, "The moment I saw the brilliant proud morning high over the deserts of Santa Fé, something stood still in my soul and I started to attend." I sat in Tomasita's, a nice Mexican restaurant in the old Santa Fé railway station and had a plate of chicken enchiladas made with blue corn and hot chilli sauce. Funny how being alone can sometimes be lovely and sometimes devastating. This had been such a good day. I felt fed by the heart-to-heart contact with Meinrad – a fellow tree, a sister witch ("There are many of us," she had said, looking at me steadily, when I declared I was one). Later, in my motel room, I woke suddenly in the middle of the night, sat up in the giant king-size bed and seized a notebook and pen. I wrote this:

> *"I have black shoes on, handmade by the cobbler in our*
> *village. I saw them in the window and liked them straight*
> *away. They have silver-coloured buckles and square toes and*
> *little heels. I couldn't afford the half-crown he was asking but*
> *I exchanged them for a remedy for his aching joints and, of*
> *course, when his wife's time comes I will deliver the baby. I*
> *have a long flannel petticoat, a blouse with an embroidered*
> *collar and a big knitted shawl that I made myself, fastened*
> *with my mother's brooch – the only thing I have left of her.*
> *It is my most precious possession. Talking of possessions, I*
> *actually own my little house which is quite unusual for a*

woman. The other unusual thing about me is that I chose not to marry and have children. People think I am a bit weird but I love my freedom. I love to dance in the woods and sing in the meadows. I talk to the animals and they trust me – even quite wild ones like hares and foxes. They bring their babies to show me and sometimes, if I listen very quietly, I can know their secrets.

A raven sits on my apple tree and tells me about flight. A very small spider in the corner of my kitchen whispered to me the story of how the world was spun into being and a big toad who lives under a stone by my cottage door has told me about changing shapes. I make my medicines and I keep my promises to the gods and goddesses that live all around. I plant and I tend. I put back what I take out. I worship with my body. The people in the village come to me for my remedies. I bring new babies into the world and I lay out the dead. I stand at the threshold between the worlds. I am one of them and yet I am not. They live with many fears. I have none. They fear the state and the church and the taxman and the grim reaper. I am subject to no-one's laws and I laugh in the wind ...

And now they are going to murder me. It will be a blessed relief to die. For days they have cracked my bones and stuck me with sharp spikes. They wanted me to confess to fornicating with the devil and flying on a broomstick. It is impossible to talk to such stupid, cruel people. They know nothing of joy and magic only how to crush and kill. Soon the agony will end. I don't even fear the flames. They will transform me at last ...

So, it is over. The burning was terrible because it was slow. I didn't want to cry out but I think I did. An unearthly scream filled my ears and it must have come from my own throat. I will forever have the smell of charred flesh in my nostrils and know the feeling of my eyes melting and running down my face but now I am free. I know my time will come again and I can wait till then ... "

Whatever you make of it – and claiming that I had a past life as a witch is much too simplistic – there is a major part of my psyche that identifies with that story. The way it insisted itself up into my accessible image well from some dark, subterranean place when I was least expecting it must have some significance. It wasn't like a dream I wanted to record on waking, it was more of an imperative or narrative that I understood at a *cellular* level in the very marrow of my bones that suddenly asserted itself in my conscious mind. The story unfolded logically like a video film with a fast forward to the moment of death and again to the moment of leaving my body. I just wrote down what I was seeing. I was writing faster than I could think and I have left it unedited, just as it came out. I couldn't sleep again after that and went out to watch the sun rise over my day in Santa Fé. Perhaps my time has come again.

There is something about the good women I am meeting that keeps on sounding chords of recognition. "There are many of us ..." Meinrad said. What if ... ? I am convinced that somewhere, deep in our collective memory we remember a time when women were burned alive as witches. Women who were eccentric, unconventional, knowledgeable, women who were without the protection of a man were the ones who suffered most, who perished first. It makes for a shudder of unease around the naming of our own sacred experiences. We have been deeply traumatised. We understand that there are risks in bringing forth what we know.

Santa Fé is a town that has more than its fair share of artists and I felt quite punch drunk on all the galleries and shops full of gorgeous 'stuff' crowding the old central plaza and network of little streets. One thing that made me sad was the amount of 'Navajo Pawn' for sale. These are wonderful old pieces of heavy silver and turquoise jewellery, heirlooms and personal belongings which were pawned by their owners for money to buy booze or food. They were never redeemed so dealers have snapped them up and they have become, of course, collector's items now and much more expensive than the plentiful shiny new pieces because there is a finite supply. The only thing I could afford was a tiny black fetish bear – an animal spirit symbolising courage and introspection. In the Native American tradition the bear represents receptive female energy. To go into her cave is to heal the dark places within oneself, to attune to the energies of the Great Mother and to receive her nourishment. In other words, to go within, to enter the silence and to own what you know. (Later I was to give this little bear to my daughter, Francesca, to guide her on her own journey into the unknown.)

I found my way to the Museum of Folk Art which Meinrad had said was a must. It was. In particular a touching exhibit called *Familia e Fé* (Family and Faith) with lovingly carved wooden holy figures. The Holy Family holding hands – the heavenly ideal to which the human family aspires. Mary, the ideal mother, who stands for purity, mercy, devotion – Joseph, the provider, protector representing nobility, steadfastness, trust in God; and Jesus, the ideal child, the innocence of childhood embodying the hope of all mothers and fathers for their children.

There were delicately decorated altars and lots of paintings of Our Lady of Guadaloupe – all with the homely aura of sincere, unsophisticated devotion common to folk art all over the world. An old Italian proverb says, "*Tutto il mondo e paese"* – The whole world is a village. A sign in the museum said, "Folk art tells us there are no foreigners. Humour, spirit and aspirations are woven into one incredibly rich humanity." Right next door was the Indian Art Museum (it is correct to say Indian rather than Native American in New Mexico) and luckily for me I arrived just as a tour was due to start and nobody but me showed up so I had a personal guide for over an hour introducing me to the unrivalled collection of pots, baskets, fringed buckskin clothes and old artefacts. I thought of the craftswomen who had made these beautiful things – imbuing their everyday utensils and garments with the magic and mystery of their creative imaginations, transforming them from the commonplace into the rare. They didn't have a word for art. This was beauty for its own sake, for the pleasure of doing it, for the glory of the spirit.

I drove back to Albuquerque along the old Turquoise Trail – the original road, part of the Santa Fé Trail that brought the covered wagons, the settlers, the miners, the padrés and the near-fatal impact that the Indians would barely survive. And all such a short time ago – less than 150 years. Dazzling scenery, endless vistas of desert and mountains, mesas and riverbeds filled me up. One more night in the Monterey Motel then away to Texas in the morning.

Chapter 5

❖ ❖ ❖ ❖ ❖

*'If everything is coming your way,
you are probably in the wrong lane.'*
JOHN STEINBECK

I woke all through the night anxious that the rickety old motel radio alarm might fail me but, sure enough, dead on 6.30 it burst into a Mexican serenade. I returned my trusty Rent-A-Wreck and flew off to Texas.

A couple of hours later I found myself in San Antonio airport sitting by the luggage carousel waiting to be met by complete strangers. They were arriving on a later plane from Florida and were going to be able to give me a lift to the Well-Being Ranch, 100 miles away, out in the sticks. It was one of those occasions when I have learned to relinquish the illusion of being in control.

The Well-Being Ranch is the home of The Principle Group – a small community of people who are trying to live by their spiritual principles. They have given up their jobs in order to teach and practise their holistic philosophy of life. The train of events was this. On the advice of a friend who thought they were living an interesting experiment, I had telephoned a woman named Carol Ann Drick. She explained briefly about The Principle Group and the healing workshops that she facilitates at the Well-Being Ranch. She finished by saying, "Why don't you come to Texas and visit us? We're all going to a retreat centre for a four-day intensive at the beginning of May." Just the very four days I would be free to come. Synchronicity strikes again!

So there I was sitting by the luggage carousel as I'd been told to, getting a bit twitchy after two and half hours waiting, wondering what I'd do if nobody turned up. I had no idea how to get to the Well-Being Ranch on my own. The pilgrim's spiritual search for mysticism, celebration, kinship with the natural world, love and beauty sometimes feels like a little salmon's heroic upstream swim against a powerful current of murky floodwaters.

Finally, the delayed flight from Florida arrived and, to my great relief, a friendly couple, Terri-Lynn and Steve, came over and embraced me warmly. I was on my way again, swept up in the next instalment of the journey. As we drove to ranch – way out in a rock-strewn, parched stretch of cowboy country in the middle of nowhere – Terri-Lynn filled me in on the kind of work done at these 'intensives'. She also told me her own story in the breathtaking way Americans have of opening up to complete strangers.

Once an alcoholic, a battered wife and victim of abuse, Terri-Lynn completely turned her life around. First she joined Al-Anon, then a 12-Step Programme, and finally she met a man called Virgil Dodson who had developed a particular breathing/healing technique and cured himself of heart disease and cancer. Terri-Lynn was so impressed she felt called to carry the work on out to others in need and 14 years ago surrendered everything to travel the world teaching it. She derives no income, only travel and expenses and now there is a little core community of about eight people, including Virgil, Carol Ann Drick, her partner, Philip and a few others who constitute the Principle Group and live at the ranch. Sometimes they go out teaching and 'facilitating' – they have been as far afield as Russia – sometimes people come here and stay at the cluster of caravans that are the only accommodation. The Group make a small regular income by buying up old trailers, fixing them and re-selling them. They also raise some exotic animals, rare sheep, deer and llamas. Nobody makes a move without spiritual 'guidance' and as yet they have not been 'guided' to build a permanent structure at the ranch but the trailers are large and comfy – some as large as a bungalow -- and pretty much all they need at present.

As we drove up the dusty track to the ranch everyone came out to greet us with affectionate hugs and cries of welcome. In this land of huge distances it is a rare treat for friends to get together. There was a buzz in the air because this was to be the night when Elizabeth, one of the Group, would have a 'de-tox' done on her and she had been looking forward to it all week. It was announced that if I was to be participating this week everyone would feel more comfortable if I, too, were to go through the 'de-tox' process. It would involve taking off all my clothes and lying under a sheet on a mat on the floor next to Elizabeth (this is called, somewhat unfortunately, 'going down').

Well, I gulped a bit. How did I know they weren't a bunch of loonies looking for a sacrificial victim? Who would know where I was? Would anyone miss me? I confess to feeling more than a little anxious about lying naked in the middle of a roomful of strangers in the middle of the night, in the middle of Texas with only a sheet to protect me. Then I forced myself to trust that I had been delivered here for a good reason. I should just go with the flow. This could be interesting. People who ate organic citrus fruit probably weren't cult fanatics. So I modestly undressed, slipped under my sheet and closed my eyes. I was instructed in the breathing technique, which is to inhale deeply through the nose and expel the breath forcefully out of the mouth. All the while loud music is played and various drums and shakers thumped and rattled. The 'facilitators' may do some laying-on-of hands, massage your limbs, hold your feet, stroke your hair, put essential oils on you, whisper affirmations in your ear.

Immediately, everyone in the room began the forceful breathing – puffing and blowing like steam engines. Even though I was trying to enter into the spirit of the thing, my main priority at this stage was to keep my wits about me and not let my mind become addled by the flashing strobe lights. Until I felt safer, I had no desire for my brain wave patterns to be altered.

The idea is that you will release all the stored up toxins and mental anguish you've been lugging about, thereby purifying yourself in a safe environment of caring friends. Sometimes people cry or get hysterical and thrash about. The frenzy is carefully orchestrated by those doing the facilitating. They focus their undivided attention on the folks on the floor and bring the whole thing to a crescendo, letting whatever happens happen, being ready to step in and hold somebody if they are beginning to look distressed. They have chosen to call the process by the neutral, rather mundane, name of 'de-tox' because they present it at medical conferences and hope to gain recognition and acceptance by members of the profession, but it is actually much more like a voodoo ritual. It is none other than the ancient healing art of providing an acceptable, safe, holding space with various techniques (hyper-ventilation, strobe lights, repetitive beats) designed to encourage and enable you to let go of inhibitions and have a cathartic experience.

However, the energy in the room was not at all sinister or threatening and it finished hours later with everyone laying on the floor for a communal cool-down and meditation. Outside there was a nearly full moon looking beautiful in the midnight sky with fast-moving clouds dancing across it in the early summer wind.

In the morning we packed up the cars with supplies and set off for Wimberley, in the Texas hill country where the 'Weird Wacky Intensive Weekend', as it was described in the handout, was to be held. "Be who you really are: Intuitive Balancing, Synergistic Realignment, Unified Consciousness, Collective Examination, Essene Breath Work." The de-tox rituals, I learned, are only part of the Well-Being holistic philosophy of spiritual healing. Freshly made vegetable juice fasts are part of the cleansing process and the Group only eat good, organic food.

The location was a retreat centre called Indian Lodge – clean but functional; the dorm redolent of a thousand school field trips. By the time we had pushed the furniture about, though, and set the cushions and drums in a circle it looked much more inviting. The air was heavy and humid with the Texas summer heat just beginning to fire on all cylinders. Having started out a little sceptical and somewhat guarded I was soon touched by the courage and openness of everyone who came – people who really want to clean their lives up, people who are prepared to risk everything, quit their job, sell their home, in order to do what they really want to do – to live better, more honest lives, to 'wake up' and surrender to spirit, to 'guidance', to their intuition. It may not even be very articulate but something is definitely going on. There is a groundswell of feeling – a longing for something more than the greedy, Godless materialism of our times.

Carol Ann explained to me that the work can be done in large groups, small groups or individually. There is no-one, she says, who couldn't participate – including people with mental illness. Their credo is: There is only One Truth and that is that we all come from a Perfect Idea, a Perfect Creative Mind – artistic, undivided, absolute in every facet of our existence. All else is illusion. If, as a facilitator, you are holding the vision of perfection you are letting go into that Primary Mind knowing that everything is under complete, flawless direction and control.

Weird and wacky it certainly was. Participants had been invited to wear silly hats with the express purpose of creating a 'fun framework' to break down barriers; to look at things from a different perspective. Virgil, a large, bald middle-aged man wearing a baseball cap with a propeller on top, expounded on the theme. "Lighten up," he said. "Be one with the beautiful spirit that is in each one of us. Let it lead us in whichever way it wants. We *are* one mind, one God. As we all get to understand the truth of this we can move on." He talked about the need to examine the illusion of separateness which is nothing more than a learned societal influence. Oneness is our true state, he said, and this is where the collective breath work comes in – "opening to presence", they call it. "When we all breathe together we experience that oneness with each other, with the planet, with the whole. We become one organism instead of separate people". It doesn't matter what a person's problem is – in fact the less you know about it the less likely you are to pigeonhole and judge them – our job is to see the perfection of who they are. "To the extent that we collectively see that truth we can manifest change," said Virgil. "The essence that looks out from your eyes and from mine is the same."

The sessions were to begin the next day and I was interested in the extra dimension it could add to the healing work I already do – another way of providing a safe space, a sacred space in which people can make the changes they want in their lives and move on.

Outside the stillness reverberated with the amorous voices of countless frogs. In the eerie phosphorescent glow of the full moon, fireflies danced among the bushes – a sprinkling of shimmering enchantment gracing the summer night. I remembered being allowed to stay up as a very small child to see 'the fairies' weaving their luminous tapestry – one of my most magical early memories. I didn't know they were gradually becoming extinct until I read an article about them in a magazine where the writer lamented the vanishing of these wondrous insects of his Ozark childhood, beloved of poets and lovers, "dancing through the dark like wandering stars, like sparks from a wind-blown campfire on the shores of a summer creek." They are collected and sold for scientific research. Toxic sprays and chemical pollution have destroyed their habitat. Where there used to be millions of them, there are now few.

Carol Ann brought me a brimming cup of vegetable juice early in the morning and the first de-tox session was underway by 9am. Our collective garlic breath could have launched the space shuttle. It works like this. Six people are chosen by 'guidance' to go down (everything is done by guidance – from where to live, to what to buy for dinner, to which CDs to play in the de-tox session). Everyone else facilitates. By this time I was more comfortable with the proceedings and quite happy to let my intuition guide me to whom I should be helping . Each session lasts for a couple of hours, followed by some spirited bouncing up and down on the two trampolines provided for the purpose. This is to discharge any excess energy and get a bit of exercise.

The 'guidance' chose me to go down in the second batch and I had a nice floaty time letting myself breathe deeply and drift off to the music. Nothing startling. I just felt wonderfully present, energised and touched by the acceptance of everyone there. People held my hands or stroked my hair. Someone tinkled bells in my ear or shook a rain stick. I don't think I have any major blocks or problems to work with, but you never know. I am also aware that this is not the setting I would choose to lose control in. However, I am in a minority of one. All around me the other de-toxers were in a place safe enough to release their tears, their convulsions, their vomit in one case. Those facilitating were right there, taking everything in their stride, using intuition or buckets or tissues to help people along – whispering encouragements, occasionally two or three facilitators pulling on someone's arms and legs to provide physical resistance as they convulsed and contorted; sometimes enfolding someone in their arms.

Everyone participating in the 'intensive' has come here for that express reason and the people who do want to go for the big catharsis, hyperventilate away and get into their emotions. I was struck by two things: the permission to be exactly who you are with total acceptance by everyone else, and the feeling of unity and common purpose. Everyone is involved all of the time. There is no charismatic leader although Virgil is kind of a big daddy. It is extraordinary how the shared intent makes the experience gel. People just do what they need to do. No agonising over past history. This method completely bypasses psychotherapy. It merely posits the simple idea that *we are all each other*, that there is no difference between my pain and your pain. If we breathe together and remain attuned and sensitive we will know what to do. What I am doing for you now, you will do for me later. It can never be dangerous to work in this way because each person will be completely contained by the love and acceptance of everyone present. In between sessions we drank more freshly squeezed juice and went on until nightfall.

Alone in the star-studded, frog-croaking evening I walked beside the inscrutable blackness of the night river. I felt serene, trusting, imperturbable, relaxed. My arms and legs behaved as if I were walking in a dream – languidly through the pungent, humid Texas air scented with river smells and wild flowers. What came to my mind is that there are no contradictions in all the different strands coming together on this journey – my Jewishness, my love of Buddhism, my admiration for Cecil William's church and Lauren Artress' labyrinth, the pagans, the witches, and now this. All are committed to finding the divinity deep within our own lives, to recognising the illusion of separateness. The same clothes in different colours. Someone once said:

> *Learning is finding out what you already know.*
> *Doing is demonstrating that you know it.*
> *Teaching is reminding others that they know it just as well as you.*
> *We are all learners, doers and teachers.*

On the Sunday people told their stories and talked a bit about what brought them into this work. Virgil was a millionaire businessman who was so insecure he used to have himself paged at the airport so he could feel more important. He was, he said, "addicted to everything – alcohol, cocaine, you name it" and reached the bottom of the barrel in self-esteem. He thought all his unhappiness could be solved if he just had more money. He was on the way to his third million when he had a complete breakdown, physical and mental. Intestinal cancer had metastasised in his body and after three lots of major surgery he was told there was nothing more that could be done. That's when he 'woke up and started seeking'. Through breath-work and diet and the 12-step programme he fought his way back to life. "I saw that the physical body could make such an extraordinary recovery and I wanted to tell others: 'I *know* you can get through it no matter how bad.' I can see who a person *really* is. The joy is to have them see it too." So he gave everything up, bought the piece of land they call the Well-Being Ranch and now tries to live by his own dictum: "What would it be like if we could step outside time and space and allow our spirit to guide us?"

Terri-Lynn was a top-notch hairdresser. "Pure misery brought me into this in the beginning. I knew I had to move on and take what I had learned to other people. Watching Virgil walk that path gave me the courage. I let go of everything – the hardest was my custom-built beautiful car! When I asked for guidance, I knew I couldn't keep it. I was making $100,000 a year as a stylist, but I gave it all up trusting I'd be taken care of. The 'I' that was my ego surrendered and the whole world bloomed as I let in the passion. My whole body is *you* and I'm willing to let go of every single piece for *us*. Every ounce of me is ready for this *we*." Now she, too, lives in a trailer and feels for the guidance over a map to see where she should be.

Carol Ann resigned her job as Director of Nursing to follow the path. She had a failing immune system and a lot of health problems yet couldn't help herself. A breath session gave her a profound understanding of the connectedness of all things. "I started to change my diet and go deeper into who I am and who I am not. I realised I wanted to leave conventional medicine. My parents counselled me not to quit my job but I had to. I am making a commitment to be of service to this planet, to go wherever guidance sends me. I know, with every cell of my body that this is a great adventure of discovery. We are moving into a collective consciousness. The whole world has the same hopes, the same dreams, the same fears and the same things that hold us back. I want to learn to really trust my intuition and to get rid of attachments."

Philip was working for a government agency. He fell in love with Carol Ann and gave up his job to join her. A gentle soul of few words he works full time at the ranch fixing up the old trailers. "Trusting guidance has been a marvellous journey for me," he says. "I'm working on many issues and I would like to thank the others here at the ranch who saw the perfection in me."

Suzette, my roommate – a beautiful woman who is partly American Indian – described herself as having been "an uppity hippie involved in holistic health – a bit holier than thou – then, of course, I married an alcoholic. I had to ask myself, why was I inviting wrong energy into my life. I began to become conscious of all the things that were not supporting me in my life. I used to judge people until I saw that I was reflecting my own issues. I started working on that critical, judgmental person that I had become. I began to understand that when you 'walk your talk' you impact everyone you meet. I had to take responsibility for cleaning up my life. I started addressing my own fears, embracing them in the darkness of the sweat lodge (a Native American purification ritual). As I went into the abyss I knew that there was no separation. Whatever I *was*, I was getting back."

Elizabeth had been a social worker before she came to live at the ranch. "All I want to say is, just get rid of the fear in your life!," she said. "I am now deeply committed to following guidance. I love the Principle Group. I love the de-tox work. I have never had such support in my life. I have a life that I never thought possible. People helped me for no other reason than they wanted me to be who I really was."

Patricia Ann, who had been cooking for us, said, "I don't have a choice. I simply have to be here. I want to cut through all the 'stuff' in my life and find joy." She is a soft, pillowy woman with a body like the Venus of Willendorf. She always hated her shape, she says, having grown up, like we all did, in a world where Twiggy was the desired icon. Her life was a history of abuse and pain until, by some miracle, she found herself at a healing seminar and began to make some positive choices. She met a few people from the Principle Group and then, having bided her time until her four children were grown, seized her freedom with both hands and left home to live in her car. She is now a reflexology and de-tox practitioner. "I hesitate to use the word healer", she says modestly, "because it is somewhat involved with the ego. We're not doing anything but seeing the perfection." (This is just what Nuala Ryan would say.) On the Internet she met Mister B., a computer programmer. They found each other in cyber space and began to fall in love. Now, for the first time in her life, she has called in to herself a man who adores her exactly the way she is. She has introduced him to her healing world and they have both found love and contentment while they gently make the difficult transition from virtual reality to the real thing. It was lovely to see them together – Mister B, a big, shy, craggy guy who said very little but was just *there* for her all the time. It was a big step for him to participate in the de-tox but he did it.

In the afternoon I sat by the quiet, green river that flows softly through this part of the Texas hill country. I remembered Thich Nhat Hahn once saying, "Breath is the bridge which connects life to consciousness, which unites your body to your thoughts. Whenever your mind becomes scattered, use your breath as the means to take hold of your mind again." That is so true. Simple, conscious breathing is one of the great healing techniques available to us. It is at the heart of our relationship to God. The word 'inspiration' means 'to breathe life into', the word 'enthusiasm' means 'to be possessed or inspired by God'. So much is encoded in our language.

Out in mid-stream a family of ten turtles had climbed on a rock to sun themselves motionlessly – their old, wrinkled necks holding up their wise old heads. They didn't seem to have any problem with the oneness. The river, the rocks, the air, the sun, their bodies all breathed together. I could feel my own senses sharper, my vision clearer. Everywhere there were iridescent dragonflies, sulphur-yellow butterflies, an intoxication of birdsong. Growing wild along the lanes and tracks were riots of Black-eyed Susans, Indian Paintbrush and Texas Bluebonnets. America is such a beautiful country and so full of paradoxes. This was deep in the heart of Texas, John Wayne territory, the Lone Star State, where the cultural stereotype is the quick-on-the-draw hero living and dying by the gun, but here was this little community of people courageously trying to live by spiritual guidance moment by moment, with no security of any sort. Somehow, the two polar opposites manage to co-exist.

Earlier in the day someone in our group had said, "We have so much power coming through us collectively it *has* to make a difference." Someone else said; "As I see it, self-centred thinking is the root of all unhappiness in life. The only important thing is to help each other do what you love to do. If we're each doing what we love and not trying to manipulate each other, there can be only love. We can get to a place where there is no self, a place where we are not really separate." It seems so obvious when you think about it. How have we let ourselves get so side-tracked from greeting the God in each other, from honouring the magical spirit and taking the responsibility for being truthful with ourselves? Is it really so hard? When people elect to come together in communities such as this for the purpose of healing not just themselves but the larger whole something dynamic happens.

And then it was all over and I got a ride back to San Antonio with Patricia Ann and Mister B. They wanted to show me their city – the home of the Alamo – before I left for Florida and generously put me up in the magnificent old Victorian Guest House which they manage across the street from their tiny flat. So my time in Texas ended in style and with an unexpected special gift. Patricia Ann brought her guitar over and sang me a sweet, soft song of her own composition; "Out beyond the stars, I'll come home ...." They both got up at 5.30 in the morning just to drive me to the airport. It made me feel quite tearful. Two people who have triumphed over isolation and abuse, who have been through so much hardship, yet in spite of it all are still are able to love and to give. This is spiritual practice in daily life. A life of gentleness.

Words are not the only form of prayer. Many people pray through the witness of their lives, through the work they do, through the friendships they have and the love they offer people. Mother Theresa has said; "Be the living expression of God's kindness; kindness in your face; kindness in your eyes; kindness in your smile; kindness in your warm greeting." The important thing is to bring conscious awareness into the everyday acts of cooking, mothering, gardening, caring. To do them with *intent* instead of a kind of rushed resentment or impatience. I learned a lot from Patricia Ann – a fine woman living truthfully.

Monday May 6th

And now I'm sitting on the white coral shores of the Gulf of Mexico watching the local wildlife. Art Deco houses, the colour of sour cream and jelly beans, sleep in the sun. A bewildered-looking baby in a three-wheeled racing pram has just zoomed past on the hard, white sand pushed by a jogging woman with a workout body in an acid-green micro bikini. Flocks of clockwork sandpipers are going about their daily business of scouring the surf for things to eat. Oyster catchers stalk on twiggy legs and a couple of sleek cormorants, ace dive-bomber pilots, perch on wooden posts preening themselves.

I am in Florida where the abundance, voraciousness and fecundity of tropical flora and fauna – always with a slightly malevolent edge to it – takes me back to the South American sojourn of my childhood. If you stand still long enough you will be consumed – by rampant vegetation, by insects, by snakes or alligators – in a casual, dispassionate way. Nothing personal. Human beings are merely part of the food chain and exist here only by constant vigilance. A handy leaflet for tourists describes first-aid measures in case of spiders, sunburn, diarrhoea, stingrays, jellyfish, water moccasins, coral snakes, rattlers! Every year hurricanes and typhoons lash the land. People construct air-conditioned, screened dwelling places and drive in sealed cars but the swamp is still there, biding its time. Everything appears lazy, easy, paradisical but I am not fooled. I feel a great awe and respect for the seething powers that everywhere watch and wait. How did the Seminole Indians whose land this was, ever manage to survive? ...

This warm, aquatic land is so different, so unique – an endless river of grass blown by a wind which seems to come from out of the pre-historic past, making its imperceptible journey to the sea. The Everglades; a fragile, perfect ecosystem. There are no other Everglades in the world.

My cousin, Trish, lives in Florida and I had taken this detour to visit her for a few days. It was meant to be a bit of time out from the spiritual quest but of course it wasn't. The animals saw to that. We took a trip out to the mangrove islands on the estuary in a boat hoping to spot a manatee, the very shy, herbivorous mammals who are an endangered species. We caught a tantalising glimpse of a pair of nostrils as they surfaced to breathe, but that was it. Much more rewarding was the wonderful bird life. We came within a few feet of a nest of little baby pelicans being fed by a parent bird. There was an osprey's nest, snowy egrets, blue herons, white herons, little herons, baby herons and a solitary night heron almost invisible among the mangrove roots. Best of all was a tree full of magnificent frigate birds soaring on their great wings – the largest wing-span per body weight of any bird. They fly all the way to South Africa without ever landing on the water because their big wings would become water-logged and they'd never be able to lift off again.

In contrast, the sleek, crested cormorants have no oil in their feathers. They allow themselves to get deliberately water-logged in order to stay down longer when they fish but then they have to dry off so you see them perched about on posts and tree roots with their wings stretched out like a couple of washing lines hanging with damp feathers. Then, oh joy! We were returning back towards the dock when a pair of dolphins leapt out of the water near our boat. Then a third. Sleek as silver spume, they danced around us for a while like messengers of the Gods, then vanished into the horizon. A fried oyster sandwich at the Lazy Flamingo completed a perfect day.

After my family left California in the early fifties we went to live in Brazil where my father found work as a journalist on a Yiddish newspaper. The windows of my bedroom had shutters that I was supposed to close against the perils of the tropical night but I couldn't bear the hot, wet stuffiness so I defied my mother after she had kissed us goodnight and left it open a couple of inches at the bottom. One night a snake came to my bedroom through the open shutter. I woke sometime between midnight and dawn with the feeling of a heavy weight on my feet. There, illuminated by the February full moon was a huge boa constrictor curled at the bottom of the bed. I don't know by what miracle I had the sense to understand the importance of this magical happening but fear never entered my head. Instead, excitement, conspiracy, a feeling of having been chosen, of having a secret that nobody else need ever know. I touched his cool, dry smoothness with the tips of my fingers. The snake had chosen *me*. I covered him gently with the sheet and slept. In the morning he was gone but that night he returned and each night throughout the whole month of February my beloved animal spirit graced me with his presence – always coiled in the same place, never trying to come up nearer to me, always gone by morning. Then one night he didn't come and he didn't come and he didn't come. I thought he had been killed. I was distraught. I finally told my sister and she thought I was lying. "You're always making things up", she said. But she kept her promise not to tell. On the night of March 13th I was sound asleep and in the darkness before dawn I felt the familiar weight on my feet. I didn't need to look, I just knew it was him and I was happy. In the morning,

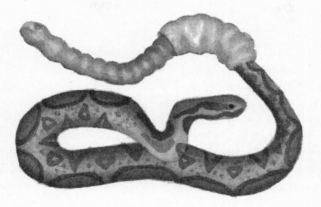

there was the circular indentation on my covers and in the middle, a perfect snakeskin. He had left me a gift (a sign? a symbol of re-birth? of transformation? All my adult life I have pondered the meaning of his gift.) I never saw him again but I kept the snakeskin for years until it finally disintegrated into a box full of dusty scales.

After our day on the estuary, Trish and I were relaxing on her screened veranda talking when there was a sudden power cut so we sat on in the delicious blackness with only a candle – realising after a while that we had unconsciously dropped our voices to a whisper. Out of respect for the powers of the night? Outside looked like Africa with no street lights or house lights. Only the stars and the night sounds of cicadas and distant dogs barking. "Pay attention", said the swamp. "I am right here. Don't think you can push me back again into some handy category labelled 'primeval past'. Without electricity you wouldn't last long. No air conditioning, no burglar alarm, no water pump, no computers. Don't turn your back on me."

After a few hours the fault was apparently repaired, the lights came on again and normal life was resumed, but we read in the paper next morning that a huge snake had got into the generator and caused the shutdown. Hail, snake medicine! Mother nature, I hear you.

In this same mood of sober respect I borrowed Trish's car and drove south to Corkscrew Sanctuary – another one-of-kind – the only place left on earth which contains such a concentration of huge old bald cypress trees. This must be what Florida once was – lettuce lakes, water meadows, cypress groves – a minutely dovetailed, finely tuned, interrelated eco-system. Tiny mosquito fish everywhere creating their own little expanding ripples looking like a million raindrops falling on the surface of the swamp water. They feed on the mosquito larvae thereby virtually eliminating the mosquitoes. Many creatures live in this habitat but there's no telling which ones will choose to show themselves to you. I saw red cardinals and white ibis fishing for crayfish. I saw three otters, a large alligator thrashing about in a pool and another, smaller, one dozing on a log inches from my feet. I saw a pileated woodpecker with a bright red crest, a nest of noisy wood storks and a breathtaking pair of barrelled owls just sitting and watching. We looked at each other for a long time and I felt that extraordinary deep sense of privilege at being allowed to be included just for an instant in their world. Suddenly, there was no difference between my body and the body of the owl. I blended and merged – my eyes simultaneously looking into and out of the deep, unblinking pools of owl eyes. My spine breathing like a tree, a million particles of golden light coursing through my veins, the late afternoon sun filtering through the forest canopy, the humid, tropical warmth damp on my skin. "I am the swamp. I am the moss. I am the otter, the tree, the sky," sang my bones. "I am the heartbeat of the Earth. There is no 'other', only this oneness." The sensation lasted only a few minutes but the rhapsody of it will stay with me. I was happy – filled up with majesty, with love for this world.

There is a poem by Rumi, the 13th century Sufi mystic, which describes exactly how I felt at that moment:

> *As salt is resolved in the ocean*
> *I was swallowed in God's sea*
> *Past faith, past unbelieving,*
> *Past doubt, past certainty.*

Valerie Andrews, in her lovely book, *A Passion for This Earth*, writes: "Each day I remind myself that we are not here to control the environment, but to learn lessons of humility and surrender. When I am capable of that, my life takes on a wholly different meaning. I no longer feel so small and separate. It is as though I am being held by a power that is both infinitely great and infinitely tender."

Flying along in mid-air en route from Miami to Pennsylvania a voice came over the intercom: "Hi there, folks! We're still up the front here doing all that pilot stuff for you. The plane you're riding in today is a 727, take-off speed so and so, flying speed five hundred and something miles per hour. That's considerably faster than a bullet shot from a Colt 45."

No wonder we feel weird after a four-hour flight. As we make a perfect landing the voice purrs, "Don't you wish you could do that!" As I left the plane, he was standing by the exit looking like a toothpaste ad. "Great landing," I said, with a rather feeble impromptu attempt at irony, "and extra points for modesty." He laughed. "I don't need to be modest, I'm a pilot."

Philadelphia; the historic City of Brotherly Love and of the Declaration of Independence. More recently it is also the birthplace of the Jewish Renewal Movement. I arrived on a Friday and took a taxi straight to Rabbi Julie Greenberg's apartment. Julie's name was given to me by a friend in London and when I'd telephoned her she spontaneously invited me to Shabbat dinner, the Friday night Jewish tradition. I was welcomed by the three delightful and extremely bright Greenberg children, Rosie, Rafael and Zoe.

The Sabbath commences one hour before sunset and it would be hard to exaggerate its importance in Judaism where it is compared to a bride (the indwelling spirit, the Shekhina), coming to greet her bridegroom, (the Jewish people). More than anything else, it is the Sabbath that has held the Jewish people together through all their vicissitudes. We began by each lighting a candle and sending the Sabbath light to somewhere special. We sang a prayer, we blessed and broke the bread, we ate the vegetarian lasagne and salad, we sang more songs and played games with the children. It was such a lovely evening. The atmosphere of joy, fun, lightness and goodness was sparkling and embracing.

A very slight young woman with a radiant face like Audrey Hepburn, Rabbi Julie Greenberg is a radical, lesbian feminist, the founder and director of the Jewish Renewal Life Center which offers a unique training programme in Jewish spirituality and community building – encouraging participants to explore and deepen their understanding of what it means to be Jewish. She is learned and able as a rabbi as well as having a fund of energy for promoting awareness and change from within – finding ways to interpret the ancient Hebrew religious texts which are appropriate and acceptable to today's communities of unconventional and non-traditional families. Her own is certainly the latter.

Julie is a dedicated and brilliant mother, currently negotiating to adopt a child from Guatemala, and I have rarely met such open, friendly, confident children as hers – proving, if proof were needed, that love and community are more important than convention. Over the next few days I would have the chance to get to know her better and hear her views.

The Jewish Renewal community do not have their own synagogue. They rent their sacred space from the Summit Presbyterian Church. I joined them there for the Saturday morning service conducted by Rabbi Marcia Prager – assisted by several others – a guitarist, an Indian tabla player, a young man who teaches Otiyot Khayyot (translated as Living Letters), a Tai-Chi-like movement meditation where the practitioner forms the Hebrew letters of the alphabet with her body.

They began with a beautiful opening song which acted like an echo-sounder in the ocean of my racial memory and my eyes instantly pricked with tears. Everyone was adorned in rainbow-striped prayer shawls and jewelled, embroidered Indian caps – the festive air reminding me that worship is supposed to be joyful, at least some of the time, and not solemn as it usually is. It was a scene of cheerful confusion – babies were squalling, kids charging about, a mentally handicapped child who loved the music joined in, unself-consciously, with a loud tuneless drone practically drowning everyone else out.

"Any distraction," said Rabbi Marcia, beatifically, above the din, "can be turned into a way to *feed* your prayer. Build it into your foundation – the place from which you call out your songs of praise; your songs of love. These are the new ways in which we davven (pray) – so opening, so delicious! When we stand in the light of that love we *get it* – the oneness! Prayer is about coming home to oneself, to a place where there is no separation, where we are not alone, where we are welcome at any time, where there is always someone to wipe away the tears.

> *"Blessed is the Source of Life of all the World*
> *Whose Image is mirrored in my own*
> *Whose Freedom challenges me to be free*
> *Whose Teaching makes of me a Jew*
> *Whose Wisdom opens a blind eye*
> *Whose Compassion commands us to clothe the naked*
> *Whose Justice bids us to free the captive*
> *Whose Love calls us to lift the fallen*
> *Whose Unity demands that we care for all life*
> *Whose Being provides us with infinite possibilities*
> *Whose Torah guides my every step*
> *Whose Wonder removes sleep from my eyes,*
> *that I might wake to the wonder of life."*

The special event of this Sabbath day was a naming ceremony for the newest member of the community, a baby boy, Morry, born to a lesbian couple, Susan and Moon (by the kind contribution of donor sperm provided by a family friend). They already have an adopted Chinese-looking toddler and together they made a beautiful little family. Everybody showered blessings on the baby and sang to him:

> *"For each child that's born*
> *a morning star rises*
> *and sings to the universe who we are.*
> *We are our grandmothers' prayers.*
> *We are our grandfathers' dreaming.*
> *We are the breath of the ancestors.*
> *We are the spirit of God"*

"We welcome not only the new-born child but all our new-born souls on this new morning," said Rabbi Marcia. "For each one of us a morning star rises, singing to the universe, proclaiming what we may not yet know which is *who we are*. We are the God Walkers. Not just talking the talk but walking the walk – holding the love that flows from Creation to us and back. We stand in the oneness." She talked about the four-letter name of God – YHWH or Yah – "those aspirant consonants which, in the absence of vowels, can only be pronounced by breathing." This 'breathing of the divine name', freed from the shackles of gender, informs the community's frequent translation of 'God' as 'the breath of life'. Divinity is immanent. It is the indwelling spirit. It is all around us. It is the essence in which we exist.

There was more davvening and lots more singing and dancing. When I hear those old Yiddish folk melodies something atavistic happens. I am back in the shtetl of my grandmother's grandmother – the joyful yiddle diddle di di, the sobbing voice of the cantor that tears the sky and wrenches your heart open – I feel it in the deepest place where I live. Other spiritual paths are attractive and stimulating but this wonderful, light-filled, un-dogmatic Jewish renewal stuff gets me in my bone marrow. It is everything I always wanted Judaism to be, so generous, so inclusive – bringing all the gifts of the feminine into the language and blessings of Jewish spiritual life.

The tears just kept coming – an ancient well of bottomless grief – and I knew with sudden clarity that one of the reasons I write is because my father never lived to finish what he set out to write. He never wrote beyond the pain barrier. He wrote once removed, and now he is removed completely although, like today, he comes back in the music he used to sing and I hold his hand in the chain of ancestors whose breath I am, whose dreams I am. I write because I want my voice to carry over the seas and over the land stained red with the blood of all my kin who died – children, shopkeepers, poets and fiddle players. They can't shut me up like they did them – starved, shot, gassed, bulldozed into mass graves, incinerated.

Once when I was about 12 years old my father sent me to fetch his pipe from where he'd left it in his desk drawer. I saw a little bundle wrapped up in a handkerchief tucked at the back of the drawer and unwrapped it. A small bone fell out. "What's this?" I teased my Dad, "Planning to get a dog?" His face crumpled. "Oh Lali, I didn't mean you to find that. It is a child's bone from Auschwitz." Mortified, I didn't know what to say as my father sobbed into his hands. I wish we had buried it. If I had known then what I know now I would have done something to lay the past to rest but neither of us knew how to help the other and the unquiet ghosts looked on.

I write because I want to get hold of the world, because I want to heal the wounds, to bury the bones, to gather up and make sense of the fragments of me that are scattered around the globe. Who are the women who live inside my body? The madwoman and the goddess, healer and the whore, the witch and the lover, the murderer and the mother, the concentration camp guard and the saint? I write because I want to know them, because I am Everywoman.

Someone who noticed me weeping came up and quietly put an arm around my shoulder. I turned towards her and buried my face against the soft cloth of her dress. She held me and we stood there in the oneness, holding the love that flows from Creation to us and back. It was one of those precious moments, an affirmation of the legitimacy and beauty of feminine spirituality as manifested in kindliness and motherliness, a reflection of the sacred healing power within women and nature. If the Shekhina is the Jewish Goddess, the indwelling spirit, the Sabbath bride – I felt the brush of her wings in the arms of a stranger.

Anyone, man or woman, who wanted to was welcomed to come up and read from the Torah – an activity traditionally reserved for men only. Wrapped in their beautiful prayer shawls like a flock of tropical birds, members of the congregation gathered around to feed from the holy scriptures. It seems crazy that gender should ever have anything to do with this. The only criterion should surely be whether the person is or is not willing to participate in the mystery. Traditional Judaism has committed many crimes of patriarchal injustice against women. What the Jewish feminist rabbis and scholars are accomplishing is a revisioning of what Judaism might be. In fact, it is nothing less than a revolution. It has never been static anyway. As Julie Greenberg said, "I have such faith and trust that Judaism will evolve. 3,000 years ago what Judaism looked like was slaughtering animals in the temple. It has continued to grow and change and evolve since the beginning."

> We prayed:
> *"As we bless the Source of Life*
> *So we are blessed.*
> *And our blessings give us strength*
> *and make our visions clear.*
> *And our blessings give us peace*
> *and the courage to dare.*
> *As we bless the Source of Life*
> *So we are blessed."*

Not a word of the old patriarchal stuff during the entire service.

After the rituals and the singing, that other cornerstone of Jewish life, a wonderful feast, was provided with bagels and cream cheese. I was in heaven.

When I met up with Rabbi Julie a few days later I wanted to know what had brought her to the rabbinical path. She is such a pixie to look at and so surprisingly unlike any image you might have of a rabbi. "I grew up in a home that was not at all Jewish identified but very spiritually connected – particularly to nature," she said. "My mother was a single mom with five kids. She always had a relationship with God and there was constant ritual happening in the family – the dog's birthday, a kid coming home from camp, the burial of a pet mouse – lots of celebrations and observances. I never really grappled with, 'is there a God or isn't there?' I was just a person of Faith with a capital F. I always had a sense that wondrous things like the intricate structure of DNA were *beyond random chance*. Such complexity! Such perfection! All the resources are there. We have everything we need. And now? I don't think of a person in the sky – more of a flow of events, a creative force, a principle of transcendence and development at work in the Universe.

"In raising my kids Jewishly I have come across the difficulties of talking about God. I teach them that 'God is a spirit in the universe' or 'God is what makes us love each other', but then we read these particular stories where 'God says to Abraham blah, blah, blah'. I've really thought about how do you hold both those things at once. Now I feel much more at peace with it. Both those ways of thinking about God have been *metaphors* and myths of our people. Some of the stories may be violent and patriarchal but you don't have to take them so literally. You can discuss them, put them in a historical context.

"I was lucky because I was able to enter into the whole meaningful tradition in a circle of radical, feminist Jewish women. We created something we called "Dyke Shabbas"! For as long as I can remember I very much understood the need to have equality for women and for womens' voices to be 'out there'. I grew up in the Civil Rights movement and became a full-time feminist organiser. As an adult I began to put all these things together and re-connect with a Jewish path. As I became more identified as a Jew I became more sensitive to injustices I hadn't addressed. I know the black ghetto problem in the U.S. right now is much worse than the anti-semitism but I also know that it is all part of the same climate of not having respect for differences and not letting each other flourish. The root of all those problems is the same – fear and intolerance.

"In Dyke Shabbas we met together every month for years for a pot luck or a celebration, for teaching or davvening. We changed all the Hebrew liturgy into the feminine. If we thought any concept was too patriarchal we simply re-wrote it. It was so exciting and it became a more and more central part of my life. We were not very learned but we made up our own rituals and ceremonies. As an introduction it was most loving and endorsing and not merely a negative reaction. Having reached the limits of what we knew and what we could teach each other, a lot of us went on either to graduate school, or to Israel or to become rabbis. It wasn't my life's ambition to become a rabbi but I was hungry for the learning. I wanted to do my work in a Jewish context and it has served me well and enabled me to do a lot of worthwhile things."

In addition to her rabbinical practice, Julie has started a summer camp for the children of 'alternative families' – the Mountain Meadow Feminist Camp. She has a syndicated newspaper column on single parenting, she teaches workshops on 'Parenting as a Spiritual Path' and she runs the Jewish Renewal Life Centre which offers participants a year of immersion in Jewish living and learning, training in spiritual practice and community building skills. The goal is to produce more lay leaders in their own communities, to take the ideas and visions of the ever-growing Jewish Renewal Movement as a whole out to people who are hungry for it.

"Several different strands of American religious life came together to produce the Jewish Renewal Movement," Julie explained. "One of those strands was all the Jews who had been flocking into Eastern religions and, finding meaningful things there, now beginning to return and discover the hidden riches within their own tradition. Then there was a resurgence of interest in the neo-Hassidic, the Kabbalistic, the dancing, the song, the joyful stuff that Marcia Prager teaches. The *heart* and *body* parts of Judaism. The *passion* which had been largely ignored for a long time. The third strand was feminism which said women need to have a voice and women need to have equal leadership. And there was maybe a little New Age flavour as well."

For a generation of post-Holocaust Jews the Renewal movement is clearly fulfilling a crying need. It is growing rapidly and its institutions are becoming stronger and stronger. In a people who have collectively suffered so much pain and shock and hurt there is a longing for homecoming. There is a huge appeal and people come from far and wide to the Life Centre wanting to take something of Jewish spiritual renewal back with them to their own more conservative, traditional Jewish communities. Leadership is gradually being passed from Reb Zalman Schachter-Shalomi, one of the creative founders of the movement, to a younger generation of which many are women.

Respect for diversity is one of Julie's great passions. I asked her how difficult it was walking her talk and bringing up her little 'alternative' family. "I can't imagine anything I'd rather be doing than raising these three children," she answered. "It is a complete and utter joy. Of course it would be great to have more helping hands with chores and paying bills. I don't live with a partner but as to difficulties ... it depends what circles you're moving in. 'Family' is a very strong value in Judaism and even orthodox, traditional people are lending support to alternative families. Gays and lesbians are often criticised for undermining family values, but then if they try to start their own it's, 'How dare you?' so you're damned if you do and damned if you don't." She shrugged expressively. "I've carved my own path. I'm not exactly in the mainstream Jewish world.

"When I started rabbinical school there was 100% discrimination. There was not one single 'out' gay or lesbian rabbi of a mainstream congregation anywhere in the world. In a very short number of years we've made a lot of change. At this point the issue of gay rights is very much on the Jewish agenda in all the non-orthodox parts of the world. The Reconstructionist College has a non-discrimination policy for applicants, students and graduates and the Jewish Reconstructionist Federation has a non-discriminatory policy for hiring rabbis. That doesn't mean, of course, that there is no discrimination, only that the policies are in place and have come about because of lots of education, lots of dialogue, very intense struggles and years and years of hard work. This has happened between when I graduated in 1989 and now. A revolution within the past few years! And not just because of gay and lesbian people but also allies who understand that anyone's lack of rights diminishes us all."

One of Julie's support structures is the B'not Eysh, the Daughters of Fire, a friendship circle of Jewish feminists. "It has been a very powerful leaven in the bread of feminist Jewish life," she says. "We want to have a voice in shaping the future of Judaism so we have created our own 'old boys network' where we systematically invite each other to our congregations and our campuses. We ask each other to write papers. We footnote each other. And it is working. The books are getting written and the subject is beginning to reach a much wider audience." There is even a coven of Jewish witches who call themselves the Covenant Group, working to integrate Wicca with Jewish practices. They call on the four directions, the four elements and the four mothers from the Old Testament – Sarah in the East; Rebecca in the West; Rachel in the South and Leah in the North. They do rites of passage rituals and fertility rituals and birth each other's babies. The orthodoxy, of course, are terrified that the traditions will be lost and that Judaism is under threat but, as Julie says, it has always evolved and will continue to do so. If a religion is to be a living thing, it must be relevant to people's needs. It must grow and change.

There were two more women I wanted to talk to in Philadelphia – two amongst the many wonderful feminist thinkers and Jewish community leaders contributing to a fast-growing interconnected network right across the United States. I wanted to learn more about Jewish Renewal which had left me reverberating like a struck tuning fork. They invited me over to visit them in their home one evening and we sat around the kitchen table with cups of tea.

Phyllis Berman is the programme director of Elat Chayyim, a spiritual retreat centre in the Catskill mountains dedicated to providing warm, supportive community programmes where people can discover more personal meaning and joy within Judaism. She and her husband, Rabbi Arthur Waskow, a leading light in the Jewish Renewal movement, share their home in Philadelphia with Rabbi Shefa Gold, who teaches spiritual leadership and Jewish meditation and is also a performer and composer of passionate spiritual music.

"People were tired of, bored by, disconnected from formal structures that didn't speak to them," said Phyllis. "It became very hard to go into a stuffy synagogue where things felt very alienating, where people dressed in a particular way and synagogue life was often based on how much money who gave. The Jewish Renewal movement is part of the whole climate of change that came into being in the late sixties – the Civil Rights movement, the feminist movement, the political struggle against the war in Vietnam, the anti-authoritarianism, the communes.

"There was something coming up in people – a feeling of wanting to be part of a global transformation," said Shefa. "People were struggling to find what form that could take and experimenting with lots of different meditations and practices. It was sort of inevitable that people who were Jewish and were part of an awakening would realise they had some kind of heritage they could work with. They had to take whatever gifts they had and come to terms with their own identity saying, 'This is a way into the depths, this is the way I am.' With myself, first came the awakening then the question, 'what kind of form do I put this, in that has integrity?' The Reconstructionist idea is that Jews of every generation have reconstructed Judaism. In order for it to stay alive and working to fulfil peoples' spiritual needs it has to be continually recreated, adapted, relevant."

I asked, "How can something that has been so steeped in tradition evolve?"

"But it hasn't been so steeped in tradition," answered Shefa. "That's the myth. Learning history has been very liberating for me. I can see how Judaism really has changed through the ages. It hasn't been monolithic but taken different forms, different languages, different ways of approaching God. People have always made it their own. They had to otherwise it would have just become a relic."

And when I asked about the re-interpretation of texts from a feminine perspective, Shefa reminded me that there have always been re-interpretations too. "The fact that women are coming more and more into central positions of leadership means the imperatives for those re-interpretations will become louder and serve to inspire one another more. In a tradition where women were separated from men there was probably a lot of re-interpretation all along only it never filtered through to the mainstream. There is a poem about a young woman being at Mt Sinai with her brother but since *she* had a baby on each hip *he* was the one with a spare hand to write down the word of God! Women in all traditions are beginning to understand that whoever did the writing made our history and that it may only be half the story. Women hold up half the sky.

"In Judaism, the Torah (the Holy scriptures) is like a mirror. As you change you see more revealed in it. The irony is that although Judaism teaches that in each generation we need to bring ourselves new to it there is this extremely loud minority of more traditional Jews that argues against changing anything and acts as though the whole nature of doing *midrash*, of making interpretation, is un-Jewish. However," she added philosophically, "from a wider perspective, the conservatives form a good balance to the forces of change. I'm here playing my role but I'm free to do it because somebody else is playing theirs. It's a push-pull balance. From that perspective they are not my enemy. Altogether we form an organic whole."

Phyllis shook her head. "I stay pretty far away from the orthodox world because it's too painful," she said. "There are still too many places where women don't count and aren't listened to. It's like an obliteration of everything that I feel we stand for. I can speak much more easily to a spiritual person who is Muslim or Christian or Buddhist but who is also a feminist and trying to make the same changes in their community as we are in ours, than I can to an orthodox Jew. It feels to me that there are some basic truths in the world and in each religion we try to express those truths in our own ways but the realities are not so very different. One of the best of my life experiences is that I can be really at home sitting in a church or a mosque and not feel disloyal, but rather connected to a larger world. Even before I was part of this community I had been reaching out to other communities, not because I didn't find what I was looking for in Judaism, but because I found good people and wanted to know what was behind who they were. I was also interested in why, when people wander out into the world and find a pretty good fit, do they 'come home'. I asked Zalman and he said there's probably something in the memory whose sounds and smells, no matter where you go, you're most at home with."

This certainly resonated with my own delight at finding so many places where I have felt comfortable, where I have met with good people, very spiritual people from the pagans to the Christians, the Buddhists to the witches. There are wonderful people out in the world doing terrific work but when I was at their service on Saturday it made me cry because it reached something that was unfathomable. A pit of bottomless longing. It made me feel like an orphan.

"Everybody goes back home in order to heal," said Shefa. "The place that needs to cry is the place that is wounded. There is something in our development as humans that takes you back to your birth religion in order to do the healing – something about going back to the beginning to set it straight inside you."

Does that mean there is a whole generation of post-Holocaust Jews like myself who are adrift, longing to belong somewhere, to come home, to heal the wounds of the past? I asked.

"The Holocaust set us a spiritual challenge," answered Shefa. "How to find meaning? This is the context we all got born into – post-Holocaust anyone, not just Jews – and a lot of what we're doing is in response to that challenge. It's not an option to ignore it. It's part of what it means to live now – to grapple with not only what happened then but what is happening now."

And is part of the challenge to rediscover the Divine Feminine? I wanted to know.

"I don't think very much about the Divine Feminine," said Shefa. "In my own searching and experience, the highest level of the Divine is very much beyond gender, beyond duality. There is a level of wounding in myself – to do with the traditional 'maleness' of God – that I am trying to heal in order to make myself whole and bring myself back into the realm of the Divine. But it feels to me like once I have done that healing inside myself I won't need to look for the Goddess. In the deepest, deepest place in me is the knowledge that that's not where it's at. It becomes kind of irrelevant except in the imagery. I need to connect with the different images because I am a human and to be in relationship we have to be in relationship to *something* but it feels like the reality is much too big to fit into any gender confines."

Phyllis spoke up, "I feel very much like Marcia Falk, the West Coast poet who has just come out with a book of blessings. She is one of the feminists in this country who have pushed us to find other names for God besides Father and King – other blessings besides the masculine construction in Hebrew that begins the prayer 'Baruch ata ...'. It has helped me to do some healing around the damage done to generations and generations of women who have forever pictured the male God sitting on a throne and somehow seen themselves as less than that — *never* able to be like that. I feel that it is really important to have a mixture of images and of language so we don't get frozen in the Father/King picture. On the other hand, I, too, feel that the duality is not what it's about. It makes a much more cloudy and complex relationship with holiness.

"My struggle has been more about the presence of human women having an impact on the tradition — women in rabbinical schools, women being prayer leaders, teachers, writers — so that the stories that get passed down are not only from the male perspective. The notion that men were the only ones to make decisions has been so absurd to me. Even as a child I would change the words of the Haggadah (the Passover narrative) to *She* where it said *He* in the English translation. It was a long time before I realised you could do it with the Hebrew as well. I see it as expanding the gender. Making the holy names gender*ful* rather than gender*less* or castrated."

I had heard the Shekhina described as the Jewish Goddess and wondered what Phyllis and Shefa's thinking was on the subject.

"Well," said Shefa. "Shekhina in the Bible means *presence, immanence.* It became associated with the feminine while *transcendence* was associated with the masculine. For me it's not so personified. Again, it's genderless, within everything. When I am in a state of openness I perceive that indwelling spirit. The Shekhina is in exile when I am closed."

"I do think of the Shekhina in gender terms," added Phyllis. "I see it as the mothering quality — that which nourishes me. I see it in those people in my life who have been attentive, close to the earth, close to me, *aware*.

"But that can be dangerous and divisive," said Shefa. "In the realm of the Divine it's not appropriate. It's like an intermediate level of understanding."

My own feeling, when I first heard that you could think of the Shekhina as the light that you bring into your eyes when you light the Sabbath candles, was how beautiful an image that is and not divisive in any way. I can identify with it as a woman but it doesn't exclude anyone. It is another way for a lay person to feel a personal connection with an aspect of divinity which has been so dominated by male imagery. Women are claiming their right to come out of the shadows.

Also, as Phyllis pointed out, if you have a lot of women scholars studying Torah, they bring to the reading their life experiences, the perspective of the mother, the wife. It leaves a lot of room to find the stories that haven't been expressed yet or, that in an oral tradition, never got written down. "So many women in the Biblical stories are nameless or have just a tiny role ('He took so and so to be his wife'), she said. "And then there is what we call the 'white space', the unexplained transitions between one sentence and another when the whole world seems to change. These are the places in which we are invited to do all that interpretation. What happened in the spaces between the words?"

"So much of what women have done in the feminist movement has been to do with telling our stories," said Shefa. "There is a feeling in Judaism that the Torah is our story, our history, our acts of heroism. Against all the odds we have survived and the images and allusions are a language to help us understand our lives and talk about them. It's not just about what happened then, it's about what's happening in our lives now. Passover is a time when we reflect on our *own* liberation process. Part of what women are bringing to Judaism is this 'taking it personal' – talking about me, us, our lives. The stories are a blueprint pointing me towards a deeper reflection of my own life. Eliciting those stories and sharing them with each other is part of what we're asked to do as religious people."

"It seems to me that we're coming back to a much more organic way of living such as there probably was in ancient times where there wasn't a separation between going to synagogue and living one's life," said Phyllis, "where rituals and celebrations arose out of real life. Part of what we're trying to do as Jewish feminists is to make *real* what has become almost forgotten. We're asking, 'what was the spiritual function?' rather than accepting just an empty form. There was meaning to begin with and if there isn't meaning now we don't need it or we can create some. If we dig far enough, there is juice and it's just waiting for us.

"In order to make a community vibrant we also need festivals where people can get together two or three times a year to talk about the good times and the bad, the losses and the successes. We need times for celebration and remembrance. We need rites of passage. I've done wonderful ceremonies for menopause, for getting a job, for leaving a neighbourhood, for blessing a new home or a new-born child. So there are lots of vehicles although we've lost so many of them. We are revitalising both the ones that there were and the ones that there should have been that our modern lives need."

So what still needs to be done, I asked. "It's an ongoing process," answered Phyllis, "getting more deeply connected to the ground on which we stand, to the riches that our ancestors have to offer us. And as we heal the wounds of being Jewish we become more and more open to receive those traditions and not have our buttons pushed by them, to be able to transform them and pass them on to the children.

"One of the differences we've talked about a lot in the United States is between egalitarianism and feminism. Egalitarianism asks that women have equal access and equal rights in what still looks like a male structure. Feminism asks us all to look a little more broadly at what it has meant to be on the outside of a process without our input and in a feminist view of Judaism there is space for a lot of change that may not yet have happened. I'd like to see that change continue."

"For me, re-integrating religion and the arts has been an important healing process," added Shefa. "Art takes the raw feeling and transforms it into something that can uplift. It has the capacity to take religion out of the head and *embody* it. Embody, embellish and *birth* it."

Shefa and Phyllis – both beautiful, wise, thoughtful women who spoke with great depth and clarity. As we finished our blackcurrant tea and chocolate cookies, Phyllis told how one time during a Shabbat evening event, Reb Zalman started singing Jewish words to American tunes like Shenandoah. Suddenly her heart opened and she realised she could be a Jew *and* an American *and* a woman. All the separate parts of her could become whole. This is what is happening to me. The path of pilgrimage is becoming a path of healing.

Chapter 6

*'Each one of us carries a sacred space within us
and our challenge is to live from it
throughout our life's journey,
throughout our earthwalk.'*
A NATIVE AMERICAN GRANDMOTHER

When the writer Natalie Goldberg was struggling with what it means to be a Jew, her Buddhist teacher, Katagiri Roshi, said to her "When you get to the heart of Judaism you'll find Zen." Up until then she felt as if trying to understand Judaism was driving her nuts. It was like an ornate tapestry, she said, impenetrable. She got lost in the history, the Holocaust. Judaism seemed opinionated, sexist. Her teacher said to her, "Pay no attention to all that. Stand up with what you have learned here and continue to penetrate."

I understood exactly. All those Hebrew letters, like a graveyard of bones, were merely the container for the golden essence: "Let there be grace and kindness, compassion and love." There is no difference between the golden essence contained in all the divine teachings. I can be a Pagan and a Jew, a Buddhist and a Quaker. Each is a treasure of jewels. One does not exclude the other if I don't want it to. At the centre is stillness. At the centre I am connected to the great Mystery. It is possible to see beyond all the boundaries. My mind searched for a metaphor and I thought of the landscape of the Peak District of England where you can stand in a field and, as far as the eye can see, be surrounded by an immense greenness divided by a patchwork of stone walls into little plots – yours, mine, his. In the last analysis the divisions are manmade; nobody owns any of it. One day the stone walls will crumble but the immense greenness will be here long after we've gone.

In stark contrast to this loose-edged view of spirituality is the one held by the Amish, ultra-conservative Christians who have rejected modernity and still live in the 19th century without automobiles, electricity or telephones. They are a very private people who eschew contact with the outside world except to sell their produce. I would have loved the opportunity, while I was in Pennsylvania, to talk to some of the women, but it is well nigh impossible to penetrate their closed community without a personal introduction. The closest I got was driving around the small country back roads near Bird-in-Hand and Intercourse, two of their towns, catching a few tantalising glimpses of the Amish going about their business – a team of eight horses pulling a plough in a field; rows of plain, modest clothes hanging on washing lines; little horse-drawn buggies driving by at a brisk trot, barefoot kids in old-fashioned clothing in the playground of the one-room schoolhouse.

Thinking I might get close enough to speak to someone I made the mistake of paying $5 for a crummy guided tour of what turned out to be a fake Amish house and farm. I learned that they are simple, devout, family-minded people (no feminist theology or lesbian ministers here). The Amish don't believe in higher education so the children leave school aged about 12 or 13. Women wear long dresses, bonnets, capes and shawls, thick black stockings and stout black shoes. No adornment of any kind – not even buttons in case they might be too fancy. They are subservient to the men and anyone who transgresses their strict moral code or opts out gets shunned by the entire community including close family – a harsh disowning process that can never be reversed. It didn't appeal to me much, particularly the God-fearing bit, but there are obviously many virtues in a life of simplicity and honest toil in a farming community and I wished I could have heard an insider's viewpoint, but it was like trying to understand the Hopi or the Navajo by visiting an Indian reservation. You see what they want you to see and no more. Instead they try to divert tourists into their theme parks and quilt shops so that they will not be ogled and pestered and photographed. I had to leave Pennsylvania with my questions unanswered. A tourist instead of a pilgrim. I hate that.

At the airport I was so tired I checked in, went through to my gate, fell asleep and never heard the call to board the bus out to the plane. I suddenly looked up and found everyone had gone. I'd missed the flight. American Airways didn't have another until too late to make my connection to Boston. The old me might have burst into tears but, as the whole of this trip had been an unfolding in its own sweet way, somehow I felt calm and just trusted that things would work out. Luckily there was space on a Delta flight and they agreed to take me – amazingly at no cost – so I arrived in New York in time to catch the Boston connection after all and my suitcase even arrived too. Thank you, guardian angels. Thank you Delta.

I had come to Massachusetts to meet up with Linda Ward who had kindly driven an hour and a half to fetch me back to stay with her. This was another example of something which had characterised the whole of my journey – the kindness of strangers. The link was once again an introduction by a mutual friend which had led to this invitation. Linda Ward is an authority on the

Kabbalah, the ancient Jewish mystical and esoteric teachings which she has studied for 25 years. It is her life's work to demystify the body of teachings and present it to people as a set of tools for transformation. A combination of astrology, numerology and the Tree of Life, it is a system of divination and wisdom that I was hoping to learn a bit more about during the week.

The first evening of my visit coincided with a discussion group for young people that Linda has initiated in her home every month. She feels strongly about the importance of older people taking seriously their role as elders in society as well as being willing to learn from young people too. Amongst the treacherous rocks of Linda's own very unhappy childhood there was Faith, not an abstract noun but a wonderful older woman friend, a beacon, who inspired and encouraged her, so she is passing on the flame. The group consisted of about 10 young people, mostly men, in their twenties. 'Transformation' was the topic they had chosen for what turned out to be a very lively discussion. Linda's skill lay in making a relaxed, welcoming space where even the least articulate felt safe enough to speak and share their views. Like many young people I've met they seemed to have transcended the gender war and be really trying to understand and work beside one another to face the challenges of today's world. Looking round the circle at the shining, idealistic faces of kids the same age as the young men we make into killers and cannon fodder I wonder why we don't instead harness their fine warrior energy and their creativity into thinking about how to help the planet survive.

It was with these thoughts in my mind that I had an unusual encounter the following day. Linda's cleaning lady was meant to come but since she is an alcoholic and currently drying out at a de-tox clinic, her partner came in her place. George – a grizzled, scary-looking guy of about my age, maybe 60, with a long, grey braid hanging down his back, an armful of tattoos, a hard, slim body, black leather biker clothes and black cowboy boots. I was making tea in the kitchen and he was down on his knees polishing the lino when we got talking about his time as a soldier in Vietnam. He had been in the Special Forces – personally given his green beret by President Kennedy. "They had a way of hand-picking the loners and brainwashing them into killing machines," he said. "We were invincible." He had even volunteered to return for a second tour of duty. "I went back to cut off more ears and become a drunk and a drug addict," he said.

There were horrors upon horrors. Then, with a stricken look in his eyes, he sat back on his heels and told of the incident which finally penetrated even his blunted sensibilities. His platoon had been told to go into a village that had been supposedly taken over by the Viet Cong. When they got there all was eerily quiet until suddenly, from the surrounding jungle, they were attacked with great ferocity. In the midst of the chaos – flames, people running everywhere, gunfire, screaming – he noticed a woman squatting in the middle of the road and when he came near he saw she was giving birth. He delivered the baby, tying off the umbilical cord with a bootlace and cutting it with his bayonet. Picking up the slimy newborn and trying to help the mother to a safe place they ducked into a house and, inside, found a woman and two little children burning alive. He couldn't save them. At that moment he was finished with God, he said, and the image is etched forever in his mind.

Not long after, he got badly wounded in action and they sent him home to less than a hero's welcome as the tide of national opinion had turned against the war in Vietnam. In constant pain from his injuries, he became a morphine addict and increasingly violent in his behaviour. Two marriages failed – the last one leaving him with three little kids to bring up on his own. Finally he dragged himself to AA and with immense courage has arrived at the place where he is now – proud to be cleaning houses and taking care of his family. The metal plates holding together the shattered bones in his leg hurt him every minute of every day and he daren't take so much as an aspirin for fear that his addictions will imprison him again. I felt privileged to meet him – a free man. How ironic that I had been thinking only the night before about the terrible crime of sending young men to war. George was 18 when he first went to Vietnam. What to do with all the surplus testosterone is one of the great challenges of a post-patriarchal society.

In the evening I sat in on Linda's astrology class. Her students had been studying with her since the previous autumn and were already quite knowledgeable. It was all completely over my head as I don't even know the order of the star signs and, to tell the truth, have always been a bit sceptical about the value of astrology, but Linda was inspired. She was in her element – incredibly learned and able to hold heaps of information in her head, making cross references, coming at things from different angles, illuminating the esoteric nature of her subject. Whether or not the signs, the elements, the houses, the nodes, the aspects mean anything about anything, Linda uses them as a framework from which to extrapolate. She feels that she has constant guidance from a Master Protector and four Angels of Mercy, that her insights, inspiration and intuition are assisted because she couldn't possibly do it all alone.

On this occasion she talked mainly about the end of the Piscean Age, that began with the birth of Christ, and the beginning of the Aquarian Age for which we are now in a state of preparation and transition. It will be a time of hope, said Linda (although I also read somewhere that 2008 is supposed to be the year when a terrible earthquake will devastate Los Angeles). She prophesies that it will be a time of the coming together of science and the mysteries, faith and reason, technology and subtle energies. We will begin to work in smaller, more autonomous groups instead of large hierarchical, patriarchal structures. The last couple of decades have shown the illusory nature of security, she said. More people have lost their jobs and their homes than ever before. Suffering has multiplied. We've overdosed on plastic, run up impossible debts. We've forgotten who we really are – souls on a journey, not egos. We have forgotten to care for the world. We are not here to dominate the Earth but to *serve* it. The Piscean illusion, she said, is that we can somehow be rescued, saved. So we built The Church instead of finding God within ourselves. We've lost sight of our humanity but now a massive shift in consciousness is upon us. It is time for social justice, equality, responsibility. We are going to go through big changes in order to achieve a new society with a transformed purpose but this will not be easy as the old structures cannot survive in the new world. Organised religion will be replaced by the new spirituality – more equal, more inclusive – honouring all cultures, all sexual orientations. The New Age begins when it happens in your heart and we've already begun. Everyone is going to have to make a sacrifice. We have to ask ourselves: Can we work for the greater good instead of just for ourselves?

As Linda observed, we are already beginning to notice a big movement back to the Earth, feeling her pain in our own bodies, changing our relationship to her from an exploitive one to a reverential one. We are beginning to want natural fibres, organic produce, herbal medicines, less waste, less preservatives, fewer toxins and factory farms. We're starting to simplify, take more responsibility for our health and what we put into our bodies – getting to the heart of what's important rather than fighting to be right. More people will want peace, love, a morally and ethically inclusive society working towards unity.

None of this would be ready to happen, she said, had it not been for what has gone before. We couldn't learn about the heights until we had been to the depths. What we have had is an out-of-control, corrupt value system. We are feeling the effects of an obsessed, illusionary, deluded, addicted society controlled by desire and excessive greed. We are longing for meaning. Sex, power and money have all become pornographies. Once we understand that we are a sick society, the first thing we have to do is to get well, to become aware, to wake up and take responsibility. We are learning that we can't trust in banks, investments, insurance. They're all corrupt and falling apart. We're going to have to learn to live in the moment and not kid ourselves with false notions of security. We must breathe new life into the arts, culture, education, into a new sense of the everyday sacred instead of the old divisive religions. We must transcend our attachments to our old beliefs – going beyond illusion to true liberation. "Having chosen to be here at this extraordinary time in the history of the world, what part have you come to play?" This was Linda's parting question to her class. She asks them all to apply the tools, the hidden, esoteric teachings in astrology, to their own natal chart to find out what sense they can make of it all.

Linda is such a surprising person – coming, as she does, from a pretty terrible background to this blazing clarity. As she says about herself, she is not an educated or an intellectual person. It's a mystery how a stubborn little child raised in a bigoted Mormon setting had the sense to see through the religious propaganda and hold onto her own truth. She has a clear mind, a prodigious knowledge and the capability to put into words the insights she comes up with. The evening ended with me cooking the dinner for Linda and her husband Carl then the three of us flopping in front of the tele to watch the unspeakable, jaw-dropping Miss Universe pageant from Las Vegas – a hilarious contrast to portentous thoughts about the evolution of human consciousness.

Over the next couple of days Linda and I had many stimulating conversations where we carried on poking about in the themes that interest us both. She talked about the Kabbalah – a finely tuned, coded body of esoteric knowledge and wisdom that can be used to help you understand and negotiate all the obstacles and challenges that you meet on your spiritual journey. It is all in her head and she computes constantly but merely knowing the stuff is not enough. It is the spark of intuitive thinking which transforms the whole thing from a rubric – mechanical and technical – to a wondrous, spun gossamer fabric of insight and perception.

All my previous scepticism along the lines of 'how can you tell anything about a person just because they're a Leo or a Capricorn?' betrays a woefully inadequate understanding. It takes Linda more than three hours to do a Tree of Life chart (incorporating all the relevant astrological and numerological information) for someone. "A Tree of Life chart shows the evolutionary patterns of the soul," she told me. "It reveals the challenges that the soul will have to meet in this lifetime. It enables us to understand our divine nature and from that we can begin to evolve into the full awareness of who we really are – divine sparks." As her reputation has travelled far and wide, she is swamped by private clients including many famous people and several rabbis. "For as long as I can remember, all the questions I had as a child were about resolving the confusing paradoxes in life and finding purpose and meaning," said Linda. "All my conflicts were about the dualities and dichotomies in life – black/white, male/female, the darkness as well as the light – things that seem to separate people and cause them *not* to come to some kind of mutual respect. I didn't understand why religion didn't answer those questions, why education didn't, why you didn't learn them in your home. I didn't want to take sides. I wanted to celebrate the differences. I figured out that's what God was – the amalgamation of yin and yang, the balance of the polarities.

"I was also psychic but it was not possible to explore the world of the paranormal through conversations with my family. For a child who came from a family where none of this was discussed it was frustrating to have all these huge ideas and experiences and no one to talk them over with. I was called weird and strange and I realised that I would have to leave the family and the 'safety' of known reality in order to get the answers I was looking for."

It was after she finally left home and had been studying astrology for some years that she met Faith who opened the door into the Kabbalah. "She was the first person who *recognised* me. I wanted to be like her and it began a friendship that lasted for 26 years until her death. The Kabbalah is where I found my heart and soul. It embraced me and I felt as if I had come home. Everything began to make sense. It has given me a language to express all the things that intuitively come easily to me. It has assisted me at every level of my life's journey. It has been there to help me and to show me how to rise above situations and take the next step."

Z'ev Ben Shimon Halevi in the preface to his book, *The Way of the Kabbalah* writes;

> *Everyone is searching for something. Some pursue security, others pleasure or power. Yet others look for dreams, or they know not what. There are, however, those who know what they seek but cannot find it within the natural world. For those searchers many clues have been laid by those who have gone before. The traces are everywhere, although only those with eyes to see or ears to hear perceive them. When the significance of these signs is seriously acted upon, Providence opens a door out of the natural into the supernatural to reveal a ladder from the transient to the Eternal. He who dares the ascent enters the way of the Kabbalah.*

Kabbalah means 'to receive' and the centrepiece is the Tree of Life (shown as a pattern of interconnecting circles and pathways representing the attributes of the Infinite). Linda explains it as "the universal filing cabinet where everything has its place. Things that you would never think were connected at all are indeed connected by universal laws or universal themes. Once you understand it as the filing system for all symbols – the 22 major arcana of the Tarot, the 22

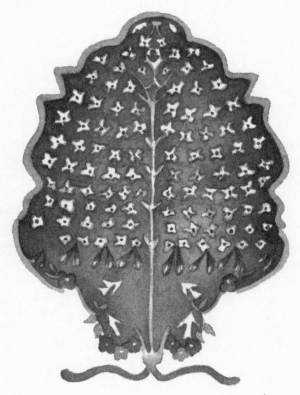

Hebrew letters, the 22 steps of consciousness – you can work out your place in the scheme of things. It is the means by which you can begin to discern the way a particular set of circumstances keeps repeating itself in your life. It is an endless revelation. Everything fits together. Each day I discover something new."

I asked how, since it all seems so terribly complicated and esoteric – perhaps deliberately so, to keep it in the hands of vested interests – the knowledge could be used by ordinary people who can't give as much time to it as she does.

"Well, numerology is the simple form," she answered. "You could start with that and from there you can progress to the Kabbalah. I didn't really know where to start. I was conscious of something but I had no awareness of what it was. It would have been easy for me to give up and stop asking the questions, but if I had shut off and conformed to what was expected of me I would not have grown in this lifetime. I wouldn't have become the person I can end up liking. I would have been bored. I would have had no creativity. I wouldn't have found the courage to be me. The wonderful thing about the Kabbalah is that it gets to the *core issues* of the individual very quickly. And with a little bit of understanding of what those core issues are, all the psychological pain and hurt seems to fall away. You are washed over by an unbelievable feeling of compassion and it's coming from *yourself* because you begin to see how courageous you were to have gotten into those experiences in the first place. It helps you to get to your authentic self – to find the value and the meaning in all the things which have happened to you instead of letting your anger, bitterness and resentment ruin the quality of your life. As you acknowledge yourself and your courage, as you *own* all those experiences that caused you pain, you transform them. They become the part of you that you can feel safe with instead of betrayed by. At the same time, you can begin to allow yourself to have the experiences you know you want and deserve.

"I used to be obsessed by the 'shadow', the dark side," she continued. "How does God deal with these things? I would ask. I had a tremendous longing to be close to some sort of Divine Essence but I could never connect with a God who discriminated against people. Being brought up in a Mormon home, you are not baptised at birth but when you are supposedly old enough to understand the significance. When the time came for my baptism, I was a bit ambivalent about the whole thing. Nobody had actually asked me. I wasn't quite sure about making a commitment to a God I didn't know yet based upon a faith I had not chosen for myself but they told me I had to – had no choice – or I wouldn't go to heaven. After the ceremony I asked the minister if the people in Africa would go to heaven if they hadn't been baptised and he answered, 'No. Even if they were baptised, *they* wouldn't go to heaven.' That's when I went into the cloakroom where no one could see me, buried my face in the coats and screamed at the top of my lungs. I had just been betrayed. I had been told I had to be baptised by a God I didn't want to know. If that's what God was, I hated him.

"Now, of course, I have formed a different impression of God. I feel as if I am being loved by a 'presence'. I don't think God works *for* us. I think God works *through* us. As we learn to live our lives in a way that's in harmony with all things, we're letting God be God within us. We begin to experience the real God which blesses and enriches us on all levels; mentally, emotionally, physically and spiritually. I've found a synthesis of those polarities I was looking for. The Kabbalah is so vast and wonderful – so inclusive and deep. It does not discriminate or alienate. All religions have their perfect place. It is only when a religion tries to own God and become exclusive that you *know* it is not rooted in love, therefore it is not rooted in unity, therefore it doesn't come from the Source.

"I've found a tremendous amount of serenity and peace now. The Kabbalah has enabled me to totally accept everything as a natural part of the evolutionary process. However it is not a cut and dried formula. You have to *live* it to see it working. You can't use it to help others until you have used it for your own clarification. There also needs to be a heart and soul connection to this information otherwise it is just words – nothing more than a mental game and a head trip."

'Heart and soul' is the dimension that Linda brings to her work. When she did a chart for me about my son she was in fine inspirational form. She knew nothing about him and yet the degree of insight and perspicacity was nothing short of astonishing. She took flight. There was a profundity in her interpretation that went far beyond the mere words into the realms of clairvoyance. By her own description, an ordinary little woman with no special education, something happens to her when she is in divination mode. A quickening. One observation after another, accurate, compassionate and helpful. It's as if she becomes another person, expanded, filled with that quality of inspiration – the breath of God – that brings the mystery a little closer.

Linda explained to me that in ancient times the Kabbalistic system was devised as a means of keeping safe the occult wisdom teachings of the Mystery Schools (Egyptian, Hellenistic, Persian) which were under threat from The Church. Using various means, such as Tarot cards, this esoteric knowledge could be hidden as a set of symbols – the language of the unconscious – that would always hold meaning for those with eyes to see. "The unconscious works through symbols," said Linda. "Some part of us will always be triggered and awakened when we look at them even if we don't completely understand. There isn't anything in the Tarot that doesn't have significance or isn't teaching you something about some universal law or theme. A good teacher's job, remember, is to help us *uncover* that which we have always known.

"All of a sudden, when it comes via the heart and soul, there's *recognition*. For me there was recognition that I had to take responsibility for my own goodness – that's how God works within us. There was also recognition of my 'soul vibration' and of my needing to become a seeker, an explorer entering the world of the unknown, honouring the bigger questions, aligning my will to something higher than needs of my ego."

So how does the feminine fit into all this, I wanted to know.

"In this area of our lives we are venturing into the unknown, into the void which is the domain of the feminine," answered Linda. "What we have suffered in the last 2,000 years is a preparation for us becoming strong and equal partners. We have to take responsibility for the part we've played in our own submission. It isn't all men's fault. How did the abdication happen? We allowed it." She drew a symbolic tree on a piece of paper. "At the top of the Tree of Life are the symbols of Hochma and Bina signifying Wisdom and Understanding, Soul and Consciousness. The mystic marriage is the marriage of wisdom and understanding. As we go into the Aquarian Age, women have a job to do. We're trying to unite these two things but in a new way, a woman's way – realising that there's strength in kindness, strength in compassion, strength in empathy. It's not a weakness to practice unconditional love. That is the Goddess. That is the feminine face of God. That is the Divine Mother loving us when we don't love ourselves, holding us when we don't know how to hold ourselves and when there's no one else to hold us. This is the age of empowerment for all – when women can empower men to be warriors and men can empower women to own what is in their hearts and souls. It's got to be mutual. I see the Kabbalah as presenting us with an idea of the Divine as embodying both male and female energies. I'm talking about a synthesis of opposites – the very thing I have been looking for all my life."

Linda's words kindled a spark of hope in me. Hope that not only she, but many other people may share these ideas. I love the idea of a 'mystic marriage' – healing the wounds between men and women, between human beings and other forms of life. It is about healing the Earth. It is the bringing together, the re-tying (re-ligio), the making whole. For me it is the very essence of spirituality.

"I also see the Kabbalah as presenting us with a code of ethics to live by," said Linda. "Not in the sense of taking the place of obsolete organised religion or ready-made, off-the-peg spirituality but in challenging us to take responsibility for our own value system. Not everybody is ready for this. It's about total accountability every moment of our lives – not so much a spiritual practice as a way of learning about the soul and its journey, about life and how it works and how things bounce off each other.

"I'm interested in using it as a tool to help myself stay on track with my own sense of integrity under any circumstance and that's important for me because I have never belonged anywhere. I didn't belong in my family or in the church. I could pretend I did but I knew I was pretending. I needed to be *who I am* – for all its loneliness. And I have found that I am not alone."

I salute her courage. The fear of isolation and ostracism makes many women distrust the truth of their own experience. We grow up trying to please other people rather than asking 'who am I?' Maybe we remember in the deepest rivers of our bloodstreams the thousands of women who were tortured and burned alive for daring to practise and say what they knew. I remembered the quote from a Native American grandmother that I once wrote down in my notebook so I wouldn't forget it: "Each one of us carries a sacred space within us and our challenge is to live from it throughout our life's journey, throughout our earthwalk."

On our last evening together, exhausted after such extensive discussions on the mysteries of existence, Linda and I felt peckish for a Cherry Tree Farms ice cream – the supremo, numero uno, best ice cream in the world that just happens to be made in a town nearby. So we drove all the way to Cherry Hill, Lunenberg only to find the little road-side farm shop besieged by other sensation-seeking ice cream junkies. We had to queue for 40 minutes being bitten alive by mosquitoes while the staff struggled valiantly to cope. The ice cream was divine when we finally got it, (if nothing else, I will have at least experienced this earthly manifestation of divinity), marred only slightly by thoughts that I must now Turn Over A New Leaf and begin to live according to the guidance from my higher self which says, 'No more ice cream and no more chocolate'.

By good fortune, also in the state of Massachusetts, lives my friend Lenore. We met as colleagues – both teaching courses – on the Greek island of Skyros a couple of years ago and I was glad to take the opportunity to catch up with her. What was originally going to be an interim respite from the spiritual search turned out to be another way of approaching it. Lenore is a beautiful, gentle person with a fine mind who has miraculously triumphed over much adversity in her life. It's impossible not to marvel that someone who could so easily have become screwed up has chosen not to be and, instead, radiates a great deal of happiness and contentment.

We walked among the intoxication of lilac trees in full bloom, along the beautiful riverside trail near her house and the mellow college campuses. In Lenore's town, Northampton, it just happened to be Graduation Day at Smith College – one of the famous women's colleges of the East Coast. The streets were thronging with happy graduates and their families. The tradition at Smith is to light 2,000 paper Japanese lanterns with candles in them and hang them all around the pathways of the college grounds. It looked enchanting and a jazz band was playing and people danced under the stars.

Lenore has recently recovered from an agonising spinal injury and told me the story of the long, slow healing process she had to go through – finally, as she said, having to learn her lesson the hard way that the Universe loves her. She has done a remarkable job of transcending the rough start she had to life. She is an accomplished practitioner of a therapy called Body/Mind Centering and loves the work she does. She paints, has wonderful friends and takes care of her health but this experience of being totally incapacitated has taken her to another level of deep understanding. As she points out, nothing that happens to you is intrinsically good or bad – it is only your own subjective response that makes it so. If you can free yourself from your conditioned reaction and just be with what *is* rather that wishing it otherwise you will experience a great liberation. Joy and happiness aren't down the road, through the gate, in the rose garden. They are here and now, doing what you do to the fullest.

She worded it all so well, but I didn't write any of it down at the time and by the morning I could remember the sense but not the words. I was sitting at the breakfast table with her feeling thick and dull, wishing I had a better memory for dialogue when she said, "I wish there was some way I could assist you with your research". I had never presumed to impose on her but her offer suddenly seemed like another unexpected gift – like meeting Nuala Ryan in California – so we borrowed a cassette recorder from her neighbour and taped a conversation. Lenore is lucid in her thinking, always thoughtful, always true. She has a wisdom and a maturity far beyond her youth and I admire her tremendously. She has done a course of study at The Option Institute with Frank Mosca and now incorporates his philosophy into her own healing work.

"When you have decided that any state you're in is OK with you because that's what *is*," she said, "then you create an environment of compassion and freedom. I can only tell you that I love it. It's been the best I've ever gotten to – not fixed but flowing."

Righteousness, she says, – the conviction that I know what's best for you – is the number one enemy of any kind of harmonious co-existence or, indeed, any kind of future for life on this planet.

"If I know that you ought to be a Christian and go to *this* church and believe in God in *this* way and read *this* Bible and I'm going to get a gun and kill you if you don't because I'm so sure I'm right, that is no different from the righteousness that says, 'you had better eat organic vegetables, you'd better cry out all those old suppressed tears or you'll never be a fully realised person.' The illusion that there's an 'in' on the truth for your emotional or spiritual goodness, is exactly that – an illusion. Once I know that I like God my way and you like God your way and that's all there is then I also know that today's a sadder day and yesterday was a happier day and that's OK too. You can't bang your head against what is. I hate that my grandmother's dead. But she is dead. How does banging my head against it serve me?

"Once you come into seeing that everything that *is* is intrinsically OK in that it has no inherent meaning or value it just simply *is*, you come out of the kind of fear-driven righteousness that has gone on behind everything we've ever learned. We've always been taught that things are better or worse than other things rather than, 'I'm choosing this because I like it for me.' How could I possibly know better how anything ought to be. We don't get to make up the universe. Stuff happens – all kinds of stuff happens. If we go around hating or judging what *is* we're trapped in a kind of righteous un-freedom.

"I can join things, go to the synagogue, revive my Jewish roots but that would just be what I wanted to do because it felt meaningful for me at a personal level – not because there was any answer in it – not kidding myself that there was an intrinsic truth or superiority in it at some ultimate level. It is the most painful and liberating information to know that you are the one at every moment choosing your response to things. No one else makes you do anything. You're not in control of everything but you do create your response to it. You don't create reality but you are entirely in charge of your perception of it. Some of what you want is going to come true, some isn't. If I go into therapy wishing things had been different, I'm going to die miserable. But if I go into therapy because I want to take charge of my moment, that's different. I've come to see planning as a pleasure you make in the moment rather than an imagined, fearful future that you attempt to control."

I asked Lenore if she had a concept of the Divine.

"For me," she answered, "it's comforting to believe that I'm a cog in a huge, huge wheel that's so big I can't entirely see it . There's something about the way the universe is going to play everything out that's OK with me. Life has been created and it's either going to carry on or cease and within that I know that I wish to take responsibility for myself but I also feel cradled in the arms of something so much vaster than me that I can't even begin to conceive of it. I find that inability to conceive it or explain it to be a great comfort – humbling and therefore comforting. I believe the world is absolutely *vibrating* with available love. The universe is made of love and I am part of that. I believe that is the nature of being and when you stop making up fear, all that is left is this vibrating OK-ness of miraculous love. I can never be alone because I am part of the great mystery of the universe and in that sense I am divinely loved. That I don't have to explain and that I can relax because I *cannot* explain the mystery of my existence is all part of divine love."

So what is this all this need for meaning? I asked.

"People love knowledge but if you believe you must *know* in order to be free it's still the same old trap – that you get to be OK later. Your greatest challenge is to know your freedom right now. The only way we can get to a global peace is by transcending the idea that, 'I have a better understanding of what's good or bad than you do.' As long as I can only be happy when you do what I want, I will never just be busy with the business of my own passions. I will only be busy with the business of trying to control you in order to get the world the way that I believe it has to be in order for me to be OK. So you've got this ping-ponging righteousness going on all the time but once I know that what *is* is OK and I've got no 'in' on what's good or bad, I'm certainly going to spend my life going after what I value."

But then, I wondered, is there anything worth fighting for?

"Yes!" she answered emphatically, "because then you admit that you're doing all of it out of your passion and out of your joy. Do I have to know that the ruling junta in El Salvador is bad in order to wish to support the revolution? No. How do I know they're bad? They obviously don't think so. I just know which one I prefer. It may sound like a very fine point, but distinguishing between your wants and your preferences, your passions and your likes as opposed to

GOOD and BAD – some kind of *truth* about RIGHT and WRONG is, to me, the path where personal and global freedom lies. This good/bad thing is crippling and distorting. People are going insane because of this drive to be right. There is so much fear and control. Also the 'in' on the truth is constantly changing – fashions in health fads, ways of bringing up children, yesterday's guerrillas become tomorrow's freedom fighters. If I think a suicide bomber is bad, I'm caught in the trap. If I want to exercise more today than I did yesterday, that is different from believing exercise is good and I'm bad for not doing it."

"So what does spirituality mean to you?" I asked.

"All of what I'm speaking about *is* my spirituality", answered Lenore. "It is the choice to re-pattern myself out of the constant, constant categorising of everything into good and bad, right and wrong, of the dread of the judgements of others, of the need to be in control. It is the choice to come to a state of challenging myself to *be* the authority. In my view, spirituality is to make of *myself* a tolerable, enjoyable, loving, caring universe – the ultimate authority on what goodness is for me, and stop trying to be good for someone else or make them good by my standards. Taking responsibility is the ultimate compassion. Nothing outside me will ever validate me unless I feel OK about myself. I believe our intrinsic nature is freedom and well being. I ask myself, 'Can you generate those qualities for yourself now?' There will always be a reason why it's scary or unsafe to do so but I can examine the reason and come into the choosing again and again and again. I can choose to be OK in the moment even though I might not be getting everything I want (job, health, man). I can say, 'Let's acknowledge those wants but live for this moment.'

"We project a phenomenal amount of disappointment onto ourselves and onto each other. A big, big part of our suffering is that it's not OK with us. We're sad that we're sad, mad that we're mad, depressed that we're depressed. It's crazy! If I *long* for something it means unhappiness now, but if I merely want something it's only a want. It could change. In the never-ending now, things are intrinsically OK. On this soul journey, this life we're in, just let be what *is*, then choose how you are going to respond. Out of this you create a life-style of compassion.

"My work is helping people to take the authority back to themselves. That doesn't mean I am entirely realised in this but that I practice it each moment. I knew I wanted to simplify my life and go for immediate beauty. There is no intrinsic meaningfulness in this but at some point I understood it to be a path of meaning for me. You can't win a competition of meaningfulness. There is no hierarchy of meaning. There is no external authority. Just the internal authority that knows it's OK moment by moment. For example: Do I believe that life is going to constantly remind me of my past or do I believe I'm free to have a fresh response? Then which one of those beliefs do I want to invest in and cultivate? I don't know what's going to happen one second from now. I only know that the things I believe in are given energetic support by the energy I invest in them. I would ask someone, 'Do you believe you can change or don't you?' At every given moment you stand at a fork: 'I'm afraid I won't be able to' and 'I believe I can'. Then you have a choice which way to go. You only have to live one moment at a time and *now* is always manageable."

Lenore is a convincing advocate, living as she does by these teachings and being the serene and generous person that she is. I had a few niggling questions about some of the more sweeping statements. There could be a danger of sounding glib. Such is the nature of the human race that *now* is not always manageable. We are frail creatures and we can be broken by pain and horror. We can be shattered by brutality. We can be driven insane by torture. However, I agree that as a general philosophy to live by for as long as you are able, it's a helpful one. I certainly think that when we are ready to face ourselves and take responsibility for our soul's journey we are on the way to freedom. When we can transcend religiosity, find our own authentic spiritual voice, live with uncertainty, accept paradox – only then do we arrive at a place where we can touch the mystery. Guidance comes in unlikely places. I once saw a quotation printed on a packet of tea which read:

> *"I am a partner with change – moving every moment*
> *to make union with all things. Nothing happens to me.*
> *Things happen."*

I am such a jackdaw – always avidly collecting spiritual titbits – that it went straight into my notebook alongside the more homely:

> *"If you always do what you've always done*
> *You'll always get what you've always got."*

Which was pinned on the notice board of my gym! Thus do we progress on the winding path to enlightenment. These themes are echoed in Gary Zukav's sane and timely book, *The Seat of The Soul*, where he talks about the very purpose of our being as an evolutionary process towards this kind of personal responsibility which he calls "authentic power" (as opposed to "external power" which is driven by fear, violence and competition). Authentic power loves life in all its forms, does not judge what it encounters, it perceives meaningfulness and purpose in the smallest details upon the earth. When we align our thoughts, emotions and actions with the highest part of ourselves we are filled with joy, purpose and enthusiasm. We have no thoughts of bitterness, life is rich and full. An authentically powered person is incapable of making anyone else a victim, or using force.

It would be wonderful if we could find again the sense of a *reverence* for life that primal cultures such as the Native Americans and the Aborigines had. As Zukav says, "The decision to become a reverent person is essentially the decision to become a spiritual person." If we truly accepted the principle of the sacredness of life and regarded every living thing and the Earth itself with reverence it would be impossible to act selfishly or greedily, we would harm nothing, we would stand in awe, we would walk the Earth with a deep sense of gratitude. His book is about choosing to become conscious of our intentions and our actions, choosing to respond to life's difficulties with compassion and love instead of fear and doubt. These are the first steps toward this 'authentic power'. My personality and my body are the vehicle for my evolution. The decisions and choices I make affect my evolutionary process. If I choose consciously I will evolve consciously.

Lenore's Options method will be a useful technique for clarifying my choices. By an internal dialogue of questions and answers I can become more aware of what's going on and invoke guidance from my 'higher self' (a term I use cautiously because it is a rather New Age, trendy concept too often bandied about without a deeper personal understanding of its meaning). In fact, my guess is that if you can formulate the questions you probably know the answers. Whenever I have asked, 'help me to see', help has come. Whenever I have asked for guidance I have received it. Lenore spoke of prayer as "an opportunity to connect with the bigness". To me prayer and reverence are one and the same – an acknowledgement of Divinity in all forms of life. An acknowledgement of Grace. Before I left, Lenore gave me a healing treatment. I felt very blessed to be so loved and cared for. She is an authentically empowered person, making conscious choices, responding to the beauty of the world, revering life.

And so … another flight, another city. New York.

A bumper-sticker spotted on Broadway proclaimed, "There is absolutely no substitute for being totally unprepared". A good motto for the Big Apple. No matter how much I think I'm ready, it always takes me by surprise.

Chapter 7

❖ ❖ ❖ ❖ ❖

'I was the channel between earth and sky
And the song poured effortlessly
Rich, sweet and rare.'
MARY WICKHAM

The urban craziness is only one aspect of New York and I am lucky enough to be staying in astonishing luxury with my friend Sue out of town. After a lifetime of bohemian poverty, Sue unexpectedly came into some money and bought for herself and her two teenage children a gorgeous house in six acres of garden with a swimming pool, an orchard, a tea house and a canopied patio for al fresco dining. Last time I saw her she was pregnant, living in a basement flat in London and trying to scratch a living as a journalist. This time she sent a stretch limo to meet me at the airport and I basked in the brief fantasy of being a star. It made a startling counterpoint to what was to come next.

Later, Sue dropped me at the train station and I rode up to Manhattan where I'd arranged to meet my eldest daughter, Femi, under the clock at Grand Central Station. It was miraculous to see her standing there looking so beautiful – miraculous that two people can arrange to find each other out of all the billions of people in the world, in the middle of a huge city, at a precise moment in time, coming from different ends of the earth. The purpose of our meeting was to travel together to darkest Brooklyn to meet up with African-American women who, although born and brought up in the United States, have found their spiritual roots in Africa and become priestesses of the Yoruba religion. A Nigerian friend in London, himself a practitioner of the Yoruba religion, had kindly given me several contacts.

My daughter Femi is a Yoruba. Born 35 years ago in a small mud house in a village in western Nigeria to a woman who died in childbirth, she was abandoned, along with her twin brother, Tim, at a little Catholic mission hospital by their distraught father who had just helplessly witnessed his wife's death. The new babies were very tiny, weighing only three and four pounds and their chances of survival were slim. Then fate and chance worked their strange alchemy and aligned my destiny with theirs. At the time I was 21 years old and newly married with a young baby of my own. My husband, Richard, had been employed as News Film Unit Manager – part of a team helping to set up the first television station in Africa and we were stationed in Nigeria for three years. I had no stomach for the indolent ex-pat life but without qualifications or work permit the best idea I could come up with to involve myself more in the life of the country was to offer my services as a voluntary helper at the nearby Catholic mission hospital which I knew was woefully overcrowded and understaffed.

On my first day there I saw the baby twins, just a few weeks old, lying in a cot on the veranda. They were sick and thin and would clearly soon be just two more wretched additions to the heart-breaking infant mortality statistics. Here was something useful I could do. I suggested that I take them home and try to get them fit and well so they would stand a better chance if their family turned up to claim them back. The hospital was glad to be relieved of the responsibility, gave me a bag of old nappies and put them in the back of my car. The rest, as they say, is history. All attempts to trace the twins' family came to a dead end so they stayed with us. At the end of our tour of duty they had become too much a part of our lives to leave behind so we applied for permission to take them back to England and, once here, adopted them legally through the British courts.

The twins grew into beautiful, gentle youngsters. Their shaky start in life seemed to have given them an extraordinary drive and determination to make the most of any opportunity they were given. Tim became a jeweller. He makes delicate things in gold and is also an excellent sportsman. He held the Amateur Boxing Association Light Middleweight Championship title for two years running and has boxed for England in many parts of the world. He now lives in Holland with his Dutch partner and their two exquisite children.

Femi trained as a dancer at the London School of Contemporary Dance and the Alvin Ailey School in New York and now earns a good living in theatre, films and television. But always through the twins' lives ran the sadness of exile. "Who am I?" "Where do I come from?" "Where do I belong?" We told them what we knew about Yoruba culture and traditions, art and customs but nothing could really fill in the missing pieces of their jigsaw. Then began the extra-ordinary sequence of events that led to the joining of the circle, the putting into place of the last bits of the puzzle.

Just before Tim and Femi's 21st birthday Richard returned to Nigeria for the first time since we'd all left, to make a film for the BBC and while he was there, decided to do some detective work into the twins' origins. Together with a Nigerian friend and colleague from the old days, he went to all the villages in the vicinity of the old Catholic mission hospital, making enquiries and speaking to chiefs and elders. They put an announcement out on the local radio station in both English and Yoruba asking if anyone remembered the incident 20 years before when a woman had died giving birth to twins as the children were alive and well and anxious to trace their relatives.

A young man named Sunday Omoniyi, who had been eight years old at the time of his mother's untimely death, happened to be listening to his transistor radio and heard the announcement. He came rushing to the rendezvous and the moment he came into the room, Richard knew he must be their long-lost brother – the resemblance was so striking. Through him we were able to trace their elderly father, the other brothers, Simon and Dayo and their sister, Julianah – herself the mother of six children including boy and girl twins. They all travelled from their homes for a meeting with Richard, poring over the photos, hardly daring to believe the miracle that the twins had not perished. There followed a feverish exchange of letters, presents and tape-recorded messages but more than anything else in the world I wanted to fix up a reunion for their 21st birthday. It seemed a pleasing symmetry as I had been 21 when they came into our lives. I wanted them to come full circle in the symbolic year of their coming of age. To enter adulthood with a sense of their true identity and a knowledge of their roots seemed the greatest gift we could give them.

And so it came to pass. Planning the trip was a labyrinth of crossed wires and last-minute panics but I never really doubted that it would happen. And when we finally stepped off the plane at Lagos airport we were engulfed in an unbelievable welcome that took us completely by surprise. The entire, extended family were there, crying, singing. Their old father came forward dancing and praising God. Femi and her sister wept in each other's arms. The love and joy were so spontaneous and wonderful that all twinges of anxiety were instantly dispelled. We were swept off in a delirious party of motley vehicles honking and driving crazily all over the road and for the next three weeks subjected to an orgy of kinfolk – a first-hand illustration of what it means to be part of the famous elastic African family – enveloped in the legendary warmth and generosity of traditional hospitality.

As guests we were given the best they could provide. If there was one bed, we would have it and they would sleep on the floor. If there was one fan, one bucket of water for washing, one piece of fruit, they would go without and give it to us. They had so little themselves and lived in conditions which most Westerners would call slums but with so much cheerfulness and good humour. I felt ashamed of the wanton wastefulness of our own society. Neighbours would leave a chicken or a few eggs on the doorstep knowing there were extra mouths to feed. What we were privileged to glimpse was something very precious and unforgettable: the age-old West Africa. Not the corrupt, inefficient, chaotic, crime-ridden modern nation but the true Nigeria, a land of family life, courteous, generous and rich in traditional values. This is the twins' true heritage, their birthright. Tim and Femi came of age in the land of their birth and now had strong roots from which to grow out into the world.

In microcosm, this is the story of the great African Diaspora and the longing for homecoming experienced by many descendants of those who were torn from their families during the centuries of exodus and captivity. Deep in my bones I understand this as a Jew. Femi understands this as a Yoruba and as an adopted child. Together, as mother and daughter, we wanted to share the experience of meeting other women who had found their own way to come home and there she was under the clock at Grand Central Station. A miracle.

We managed to get ourselves on the right train (Duke Ellington's famous 'A'Train!) out to Brooklyn – not the worst neighbourhood by any means but very down-at-heel and neglected – such a stark contrast to the opulence of the Hudson River Valley that morning. All the clichés were right there as we stepped out of the subway station. It looked like a war zone – garbage cans overflowing, an abandoned, chain-link fenced basketball court strewn with broken glass, a posse of disaffected 10 year olds with baggy shorts and back-to-front baseball caps sitting on a wall, smoking. Confidence was not restored as we passed by a young man lounging against a lamp-post on a street corner, cleaning his fingernails with a bowie knife. His tattered T-shirt proclaimed "Fuck the World". A notice above a door leading into the gloomy, beer-smelling interior of the Domino Bar said, "No Weapons, No Drugs"; a peeling church sign-board read "Crack Kills, Jesus Saves" and spray-painted graffiti on a billboard proclaimed "Niggaz With Attitude". I was the only white person to be seen. Both Femi and I were grateful to be abroad in the menacing streets with each other rather than on our own while at the same time being aware that with all the scare-mongering about walking around New York in hostile neighbourhoods the real danger is to project something that isn't there and create a negative energy vortex which becomes self-fulfilling.

I said to myself, "Either we turn around and get out of here, giving in to fear and prejudice or we remind ourselves that this is also a place where ordinary people live, where families grow up, kids play, old people sit on their steps and watch the world go by." I do not want my life to be governed by fear. Neither does Femi. We walked on, arriving at an old brownstone on Jefferson Street at the appointed time.

Iyalu Opeodu's daughter, Ayo, let us in the front door and showed us upstairs to their small apartment. Iyalu, a large-beamed, dark complexioned African American woman wearing traditional Nigerian dress and an elaborate web of crocheted hair on her head, was guarded and non-communicative at first. With such a long history of suspicion and mistrust between black and white in America – maybe I was being naive to imagine that reserve could be swept aside in a tide of goodwill and shared ideas. Once she warmed up, however, and realised our interest in her spiritual practices was sympathetic rather than hostile she began to speak about the feelings of pride and identity gained through the re-discovery of the religion of her ancestors. It has been, for her, a lifetime search for a sense of 'home'.

Born and bred in Brooklyn, Iyalu has no real knowledge of where her original forebears came from but found herself drawn, from an early age, to African music, dancing, drumming. "Myself and a few others were the pioneers although we never looked on ourselves as such," she said. "Once a week at school assembly when I was a kid they would show films on geography and so on. There would be movies about Africa and the other kids would laugh at the antics of the 'savages' but I never laughed. Here were people who looked like me, in terms of skin colour, and I was curious to know more about them. Remember, this was the fifties, the days of Tarzan and Jane, so you know what was being put out there – Africans were portrayed as wild and naked with bones through their noses.

"The first time I saw a woman with natural Afro hair, I remember thinking, 'Oh my God! When I get big I'm gonna wear my hair just like that. That's beautiful!' I think it must be part of my mission here on this Earth because I've always felt very strongly about people of colour and how we were made to look funny – the whole Amos 'n' Andy thing and the blackface minstrels. They never appeared funny to me and when I saw pictures of Lena Horne or Billy Holiday I was spellbound. They were my heroines. I knew there was a connection, a relationship between me and them.

"I loved music but at school the only choice was between the baton twirlers or the drum and bugle club. Then one day someone gave me a record of Olatunji's 'Drums of Passion'. I took it home and danced and danced until I could dance no more. I just knew it was my music. This was the culture where I belonged! I found out about some African dance classes going on up in town and there I met someone who took me to the Yoruba Temple where I was introduced to the 'Orisha' – the Yoruba deities. Up until then I had been searching, searching for a spirituality that spoke my language. I was originally baptised into the Baptist Church but that wasn't 'it' for me. I always felt like a very important part of me was missing. I tried Episcopalian, Pentecostal, Methodist, even Catholic – going with my friends to their different churches – but I never felt, 'this is the place' until I was introduced to the Orisha. As soon as I came into the Yoruba Temple I knew I was home. It has truly been the thing which has given me my identity and strength."

Iyalu's family history has been lost, particularly the connection to Africa. Her mothers' father was from one of the West Indian islands. Her maternal grandmother is 100% Cherokee and her father's side are from the Deep South. "I only know that sometime, several generations back we must have come from West Africa," she said. "One day I'd really like to do a past-life regression and find out *where*. In the meantime, whenever I'd meet anyone from the African continent I'd quiz them; 'what is it like? what do you do? tell me about your ancient traditions, your culture.' I was amazed. So much was like how I was raised as a child – the folk tales, the customs, respect your elders, it is sacrilege to throw food out or not share it and so on. I was desperate to travel to Nigeria but I had to wait until the time was right and that wasn't until after I was married to Kabaisi who is a full-blooded Nigerian."

Iyalu met her husband to be at the Yoruba Cultural Centre. He was over on a visit and dropped in to listen to a group of them singing in the Yoruba language which they were trying to learn but which nobody really knew. He said he could understand every word and was astonished at how well the language and ritual had been preserved. (I was thrilled to hear another example of a vestigial memory, at the deepest cellular level, of remnants of things repressed for centuries, bearing fruit.)

"You know," said Iyalu, "when our forefathers and foremothers were first brought to the Caribbean and the Southern plantations as slaves, they were forbidden from speaking their own language. Tribal groups were broken up so that people were unable to communicate with each other but a lot of the Yoruba language, culture and religion was preserved in places like Brazil, or Cuba or Puerto Rico where it could be disguised as Catholicism – a mixture of Christianity, Santeria, and voodoo. The Orisha could double as Catholic saints – biding their time until it was safe to come out of hiding. We are very grateful to the Cubans especially because they are the ones who really gave us back our culture – most of the initiations until recently were done through them. The first lady who transplanted the Orisha in New York was Obanjoko, a Cuban priestess who initiated somebody here so people didn't have to keep going to Cuba.

"Over here there was a lot more freedom but Orisha worship still had to remain clandestine. Orishas had to be hidden. You'd come into someone's house and see a cabinet filled with pretty soup tureens but inside were really the Orisha. Now it doesn't have to be like that and shrines can be openly wherever you want them."

The Yorubas, as I came to appreciate during the years I spent in Nigeria, are an exceptionally creative people with a vigorous culture. Throughout the years of the wretched and dolorous slave trade the people, their music, art and religion were dispersed all over but the result was that, in spite of everything terrible that happened, many seeds fell on fertile soil. In Venezuela, in Haiti, in Jamaica, the worship of the Yoruba Gods and Goddesses flourished – covertly at first but the trickle became a torrent and in recent years has rapidly been gaining in popularity throughout the United States.

"Most definitely," said Iyalu. "At one time it was basically just New York. Now you have Philadelphia, Miami, Washington DC, the West Coast. I even know someone in Oklahoma and it's there too."

The Orisha are deities of which there are five or six principle ones: Olódùmarè, the Supreme Being; Obàtálá, the God of Creation; Oshun, the River Goddess; Osanyin, the God of Medicine; Orúnmilà the God of Wisdom; Sango, the God of Thunder; Ogun, the God of Metals and Creativity; Yemonja, the Goddess of the Sea and up to 400 subsidiary ones. Iyalu is a priestess of Yemonja. She described to us Yemonja's special characteristics: "Yemonja is the Mother of all the Orisha, the Great Mother. Being the Mother, she is the giver of nourishment. She is the patron of children. When you think of Yemonja you think of the ocean and the vastness. As her priestesses we are moody – changing, like the ocean, with the moon and the tides. She is the epitome of womanhood at its fullest – mysterious and deep. Whereas Oshun, the River Goddess is Miss Pretty, feminine and beautiful, Yemonja is the creator who gives birth, out of

whom flow the rivers and the streams. She is tough love – fierce and protective. She has the power to create and the power to destroy."

I asked Iyalu why she chose Yemonja to be her particular Orisha. She explained, "We don't choose the Orisha, the Orisha chooses you. You go to a Babalawo for a reading [a Babalawo is a High Priest or Priestess and diviner of the sacred oracle], you put on the *aleke* (special beads), you serve a period of apprenticeship and then when it comes time for your initiation they sit you down to find out exactly who is your Orisha. I wasn't surprised when it turned out to be Yemonja – my mother always dressed me in blue, I love blue and blue is Yemonja's colour.

"When I am serving her as a priestess I don't exactly *become* her but the energy just sort of comes over me and it isn't me any more. Other people can see it even if I'm not aware of what's happening. My duties might consist of being present at initiations, maybe washing the Orisha, maybe making the herb water or cooking the Orisha food for feast days or holidays. Someone might want a godmother ceremony with the *aleke* or a birthday celebration. Once you are initiated you go through several ceremonies to find out what your powers are. Some people are healers and they would study the herbs and medicines, others do the work of removing curses, changing bad luck, winning back a lover. Still others have the ability to deal with the dark side. It's part of your training to be responsible with those powers although of course people do abuse them. We all have the potential to use our powers for good or evil. You can't have one without the other and it's up to each individual to know the difference.

Defending yourself is one thing. Setting out deliberately to cause harm is another. You never get away with it. There will always be repercussions."

Iyalu explained that the Yoruba religion is very earth-based and nature oriented. "We are constantly aware of our connection to the elements, to Mother Earth and to the animals," she said. "Although animals are used in ceremony, it is always with great respect. You pray over them, you ask the animal to carry certain things symbolically and you thank the animal for its sacrifice." Some priestesses can read smoke or water, ashes or coffee grinds, she told us. Some have visions or use crystal balls, others are mediums who actually become possessed by the spirit of the Orisha. "A lot of things just come to me," said Iyalu. "often through dreams or sometimes I might hear a female voice. I read and interpret the patterns in the cowrie shells. Each one of us has a duty to find out what our power is, how to tap into it, how to use it and how to value ourselves. It's partly intuition and partly being open to divine guidance."

When romance blossomed between Iyalu and Kabaisi the issue of the respective roles of men and women within traditional Nigerian society was swiftly dealt with. The name Kabaisi is actually a title which means 'Your Highness'. It also means 'He whose authority or action cannot be questioned'. "I do what I want to do anyway so why do I need to make a fuss because women are here and men are here (she indicates two levels with her hands). I don't have any problem," she laughed. "I feel happy and comfortable about my place in this life. Before I married Kabaisi I said to him, 'My only question to you is will I be able to practice my spiritual work?' And once he said 'Yes', why we can deal with other things as they come up. If he'd said 'No' we wouldn't have gotten married. So where's the problem?"

The problem could have been that back home in his village in Nigeria, Kabaisi has four other wives. "I have to admit I was a little apprehensive about going over there," said Iyalu, "because he and I had met here in the United States and I knew that the other women had a say in who the new wife would be. I'd come prepared to be defensive and I didn't know whether I was going to have to fight or run or what so I put it in the hands of God.

"It was my dream to get to Nigeria – even if I died there. I didn't care. People could have taken me off into the bush and killed me. I did not care. I was going to Nigeria at last. The Motherland. Anyway, we greeted each other and every-body was just so nice. One of the women came forward to embrace me and said, in Yoruba, 'I love you. Welcome into the sisterhood'. I was knocked out. I really felt at home. I remember one day sitting alone, feeling as if I could see my life like the pages in a book. There I was, sitting in the very same spot as my ancestors, drawing water from the well, cooking, serving the Orisha and I just *knew* I must have come from there, sometime way back in a past life, to feel such a powerful pull.

"This was my 20-year dream come true at last. The hardest part was not being able to talk with the co-wives because there's so much they could have taught me. We were all sharing and laughing, knowing we felt the same way but unable to express it. The women were very independent, especially those over the age of menopause. They had a lot more power and freedom and were proud of getting older which is something *we've* lost and I found myself saying, 'O.K. Where's all this oppression I've heard about or is it just Western concepts?'

"When it came time for me to leave, everyone was crying, even the children. Being a water child myself, tears came easy. It was horrible. I didn't want to go. Before I got married I have to say there was part of me that was thinking, 'What are you getting into, girl?' But now after three years with my husband I find him to be one of the most understanding people I have ever come across – very kind and compassionate. He's a priest himself on the Ifá level [higher than a Babalawo, one able to decode messages from Olódùmarè the Supreme Being made manifest to mankind by Orúnmilà, god of Wisdom]. He's a traditionalist so he knows such a lot and can put up with things like 50 chickens sitting in the hall when he comes home! He respects my role and we can help each other."

Iyalu took us into her little shrine room. The deity Ogun, guardian and warrior stands by the door – his essence represented by pieces of iron, nails, horseshoes and stones in little cooking pots. The altar to Yemonja, the Supreme Goddess, Mother of all things, has offerings of shells, starfish, bowls of salt water and other things to do with the ocean. There is a 'spiritual table' to honour the diversity of other influences – European and Native American, Jewish and tarot cards – and a family altar of *Egungun* – ancestral spirits.

I asked Iyalu if Femi and I could request a blessing from Yemonja for our endeavours and our travels. Yes we could. She would be happy to do it. First she poured a libation, took a couple of swigs of it and spat it forcefully and dramatically all over the altar. Then, she invoked Yemonja, talked to her, prayed, picked up a rattle and rhythmically shook it. She chanted, she sang, she asked for many good things for us. As she invoked the Goddess, a change indeed came over her. It was as though the force which inhabited her body was somehow bigger than her although not separate from her. To speak of possession somehow smacks of frenzy, of being out of control. This was anything but. Iyalu became possessed by those qualities and energies that Yemonja represents and they flowed from her like magical tides as she sprinkled the salt water on our heads. Then she knelt and touched her forehead to the ground, inviting us to do the same. We gave thanks for the blessing and that was that. We hugged warmly, all awkwardness long since evaporated, and set off into the darkening twilight with Iyalu, in motherly mode now, making us promise to phone when we reached home safely.

The next day I arrived a little early at Grand Central Main Concourse – that huge cathedral of a station where a hundred thousand people a day pass through. A small middle-aged woman with frizzy orange hair and a defiant straw hat with flowers in it was setting up an amplifier and speakers. She took a guitar out of its case, tuned it slowly and carefully then began to play and sing, in a most wonderful voice full of heart-break and longing, the theme from Black Orpheus. Many bustling commuters stopped in their tracks, beguiled by the melancholy beauty of the Brazilian favelas filling the vast, cavernous space. That music was so much a part of my early life. I was 13 when I went to live in Brazil and first heard about the African faith which had crossed the ocean in the slave ships and survived, transformed into *candomblé*. I was moved, way back then, by the deep indestructible wellsprings that bubbled forth in the music of carnival, in the drums, the candlelit processions, the mysterious rites and ceremonies that were tantalisingly just out of reach. As I listened to her song, the 'saudade' (an untranslatable Brazilian word encompassing nostalgia, sadness, regret for time passing and bittersweet memories) got to me and my eyes overflowed. I kept having to dab at them with the napkin from my muffin. By Grand Central Station I sat down and wept for everyone who is exiled and homesick. I gave the woman some money and thanked her in the remnants of my Portuguese. She smiled and our eyes met and some mysterious shared heart-energy passed between us.

There was Femi again underneath the clock and we rode the 'A' train back down to Brooklyn to keep our appointment this time with Omi Olayinka – another priestess of Yemonja. A very bright articulate, woman, she welcomed us warmly and invited us into her study where she has an extensive library of books on Africa, on Black Studies and related subjects. Omi is a professor at Brooklyn College where she teaches classes on 'The Black Family' and 'The Black Woman in America'. She is the co-ordinator of a research project called 'Aids in Afro-Americans – It's Time for Action' and another on education in the inner city. She has published research papers on such topics as Marcus Garvey, the Bantustans of South Africa and Mythical Nations. She and her husband Baba-Adé who is a Babalawo have created a homely little temple and centre for Yoruba Studies in their house.

Omi has strong views about how the cut-backs in the education system have forced some of the Black Studies courses to close. "So much knowledge has come to light since the degree courses were established in the sixties," she said. "There's still a need to really re-write a lot of our history – to question what has generally been said about people of African descent but then, of course, the more informed and empowered we are the less we can be pushed around.

We need to know that we all have a cultural heritage to be proud of. African-American culture is really rich. My grandfather, for example, was a ragtime jazz musician who played with Scott Joplin and Jelly-Roll Morton. He taught my father how to play piano and my father taught the five of us brothers and sisters how to play piano. We each also had to play another instrument (I play bassoon) and we all entertained each other. My father was an artist and our house was always full of other artists and intellectuals from all over the world. Then came Civil Rights and my parents were active all the time. Everyone was. It was just a matter of time until exposure to an African-based religion would come our way.

"Being a musical household, we were well grounded in the gospels and the spirituals and there were also constant debates going on about which aspect of Christianity was the most preferred. My parents made it clear that whichever system we chose was alright by them so long as we were upstanding citizens living righteously. Discovering the Yoruba religion was, for me, more of an Afro-centric link than a spiritual one. Like most people, that discovery came when I went for a 'reading'. The reading was phenomenal. The person who did it was an African-American priest of Sango. He drew shells – 16 shells – and was able to tell the whole experience of what I was going through at that time. How could he know all that? How could the shells tell so much? I had already been exposed to the I–Ching as a system of divination but seeing this other dimension with the 16 cowrie shells was another step again.

"Orisha worship! Here was something more tangible to me than the Christian experience. I can understand thunder and lightning. I can see and feel the change in the seasons. I can sense the sacred in all these things, God in everything, everywhere – the physical manifestation of the Orisha in terms of what we see – the ocean, the mountains, the rivers, the trees and the rocks. The powers behind all these natural forces, in our Yoruba culture, are the deities – the Orisha. I can tell my children when there is a storm; 'Oh that's just Sango speaking. Don't be afraid', and we can sit in the window and watch the lightning.

"After getting a series of readings, the next step is receiving the *aleke* – the beads. This is like a baptism. It is a beautiful symbolism. In actuality the *aleke* represent circles of light surrounding the person. I was initiated as a daughter of Yemonja. Wearing her beads around my neck means that Yemonja extends her reach around me and through Yemonja, all the other Orisha encircle me with bands of light. I now walk with protection. If my beads should break that would be a warning, like; 'Don't get on that bus or train! Go home!' You're really trusting your guidance."

The reading of the cowrie shells has so many parallels with our own ancient system of divination, the runes, or the ancient Chinese way of the I Ching. It's a way of trying to interpret while at the same time feeling a deep sense of connection to the natural cycles and energies of the earth and the cosmos. They are a tool for self-realisation and a way of revealing the truth of the present moment and of ourselves within it. The Babalawo, like the shaman of ancient Northern European tribal societies uses the cowries to impart wisdom and guidance.

Omi filled us in with a bit more understanding of the Yoruba religion: The Babalawo (who can be male or female) revere Orúnmilà – the God of Wisdom – a spiritual being who descended from heaven, sent by Olódùmarè – the Supreme Being – to teach the art of proper living. Orunmila was never born on Earth and had no earthly parents. He led an entourage of Divine beings – the Orisha – and when their time was up they did not die but ascended back to heaven leaving their tools behind as symbols of their great work. These sacred tools were kept in pots and calabashes and are worshipped today as symbols of the spiritual forces or Orishas whose gift they are.

The teachings are in the form of stories and parables, chants, songs, rituals, dances, prayers, even drumbeats depicting various aspects of Yoruba life passed down by word of mouth, generation to generation by the Babalawo. The Yoruba religion is a very ancient, complex system of worship that survived the great slave trade Diaspora and transplanted itself in the New World in spite of all attempts to suppress it.

Chief Mrs Adewale–Somadhi, a respected priestess has written in her book, *Fundamentals of the Yoruba Religion*, "All attempts to destroy Yoruba religious life and culture have failed. The Yoruba gods, the Orisha, could not be killed. The Yoruba descendants continue to survive and Yoruba culture flourishes in the Diaspora."

This is an example of a Yoruba prayer which I found very beautiful – a simple declaration of reverence:

> *"My reverence to God. He that spreads over the universe*
> *My reverence to the dawn of the day*
> *My reverence to the sunset*
> *My reverence to Mother Earth*
> *My reverence to the Witness to Creation, the Wisdom God, Orunmila*
> *My reverence to the Divine Beings on the Right and Left hand sides*
> *   of God*
> *My reverence to the Wisdom God's first students*
> *My respects to the Beautiful Mothers (the Witches)*
> *To my ancestors*
> *To my mother*
> *To my father*
> *To my Godparents*
> *My respects to all Babalawo and all Orisha worshippers worldwide*
> *I give praise to the waters*
> *   to the fire*
> *   to the earth*
> *   to the wind*
> *   to my roots, my beginnings*
> *   to the ancestors I have lost*
> *   to the one who comes to see*
> *   to the one who sits and watches*
> *   to the one who gave me knowledge of divining*
> *It must be so!*

"The first thing you get from a Babalawo is protection. You are blessed," said Omi. "Once you put on the *aleke* you will always be in the path of your destiny. Then your responsibility is to *listen* to that guidance and to lead your life in accordance with the correct way of acting."

I asked Omi if it was important to her, as a woman, that the deity to whom she is a priestess is a female deity.

"You know, for me," she answered, "far more important than the presence of female deities was the fact that it was an *African* religion. Male versus female took second place to African versus Western. In this country racism has had a much bigger impact on our lives than gender. First things first. But now that you're talking about it, the female deity aspect is something I need to ponder and yes, I am happy that I have a female deity. I love Yemonja and what she represents. She is the Great Mother, the nurturer. She holds her children. I guess I would say that it is very empowering and strengthening to women to have a deity who represents something so wonderful instead of the Christian tradition with a God figure who is always male, which leaves women feeling as if they don't count. Yemonja is feminine. If ever I am troubled I can always go to the ocean and bring a watermelon to give to her and she will take care of me. Same with Oshun, the River Goddess. You can take five oranges to her. She is the weaver of culture and society, art and music. One of her symbols is a needle and thread. She is the patron of anything creative.

"What I love about this religion is that you learn to understand the power of womanhood. The power of the feminine. Women have a very highly respected role in Yoruba society. One of the important consequences of the black feminist movement has been the revisioning of our history. In my course at the university I teach that, yes, we came to the United States as slaves but we are descendants of queens and queen mothers and priestesses of power. Our cultural link was with a very strong, powerful feminine reality. Prior to colonialism African women were the strongest and most socially organised women in the world. They always had a sense of control of their universe. We came to America with a deep memory of that link.

"What many people don't know is that there were always free blacks in this country," she continued. "There were always some *powerhouse* women providing food, clothing, social services to help their people. They were a dynamic force in the abolitionist movement and in the underground railroad. In 1895 it was women who organised the National Society of Coloured Women's Clubs out of which came the NAACP (The National Association for the Advancement of Coloured People). What we never had, as African American women, was the opportunity to stay at home and care for our children. We've always had to work – usually doing housework for white women. There's a wonderful poem that goes: 'Nobody opens no carriage door for me and ain't I a woman? … Life for me ain't been no crystal stair.' But we always had a sense of our own strength as women, as mothers, as those who kept the community and the church together. We knew the power of womanhood. In the forcibly broken families it was the women who had to hold things together as best they could.

"Only today when we are seeing the tragedy of a major breakdown in society it is because the women are losing it. More of them are addicted than ever before, to substances. Family cohesiveness is disintegrating. Our men have been adrift for much longer; casualties, unable to provide for their families, would be a better way of saying it – caught up in a pattern of generations of enforced powerlessness and hopelessness endlessly repeating itself. That's why the 'Million Man March' was so profound. [Louis Farrakhan's Million Man March that took place recently focused on the issue of men and committed, responsible fatherhood]. It is a crucial challenge. The men were saying, 'We need to stand up and be counted'. The issues are so huge but it is my opinion that the Yoruba religion can lend a sense of cohesiveness to our lives, giving us back our spiritual identity, our culture, our sense of self-pride. It can be a powerful force for good – a real renewal movement."

In spite of the rapid growth of the Yoruba religion in the United States – now over a million people – it is by no means mainstream as yet. Omi and Baba-Adé have had to put up with a lot of aggravation from neighbours and others who are troubled by practices they don't understand. There is a legacy of fear and misinformation about 'voodoo' (much as there is around 'witchcraft' in the European tradition) which continues to be augmented in the media.

"People still have that old Hollywood image and they are fearful," said Omi. "It's understandable. The stories that are put about are often negative – zombies, graveyards, skulls, superstition and so on. If that's all people see they are bound to criticise us without bothering to find out what we do. What we hope is that when the neighbours have been able to observe us for a while they will see that the type of people who come in here are not on drugs. They are not slovenly or dressed poorly or cursing in the street. They'll see that we're not a 'cult', that we don't solicit people to join. Empowerment comes from *owning* your history and your traditions, *knowing* you can make a difference. What we have here is a spiritual community providing an alternative to the perilous street life which has absorbed so many."

Omi feels that the interpretation of the ancient teachings coming from Babalawo with a Western exposure has given them new life. "All this cross-fertilisation in the world must end up doing some good," she said, laughing. Her dream is to come to England to give courses in the Yoruba religion – perhaps a symposium that combines workshops, discussions and lectures on aspects of the Orisha along with music and dance. For the moment it is just a dream but even as we spoke a Yoruba Arts Festival, called 'Dance Africa' with drumming, dance classes, a market place with clothing, books and jewellery for sale was getting underway Downtown.

Femi and I, our heads buzzing, took the subway up to Broadway and just managed to get standing-room-only tickets to the hottest show in town, 'Bring in Da Noise, Bring in Da Funk!' – a tap dance musical about the Black Experience in America from the days of slavery to the present day. It was a thrilling show with dazzling, breathtaking dancing. The rhythm, the energy and the important theme were so good and it was impossible to stand still. Particularly after talking with Omi about black pride and identity, to see this explosion of brilliance, originality and confidence, of uniquely African American folk forms burnished to such exquisite standards was truly inspiring. I only wished that every kid from Harlem or Brooklyn could come and feel that same sense of inspiration. We adored it and were quite hoarse from yelling and whooping. That night we stayed in town, dossing with a friend of Femi's in Greenwich Village, so that we could be up early for the Festival of Obatala – the Yoruba God of Creation – the following day ...

The day dawned hot and bright. For this event we had to dress all in white and make our way to Pier 9 on the East River where the Festival was being held on a river boat. Luckily we were early and got a place reasonably near the front as at least 500 white-garbed people converged – a hugely important indication of the fast-growing nature of this movement. It was a very African event – late to get started and slightly chaotic but jolly and relaxed and a wonderful opportunity to talk to many initiates from different walks of life.

Like Maria Rosa – a Santeria medium who communes with the spirits. Maria Rosa is a young woman from Puerto Rico, she told me that she was a 'Daughter of Oshun', training to become a priestess and I heard again how the 'Spanish People' (the Cubans and Puerto Ricans) had kept the Yoruba religion safe all these years hidden inside Catholicism where Our Lady of this or that was none other than Oshun or Yemonja in disguise. I also spoke with Blanche – an enormous Cuban lady who told me how she came into the religion 10 years ago as a refuge after both her parents died. Through the Orisha she found a way to connect with them and with her ancestors in an endless procession back through time. It has given her a sense of belonging and a way to counter the grief and the desolation.

Inside the boat I found myself sitting next to an old lady with a headful of tiny grey plaits – Mary Robertson, aged 70, priestess of Obàtálá and much-respected elder. Everyone who came across to greet her stooped to touch the ground with one hand or even prostrated fully in the traditional Yoruba gesture of respect. Mary Robertson accepted their tributes with grace and serenity. Raised as a Catholic herself, she told me she has been following the Yoruba religion for the past 25 years or so – ever since her first exposure to fragments of language, rituals, chants, prayers caused thrilling echo-soundings deep in her psyche. Then when she was introduced to the Orisha themselves she knew immediately that this was for her and has embraced it all enthusiastically ever since.

"You have to understand," she said patiently, answering my constant questions in a golden honey voice as sweet as Ella Fitzgerald's, "In the time of slavery, the people were kept deliberately apart. Members of different tribal groups were purposely mixed up so they wouldn't have a common language. Communication and assembly were forbidden. Even drums were not allowed. Punishments were terrible [There is one well-documented case in 1721 when a woman slave, alas nameless, who had been part of a rebellion on board a slave ship, was hoisted by the thumbs and whipped and slashed with knives until she died while the rest of the slaves were forced to watch]. People were set against one another.

The men were kept apart as studs to impregnate the women. What kind of legacy is that? Why do you think our people today have had such a hard time building communities where folks take care of each other? Look at the Koreans. Look at the Vietnamese. One generation and they're out of the slums. Look at the Jews – even in the ghettos, even in Egypt, way back in Biblical times, they had their spiritual leaders with them, their families, their rabbis. We had nothing. Families were torn apart and sold all over the place. We were taught to be afraid, suspicious, to trust no-one. Men were not able to protect their wives and children. Those of us who weren't driven crazy became numb. Our self-esteem was eaten away. We were forbidden to practice our religion so now, rediscovering the old Yoruba religion is giving us a strong basis for rebuilding our communities. It is beginning to unite us." (And not a moment too soon. In Brooklyn I saw a billboard poster which read, 'What do you call a man who makes a baby and disappears?' and someone had scrawled across it cynically, 'Don't they all?')

Mary Robertson's four sons are all initiated priests, her grandchildren are learning African dance and wearing the beaded necklaces of the Orishas. Before they go away to college they have special protection ceremonies to keep them safe from drugs and other temptations. There are rituals and ceremonies for the rites of passage through life. Gradually a structure of meaningful continuity is being built.

One of the most interesting aspects of the day was to see the coming together of the two rivers – the Hispanic and the African – creating a mighty confluence of diversity and unity. There were also a significant number of other ethnic groups present – Caucasians, Japanese, West Africans, Caribbeans – The Yoruba religion is very welcoming and all-embracing. It does not require that its followers give up any other religion. It can co-exist quite comfortably with Catholicism, Judaism or anything else. It is only the other religions that seem to have a problem co-existing with it.

Into the midst of this rich human brew, Obàtálá, the God of Creation, who has both a male and a female aspect was carried in – his/her effigy borne aloft at the head of a procession and placed on an altar surrounded by piles of fruit and flowers and little meat pies. Then a seemingly endless line of worshippers – light skins and dark skins, children and elders, men and women – formed to come forward one at time and offer obeisance, prostrating before Obàtálá, ringing a handbell, offering gifts of food and uttering prayers. When the individual respects had been paid to the God of Creation, the Master Drummers of Brooklyn arrived to drum prayers to the Orisha in general. Everyone stood up except the very old and infirm. It was an emotional moment and many people had tears in their eyes. Then the singing began. Like the feeling I had when my ancestors' voices shivered my timbers as the Jewish prayers were sung in Hebrew at the Shabbat service in Philadelphia, these descendants of African queens and priestesses, farmers, hunters, medicine people, builders, artists and chiefs are waking up, after their long sleep, to the sacred ways of their ancient ones and finding themselves anew.

Everyone seemed to know the Yoruba words. The mystery of the preservation of the songs and chants, in spite of the draconian proscriptions against the language is as wonderful as the flight of a phoenix. I thought about Ivy, the woman I met at the Pagan gathering in Washington State saying to me, "I make up the rituals I use and when I close my eyes and go within for the prayers and blessings and incantations it's like I'm *remembering* something." Remembering something only half-forgotten. The human memory seems to be able to store things dormant, through several generations, maybe for hundreds of years, like the seeds of certain Australian plants that can *only* germinate after the intense heat of a bush fire has burst them asunder.

When people asked me why I was there at the Festival of Obàtálá I said 'I am a mother of Ibeji'. Ibeji is the Yoruba word for twins but Ibeji, the twin figures, most often seen as a matched pair of wood carvings bedecked with beads, are also Orisha. There happen to be more instances of the birth of twins amongst the Yoruba than any other people on Earth and effigies of Ibeji would have been commissioned by any family lucky enough to be blessed with twins. If one twin were to die, the mother would carry the carving of the dead twin tied to her body next to the live baby so that the survivor would never feel lonely. When Tim and Femi left home as young adults we gave them each an Ibeji figure. And there I was with my Femi. In fact she was really my passport to be there at all. Even though the Yoruba religion itself doesn't particularly resonate with her (she has been a Buddhist for years) she said that for her to see the passion and intensity with which her native culture is embraced by people who have taken several generations of sorrow and suffering just to get back to where she started, has been an eye-opener. It was a profound experience to share it all with her. Both of us were feeling quite awed by the enormity of the strange destiny that brought us together as mother and daughter in this lifetime.

Gabrielle Roth, the great dance pioneer, is a person whose work I have admired ever since we met as co-contributors on a television programme about The New Age years ago. I remembered her saying that her first opening to God, to bliss, was when she surrendered herself to dance. Ecstasy was her experience of God. Ecstasy was her healing. Teaching the dancing path to ecstasy has been her life's work. I watched her dance. She danced all the time. It was if it pained her to stand still. In the middle of a conversation with someone she would suddenly become a bird or a tree, a stand of bamboo or the ocean. She seemed to be a person whose spirit was only barely contained in her body – a person who trod very lightly upon the Earth. I knew that she lived in New York and had written asking if she would have time to meet and talk. She is one of the few famous people who unhesitatingly made time to see me.

Gabrielle Roth is a dramatic-looking woman with cheekbones to knock your socks off. Tall and thin, like a dancing flame. An elemental sort of person

– more energy than matter – she lives in a gorgeous converted warehouse-type apartment off Union Square filled with plants and music. Coming to see her hot on the heels of the Yoruba experience was good timing. So much of the release of energy, the tribal trance-dancing and shamanistic practices which Gabrielle has refined are a direct legacy of the seeds planted on these shores from Africa over the past three hundred years.

Gabrielle believes that everyone is a dancer. Her book, *Maps to Ecstasy: Teachings of an Urban Shaman* and her albums of music have been hugely influential in helping others to venture into that unknown territory where the dance is, where their power lies, where buried within each of us are the keys to our unique creative expression, where body and spirit become one.

I wanted to know what had started her off on the ecstatic, shamanistic path.

"It all happened to me so young," she said. "I wasn't conscious of any of those things. I had no big mission. I was very poor and needed to put myself through school. The only thing I knew how to do was dance. I danced as a release; as a relief, by myself, all the time. I got my first job working with children and senior citizens and, eventually, another job doing improvisational movement and theatre with schizophrenics in a mental hospital. Those three worlds stayed with me all the way through college. None of the people I taught were dancers so I wasn't teaching them form. I was really following the energy and giving it some kind of structure. I was relying completely on my intuition and imagination. These groups were like my Zen masters. I learned by being witness to their process, to their inner dance. I learned to help them put their realities in motion. I followed them into the moment – drawing them out from where they were. It was an instinctive thing on my part. I had no idea I would be doing it for the rest of my life.

"The work had a spiritual component in it right from the start. I was able to see bodies and to see energy and always felt it was my job to keep things moving – channelling that energy. It was as if I was being trained to work in a shamanic paradigm by the spirit of energy itself. By the spirit of children, the spirit of elders, the spirit of the disenfranchised, of the out-of-step, the emotionally disturbed. By the time I left college I already had a substantial body of work growing inside me. I was inventing it as I went along. I could see a lot of pain and suffering in the bodies around me and I had a lot of pain and suffering in me. It prompted me to ask the questions; How do we let go in a way that doesn't require language or analysis? How do we *move through* instead of hold on to the things that are disturbing us? How do we celebrate?"

After a few years in Europe, being an artist's model and a period teaching dance and drama in high school, Gabrielle fetched up at the Esalen Institute in California during "that wild, ferocious laboratory of the sixties" where she learned massage and was invited by charismatic counter-culture guru, Fritz Perls to teach movement to his Gestalt Therapy groups. "I loved it," said Gabrielle. "I felt like a dolphin who had suddenly been released into the sea. Esalen provided a therapeutic and spiritual context for this amazing search we were all going through. This *longing* for things to be different – somehow more real. They were very exciting times. I found a whole new language of dance beginning to spring up and take shape from within me. I began to pay attention to the little girl in me who used to go into her bedroom, shut the door, turn up the music real loud and just 'go for it'. I began to shift into really ecstatic levels of consciousness. I would go into deep trance states where I would receive information. It was my connection to some sort of Divine guidance. It cleared out everything else – a constant shedding of skins as I got closer to the bone of soul and closer to the language of soul and closer to the essence of our humanity through the dance. I had to let go of all the rubbish.

"I saw that *movement* was my medicine, my metaphor, my master. It was all things to me and over time I came to realise that God *is* the dance. But I had no words to explain any of this and because I was a woman and young, the guru figures – the benevolent, mostly male, dictators of consciousness in the human potential movement – looked upon what I did as merely a recreation ("send them over to Gabrielle and let them move around a bit before we do the real work"). Well, since my whole ego complex was based on inferiority – not being enough, never being good enough – I colluded in that idea of me and my work. Like the Woody Allen joke – if I was doing it then it couldn't possibly be important. I didn't give value to my work or to myself. All my early training and conditioning had been to distrust and deny and destroy so the 'wounded healer' journey for me was to learn to turn that around and begin to trust my body. I feel that the whole body of my work is a map to this amazing journey that I personally went on."

Talking to Gabrielle I was profoundly moved by the way the soul can triumph against all the odds. To hear, once again, that out of the most difficult of circumstances the flower of integrity can somehow find a way to survive even at tremendous cost. It seems as though one is *impelled* towards wholeness – that there is a deep inner knowledge of what we need to do to get well even though we may be completely unable to articulate it. What had enabled her to keep going and, indeed, driven her on?

"I think it started from a deep sense of service," she said, "of simply wanting to make people feel better, have more *fun*, to seduce them into lightening up a bit, to give them permission to say 'Fuck it!' to all those people who said 'you shouldn't'. I didn't really love myself and that's what *I* had to learn. I wanted to share the things I knew and the things I didn't know while trying to find my own way through the labyrinth of soul and psyche – while trying to find the threads that connect my body to my heart to my mind to my spirit.

"Moving my body in a way that was organic took me to my heart – emptying out my sorrows, my fears, my anger – helping me to connect my emotional nature to my physical nature. By helping others I was providing a space for myself simultaneously. We were all healing each other. Together. I think this is the power of my work. It is not didactic. It's 'how do *we* unfold?' I have always felt that the work itself is the teacher, the participant is the healer and I am the catalyst – the person who keeps it all moving, flowing, in motion. I have this tremendous faith in our instinctive, intuitive abilities, in our imaginative powers. We can *re-create* ourselves. We can transform. Nothing is too big or too awesome for us to move through. All we have to do is make a commitment, give ourselves permission and find a place where we have a tribe, a collective, a group mirror. We are not the isolated Lone Rangers we might suppose.

"I feel I have given birth to a very feminine spirituality", she went on. "One that is very tribal and non-hierarchical. People may be at different levels of the path but all those levels are contained in a circle. Nobody is superior. If there's a chief then I am that chief but I'm still flowing and unfolding and falling apart and coming back together myself so I hope that protects the work from any kind of rigidity or *power over*. We've had enough of that. That has been the patriarchal system. Power over – in other words, abuse. Even in the spirituality movement we have had all these revelations of supposedly spiritual gurus molesting young girls or having sex while their whole community was expected to be celibate.

"As we women begin to wise up and come into our own era we begin to bring the feminine into balance and to show a new way of expressing our connection to the Divine Source. All things come from the Mother. That's what the body tells me and the body is my Bible. We came through her so we are part of her. We come from the womb so the Earth is like the womb of the soul. The feminine is no more nor less important than the masculine. They just need to be in balance."

I asked Gabrielle about her relationship to this Divine Source. "As I see it there are three levels of relationship", she answered. "Firstly there's my relationship to myself which is my own meditation where I listen to God speaking to me through spirit. Then when I pray it's an expressive event where I *dance* and thirdly there's that place where I want to share and be in communion – a place to experience the power of collective prayer, the power of collective meditation. The power of flowing and moving together in the dance. This is very important. A church is supposed to provide this place of collective communion but, for me, it was never quite right. They wanted control over the entire psyche, over the body, the heart, the mind, the soul. They divided spirit from flesh so we were left *dismembered* in the name of God and that is what has to change. Maybe the churches can remain but the spirit that infuses the churches has to be different. Has to be feminine. The feminine is the only thing that can provide this healing – the feminine in women *and* in men – as we come into that space together to re-member the Body, to remember the Earth, to remember the Source and to honour and revere. To look upon life with awe and wonder instead of this pompous piety, this pompous, pretend, know-it-all 'dominion over'.

"We all share the wound of fragmentation," said Gabrielle. "In so many situations I see our inability to relate, our inability to communicate from the heart, to overcome our distance and alienation from one another, avoiding each other's eyes, at a loss to know what others need. I see people searching for direction, trying to summon up their personal power, longing for the strength to be independent. But we can all share in the cure of unification. Healing lies in the unification of all our forces – the powers of being, feeling, knowing and seeing. We are all struggling to know who we are and what we need – to like ourselves, rather than wanting to be somebody else or somewhere else. Spiritual healing means taking responsibility for being authentic – for being a whole person. For me, movement has been the medium of change and my shamanic work is about dancing from within."

What healers and holy people have discovered since the beginning of time is that when you dance your own dance, you become a partner in the cosmic dance, you become, in T.S. Eliot's words "the still point of the turning world", you reach the place of ecstasy where you are no longer confined by the self. As Gabrielle says, "At this level you realise that no one can organise your perception of God better than you can."

Gabrielle has evolved a method of teaching her work based on what she has defined as the five sacred rhythms inherent in all our actions and the five life cycles that lead to enlightenment. The five rhythms move from Flowing, through Staccato, Chaos, and Lyrical, finally arriving at Stillness – the inner dance – "where each movement arises from the ocean of our being". These five rhythms lead us in a symbolic journey, which she calls The Wave, from Birth, through Childhood, Puberty, Maturity and finally Death. We are also journeying on the path to Ecstasy through five levels of consciousness from Inertia, through Imitation, Intuition and Imagination to Inspiration where we "transcend conscious effort and begin to operate with spontaneous creativity out of our spiritual centre".

I asked Gabrielle how the theory of the five rhythms had evolved. "It evolved out of the recognition of what I was seeing in the bodies of the dancers," she said. "It evolved out of what I was experiencing on my own trance journeys, what I experienced when I had a baby, when I had an orgasm. First I began to isolate the rhythms one by one then it came to me how they were connected, how they created a wave of energy that represented the entire creative process. I believe that had I not been a woman, had I not been a dancer I probably never would have discovered it. Only by paying such close attention to the *body* – mine, other peoples', to the earth, the cycles, the waves – did it come into articulation for me: that *rhythm is our mother tongue*. Slowly but surely I began to see that because this philosophy was really rooted in energy it therefore had no dogma, no judgement, it just simply *was*.

"I began to see that these elemental vibrations could be a context for understanding and embracing all the movements of life itself. The <u>Flowing</u> energies of the birth process, the <u>Staccato</u> energies of childhood, the <u>Chaotic</u> energies of adolescence, the <u>Lyrical</u> energies of maturity, and the <u>Still</u> energies of our elder time. They are a context for understanding that the soul goes through the same journey on its way to reach the place of Divine Oneness. I think that life itself has created the map to enlightenment and it is by going through life with awareness, with consciousness, that we come to the stage of

enlightenment organically. It's nothing you have to pursue so much as something happening inside yourself that you have to pay attention to all the time.
Evolution is our birthright. It's not something for the special few people who
have the time and money to go to India and sit at the feet of some guru for
six months. It has to do with a way of being here and being fully awake."

Gabrielle believes passionately that to follow slavishly any leader is to become
stuck in the Childhood phase of our journey, that our individual destiny is the
realisation of our unique gifts. When students have said to her; "I wish I could
dance like you", she tells them, "Great! Then dance like you. If you don't do
your dance then who will?"

So how, I wondered, could she avoid becoming one of those gurus herself
– expensive, remote?

"The work has taken on a life of its own," said Gabrielle. "I've birthed it but
now it is a much larger presence in the world than my skinny little body! There
are new problems and challenges. I have had to learn how to facilitate the
movement of my work out into the world, how to protect the integrity of that
which I have spent my whole life developing without controlling it. There are
others who are teaching it and many more who want to. In order to stay true
to the spirit of the work and its organic, feminine nature it has to be *embodied*
by each person who teaches it. Of course the very fact of its feminine nature
makes it easy for it to be exploited in the way that women are easy to exploit but
at the same time the work has got a certain resistance and a kind of vulnerable
strength because, at heart, it is a way to empower people, not to gain power
over them by becoming a guru."

It's as if the world has finally started to catch up with Gabrielle. She invented
the rave culture 30 years ago. As she says herself, "Ecstatic trance is where I started
out. Now I've finally found my people in the tribal spirit of the age as the old
structures are breaking down and we are coming into a new way of being".

As we said goodbye and I reluctantly left her beautiful apartment, Gabrielle
generously gave me the complete collection of all her marvellous CD's which
have inspired me to dance myself silly on several occasions since. I love to dance
anyway – for me, it has always been one of the most powerful healing tools
there is. I so agreed with Gabrielle when she spoke about the need for
communion with one another. When we meet in the dance, the great dance of
life we can see clearly that there is no difference between healer and healed.
We are all each other. We are all God. We are all Divine. There is nothing more
wonderful than the acknowledgement that we need each other and can come
together in the liberation and the ecstasy of the dance.

Chapter 8

❖ ❖ ❖ ❖ ❖

'Without darkness nothing comes to birth
As without light nothing flowers'
MAY SARTON

There was one more person in New York that I wanted to meet before I left. I had spotted an advertisement in a resources magazine, for something called *Awakenings,* a programme of workshops on spirituality for women, and was keen to follow it up. By one of those handy coincidences that are probably not coincidences at all, the address happened to be in the same town as Sue who had kindly arranged an appointment for me with Bernice Marie-Daly, the founder of *Awakenings.* She is also a director of the Institute for Spiritual Development, and the co-author of a scholarly book; *Created in Her Image: Models of the Feminine Divine.* She has a PhD and is a professor at Fairfield University. We met at a coffee shop in New Canaan, Connecticut and sat outside in the sunshine. Bernice turned out to be a terrific person, passionate, articulate and thoughtful. Another strong woman playing her part for healing in our world. Alas, *Awakenings* is having to fold for a while as it wasn't working out financially but Bernice is planning its rebirth, possibly in a different form.

"*Awakenings* was a container for so many things," said Bernice in answer to my first question. "It ranged from a group art project through song, dance and ritual but the main focus was on *reclaiming women's sacred imagery.* In the Judeo-Christian tradition women have been deprived of an image of Divine Presence that affirms our being and dignity. We are not only hungry for it, we are desperate for it. I come from a Catholic tradition myself where at least there was Mary – the only fragment of Goddess energy that we have left in the whole of the West, which is a pretty tragic statement. Of course she is not a Goddess theologically, but in the hearts and minds of millions of people all over the world she is and the Protestants don't even have her."

Bernice reminded me that the original meaning of 'virgin' was *complete within herself* but over the centuries the church has chosen to make Mary into a sexless, sanitised figure. "She embodies the feminine so obviously missing from the current Christian belief system but she isn't allowed to be *real*. She's too passive, too skinny. She doesn't have dirty fingernails. She isn't like us."

So, where is she, the Goddess complete within herself? What happened to her? How can we find her?

"I'm looking within the psyche," said Bernice. "Which means visioning, dreaming, being in touch with the imaginative processes, going way back into history and reclaiming the ancient Goddess figures. The point of going back is to go forward – to ask ourselves: What would it be like to live in a society that actually honoured women? What would it be like to walk down the street at night and not have to feel afraid? Would we continue to rape the Earth if we truly saw her as the place where the Holy Spirit is embodied? I feel that to get to that place is a spiritual process which is not contained in a religious tradition of any sort. The challenge is how to re-imagine Goddess energy for the 21st century so that is where I am right now. My journey has brought me this far from my Catholic cradle!"

I asked Bernice about that journey. "I was always very religious as a child," she said. "I went to mass every single day right through high school. I had a strong connection to the mystical and to the liturgy (which of course is what ritual is about only I didn't make those connections at that time). Then in college, although I was still drawn to the beauty and richness of it, I started questioning the institutions. At the same time the women's movement was gathering momentum throughout the country. There was an awareness of the need for 'inclusive language' – he/she – and a move towards pushing for the ordination of women. But the more I thought about the God language – the more I began to see that equality was not about the ordination of women. It was about nothing less than the nature of God.

"When I first found out that the Hebrew word for spirit (ruah), in the opening passage of Genesis, is *feminine* I was flabbergasted. 'And the Spirit of God moved upon the face of the waters'. There She is! In the Old Testament, that feminine term; *ruah*, the Spirit of God, the holy breath occurs 378 times. She is not named but She's there. It changes everything. Also in Genesis God says, "Let *us* make humankind in *our* image after *our* likeness." The plural. "Let *us* ..." God is referring to Godself as *us*. What is that about? So many things begin to fall into place. A powerful contemporary metaphor for women's struggle against the oppression of patriarchal culture is that of 'finding one's voice'. *We must never underestimate the power of language.* The process of beginning to name the Creator helps us to clarify our own self-image and our place in the cosmos."

In her *Awakenings* seminars Bernice would begin with an overview of the polytheistic traditions in all indigenous cultures when the Goddess was alive and well. "I would give this incredible sweeping thumb sketch of Her vibrant presence throughout the ancient world and trace what happens to Her as we get closer and closer to the patriarchal age and then what we are left with in terms of Christianity and Judaism today. I put feminine words like *ruah, sophia* (wisdom) and *shekinah* (the presence of light) on the board. I track how the feminine Divine becomes either neutered or masculinized until She is erased altogether. By the time I'm finished, She's gone. The impact is devastating. It's visceral. Women are baffled. They are incredulous. They are angry. There's a lot of struggle about where they are within their own tradition. Some stay on and fight it out. Others leave. I've done both. I stayed with my church for years and years and years until I finally knew, 'I can't be here one more day. I can't'. And that was the end of that."

And then what? I asked. How do you fill the vacuum?

"It is scary for women to be breaking with traditional religion and going it alone", she answered, "but it is also massively empowering. And it's healing. Very healing. We are rediscovering and inventing rituals. There's a lot of creativity and commonality. We're finding all kinds of wonderful things that we can expand and explore – a love of the natural world; insights from African cultures; from the Celtic traditions; from the Native Americans. It can be an incredible liberation."

As I thought about it I realised that just about every woman I know makes some kind of little altar in her home – a few pebbles, shells, crystals, flowers, – things that represent the Earth, our Mother, all those things that we want to bring into our lives, to honour and cherish. There is indeed a commonality. Bernice talked about the growing accumulation of evidence for a matricentric age that was meant to have flourished about 7000 B.C., before the patriarchal age. It was an age characterised by peace and partnership where our ancestors worshipped the Great Goddess – the cosmic life-force principle. Actually, I'm always a bit wary of such assertions and one of the questions I wanted to ask Bernice was, "Were things necessarily any better? Aren't we in danger of romanticising those times?"

"Of course there has been a tendency towards idealisation," she said, "however there are certain qualities that those societies appear to have had or that we have projected onto them that we need desperately now. It's really about *now* and the future rather than arguing about what did or didn't happen," she said. "Sure there were cultures where men were not treated well but nothing compared to what we're living with today – or for the last 5,000 years during which women have been deprived of education, political power, economic resources and religious authority, as well as being denied a knowledge of their history. Why is the Goddess tradition referred to as a 'cult' instead of a religion? Why are the holy, sacred women of the Goddess, described as temple prostitutes? The power of language has a huge impact on our self-image. We have to free ourselves from the patriarchal framework that has conditioned our very being and that means questioning the nature of the sacred and the revelatory experience itself. As we have said in our book [*Created in Her Image*], the Goddess – as life-force principle, as representing a cosmology that envisages our relationship with the Earth and all living things as one breathing organism – is *cross-cultural*. She appears all over the world under different aspects and with different names and yet, within Her diversity, she remains One. She affirms the legitimacy and the beauty of female power."

I wondered if Bernice believed that what we are witnessing is the beginning of a great evolutionary leap of consciousness even if it is only happening in Connecticut coffee shops?

"That is definitely what I believe," she said, laughing, "and unless there is a return to and an embracing of the sacred feminine we could very well self-destruct. Darwin was right about one thing. If we don't adapt and evolve we'll die out. The form that the evolution is taking is *consciousness*. I also happen to believe that the changes that are happening are coming through Her. There is Divine inspiration to bring back a balance between masculine and feminine – to heal the old, old misunderstanding of what we even mean by words such as masculine and feminine. The yin and yang model is perhaps the closest. Masculine, for example is not just phallic, one-pointed energy but testicular – round, holding, nurturing, steadfast – more 'yin'. Also, although woman is the traditional nurturer, no one would have ever been born if a woman didn't know how to *push* – to expel. That's 'yang', exertive energy. Neither is subordinate to the other. By complementing one another, their power is doubled.

"We're talking about a humanity here that is much more whole than the fractured pieces we keep trying to jam together. It's time to move beyond the stereotypes. It's exciting, thrilling and scary as hell! Women must be willing to risk everything in order to challenge the status quo. The world's survival depends on the rediscovery of the feminine Divine. There is no speck of dust, no grain of sand where She is not. No corner of the universe in which She is not present. She gives life and She values creation as Her own body."

So, The Goddess, by which we mean not only the feminine aspect of the Divine but also a way of symbolically representing energy patterns in the lives of women, is beginning to make Herself visible and who better to act as care-takers, as Bernice asks, than those who are created in Her image? But women cannot do it alone, she says. Luckily, neither do we have to. In contrast to the male hero's journey, women travel together toward personal and group trans-formation. What we accomplish is not for ourselves but for the wider culture. We are the flow, we are the ebb. We are the weavers, we are the web. The Goddess lives. Her presence is made manifest in all those situations where love and tenderness are forthcoming, where diversity is honoured, where injustice is challenged, where creativity and laughter flow.

Certainly, my greatest joy on this journey of spiritual discovery has been the love and support I have had from other women – travelling together, sharing wisdom, encouraging the luminous and the numinous in each other. Perhaps the greatest challenge to all women is to trust our own inner truth, to trust ourselves and not be afraid to claim our power. And to know we are not alone. If we can dream it, then it can come to pass.

Awakenings is taking a little nap but will re-awaken, says Bernice. "It must, the work will go on."

I came home to England feeling very blessed by the many meetings I'd had with remarkable women – all trying to make sense of the mystery; finding new ways of seeing; new ways of being; old ways of helping each other. Some paths have been gentle unfoldings and others like my friend Mary Aver's have been baptisms of fire.

Mary's daughter, Cara, died shockingly, suddenly, alone in her room one night – a tragedy that would have destroyed some people but the very first time I met Mary she said to me, "You know, my spiritual journey started on the day when Cara was born but it has taken off in an extraordinary way since her death. I have discovered the new religion of the heart." Mary is an Irish woman possessed of that inimitable, lyrical way with the English language which fills me with envy. Everything sounds like a poem. Now, a year on, and especially in the light of the discovery of my own daughter's cancer and my struggle in coming to terms with it, I wanted to ask her if she would be willing to talk more about that spiritual journey so here I am sitting in her London flat.

Mary's story is one of chaos and pain and redemption. Within two years of Cara's birth, Mary's husband had gone off with her best friend. Mary was addicted to alcohol and in a mental hospital. In recovery with AA and trying to put her life back together again she spent some time in Muktananda's ashram in India while her ex looked after the children.

"In retrospect, I was yearning for some spiritual depth and I didn't know at all what I was looking for. I had rejected Catholicism quite early on – terrified by all that hellfire and those appalling sin and damnation priests. I didn't believe them. I thought, 'there must be another way – life is too beautiful'. I loved the animals and the earth. In Ireland my father walked behind the plough and my job as a child was to meet the cows at the well and bring them home at the same time every evening. Now in rural India I felt curiously at home and I lived in that between world for sometime. Although I was shocked at the death of my marriage and my old life, I fell into the comforting ritual of ashram life. It called me and I knew that with the meeting of this holy being, my spiritual life was back on course. I came home to a part of myself that was really me."

Back in Europe, bringing up two kids on her own, Mary, already a qualified nurse and 're-birther' began working as a healer and a psychic.

"I knew I could do it from childhood," she said. "In Ireland a lot of people are like that. It doesn't seem too unusual. I look at people and I get pictures. Pictures of energy. The energy speaks to me. It has different shades and tones. That's what I read and put into words. Sometimes I see definite forms beyond the physical. People ask me to look for patterns in their lives and since I have always been fascinated by the moment of birth I find the tool of astrology very helpful as a way of mapping out our connection to the cosmos and how our personalities are put together. How are we formed? What do we bring? What is our uniqueness? Systems of divination are methods of *amplification* and astrology is still a wonderful bridge for me.

"I am very committed to and excited by the 'journey' although the pain of it sometimes eclipses the growth. I know that my wisdom has come through, that my study has provided me with a language. I'm shown things. Things like glimpses of the mystery and sacredness of the life of the spirit. I feel a definite guidance around – a *knowing* that comes when I'm not trying to be too smart or work things out. It comes when I surrender to that timeless wisdom. It's like a birth – you just ride it."

I asked Mary what were the sources of strength that she drew upon "Strength?" she mused, and paused a while to think. "I believe in simple things – in love, in humanity, in nature, in my garden. I trust in the fact that birds sing and flowers grow. There's a faith in *goodness*. There *will* be peace in Ireland. The Divine is the acts of love and kindness we do."

And what about the Divine Feminine? "Oh, I feel her powerfully. Especially around the mystery of life, conception and birth. Having my children was the best thing I ever did. There is a chant which goes; 'Only within is the fire I kindle. My womb, the altar.' The female body is so extraordinary. We must acknowledge it and care for it better than we do. Cara is not in her body any-more. She'd done what she came for and she left. I can say that when I'm not in pain. She died on her own. She left in the night. It's so hard not to see her ever again although I often feel her presence and she's said to me, 'Mum, there's only one body in the way now. We're closer than ever'.

"I live very close to the veil and I'm aware that it's always been thinner for me than for some other people. I had such a glimpse of the beyond when Cara died. I was shown lots of things. I followed an invisible map and even though I fall apart quite often the map remains whole. I've met her – not in the physical form, I just know it's her energy – but I don't go looking for her. In fact I asked psychics not to do any readings or try to make contact but just to pray. She made contact in time, when she was ready. She visits and then she doesn't visit. I need to stay attentive all the time. She's passed through that veil and I know that it peeled off layers around my heart. It has taught me a level of depth and compassion that was never before available to me and often it feels as if there's still a well inside that I haven't even touched. It's taught me a huge surrender and humility. Nothing else could have thrown me that far out. My heart broke and yet ... it's very complex ... the best part of her lives on in me closer than my skin. It transgresses everything I might ever feel. It takes me beyond – into other realms.

"When she left it was *vital* that I took care of her in spirit with whatever strength I'd got left. It's very poignant and paradoxical. Would I have known as much love had I not had this experience? Did I know I was capable of loving so much? Losing Cara was the deepest pain that I could ever have and yet if you can, as Stephen Levine puts it, keep your heart open in hell, you can know a level of love that maybe others don't. All the veils lifted. All the places where I was hiding dissolved. All the strands of my life came together for her wake. It was very rich.

"The one thing I would like to contribute to other women who have lost children is to stress the importance of ritual – a way of meaningful prayer and ceremony, a way of being and doing together. We need each other, we need our mothers, we need the wisdom of people who have been through it. When Cara died, the women came. They made a rota. They cooked, made my bed, ironed my clothes. They did whatever needed to be done. It is a very ancient comfort to be able to tear your hair and wail and moan and to be held by the women. They helped me by their *beingness* – being willing to contribute even if they didn't know what to do. For all the agony, it was a blessed time, a sacred time, a time when there was a gateway open and how easy it would have been to miss the gateway because we were in such pain. In the midst of everything there was a certain 'rightness' about it, if I can use that word. I learned that Cara was a being I could serve, that she wasn't *mine*, that I mustn't try to hold onto her. I really understood that. It was the closest I have ever been to the light, to God, to that other world. I'm close all the time now to spirit. I'm crazy for it in my life. When I get distracted or I'm worried or I forget, then I'm brought back with a gasp to remember to return to that place of one-pointedness.

"I belong to a women's group now which meets every month on the night of the full moon. A gentle group. A wise woman group. We dedicate the evening to whatever is occurring in the world, we make up rituals with drumming and chanting and we have a fire into which we discard our negativity. And then we ask for grace. When we did a remembrance of Cara I invited a mixture of people who'd lost loved ones and we just drummed. We drummed past the place where words are not enough. There was a miraculous point when everybody came together and we asked the Great Spirit to reach us and to guide us and to take care of the people who had died. Something ancient was being triggered. A deeper knowing prevailed.

"Women are noticing that the places within them that have been asleep are waking up and I think not only women but men are starving for ritual in their lives. They just need a little nudge. Men are seeking communion with other men – an honouring, a blessing. We are all longing for 'communion', discovering the new religion of the heart. When you allow it, it teaches you extraordinarily."

Mary's courage touches me deeply. How brave are the women who carve their own way through the forests of unknowing.

Now that I am back into my home-life routine I find myself looking at everyone and everything through sharper lenses. With each woman that I meet, I want to know about the spiritual dimension of her life. How is she finding her own way through the labyrinth? How is she getting in touch with her substance, her depth and her ability to act powerfully in the world? What does it mean to come to the end of searching outside oneself for the truth? What does it mean to come into the garden? To come home?

Janette Browne teaches yoga at my local health club, beginning each class with the serene chanting of a Sanskrit prayer. Ever since I first began attending her classes I was intrigued to know what had brought this young West Indian woman to choose yoga as her discipline and to follow the teachings of an Indian guru. Watching her teach I thought, 'Yes, she's got that inner sense of having found her way through the maze'. Originally from the island of Nevis in the Caribbean, she has travelled a long way from her origins both physically and spiritually. I invited her over to my house one autumn afternoon to share some of her journey with me.

"I was brought up a Methodist and went to church every Sunday," said Janette. "I remember trying to be a good Christian, being fascinated by all the stories, wanting to love God and Jesus. It was just the background to our lives but I didn't really understand it. When Jesus said, 'The kingdom of heaven lies within'. Within what? Nobody explained. Well now I know it means within *me* – peace, strength and love within myself – but it is only since becoming involved with siddha yoga that these things have fallen into place."

Janette came upon yoga in a book when she was 16 and practised it on her own without a teacher until she met her guru of whom she has been a disciple for the past 15 years. Siddha yoga, Janette explained, means 'perfect' or 'complete' yoga within which there are eight paths for union with the Divine or with your own self ("which are one and the same really") – meditation, chanting, breathing, service, knowledge ... One of these paths is Hatha yoga – physically working with the body's energies to attain a certain state.

"As a child I didn't have a lot of confidence in myself," said Janette. "I suffered a lot from being nervous and worried about things. I was always a seeker although perhaps I didn't know it when I was young. Mine was a conventional Christian background but I was the odd one out. People thought I was weird. I knew things inside me that I didn't consciously understand. Then I discovered yoga. I started more as a way to make me look and feel good. I wanted to lose weight and get fit.

"I was interested in the spiritual side but not in a very profound way. It deepened through my practice which has become stronger and stronger. Siddha is a path that unveils and expands *all* teachings. We use the Bible and the Vedic scriptures. You begin to see the connections. Working with the physical helps me understand the philosophy and vice versa. They work hand-in-hand and feed each other. I stuck at yoga because it worked and now I find it's given me what I always wanted. It is a kind of therapy – a dynamic, bodywork therapy for healing the fundamental sickness of the spirit. It cuts through all the mental stuff and gets to the heart of the matter. The fact that you have to put in a fair amount of effort makes it much more powerful than just going to a therapist and passively expecting someone else to sort you out. I like it because it honours all paths and hasn't alienated me from what I was brought up with. It merely answered the many questions. The Ten Commandments, for instance – not just what are they but how do you *live* with those rules? Well, if you do the practices – the hatha, the meditation etc., the good qualities just arise from within. Bad comes from hurting. When you can get free of the hurting, the good qualities already exist within you – non-judgement, detachment – they're *revealed*. It's like, 'Oh yes! Now I see how to live with the Ten Commandments.'"

Janette was a hairdresser by training then, four years ago, feeling low and depressed about her life, knowing she wanted to make some big changes, she went to the ashram to visit her guru looking for help and guidance.

"One of the things that came out of it was to be much more serious about my practice and that eventually led to a teaching job. My guru is a woman. Guru Mai. Having a woman for my spiritual leader seems natural to me and it has made me feel stronger as a woman – given me an inner strength – although I have to say it's hard being a strong woman in relationships. Most men haven't found a way of relating to awakened women. They're terrified of them! They fear they won't be in control, so they run a mile rather than trying to create a partnership. Eventually they'll probably come round to it and ultimately it will be everyone's liberation but it's my generation that are the pioneers bearing the brunt!"

I asked Janette if, as a woman, she had strong views about the patriarchal nature of the main Western faiths – 'God the Father' and all that.

"Yes I do!" she answered, vigorously. "I have especially strong views about the Catholic religion. And the Church of England isn't that much better. To be honest with you I just think it's terribly sad that they're not giving people what they really need to be uplifted. What upsets me most about conventional religion is they lay so many dreadful trips on people. In every village there's a big, beautiful church which ought to be a place of incredible spiritual growth and solace and self-discovery but it isn't. The context of 'you're a miserable sinner', means people are not being nourished. I *know* I am not that. Inside us, in a very deep part of us, we know we are not that, so it's a crime to make us think it. It's depressing to go into a church – the guiding light, it's supposed to be – to find they're going against what really is you.

"For women in particular, a church with no female deity means you have nothing personal to relate to. The only way to be a holy woman is to be a weeping virgin or a dead martyr. No strong women. Never God the Mother. I think, going back to Adam and Eve, that Eve discovered the spiritual side of life and that gave her tremendous power. The man saw this and was shocked. He couldn't cope. It was too challenging so he had to find a way of destroying it. Woman became the evil party. She was put down. Her sexuality crushed. That's my main bugbear. In Eastern thought the feminine principle is the awakening of the Kundalini – an unfolding of spirituality and sexuality coming together. Now doesn't that sound like a better idea to you?"

It does. To live in this precious animal body on this earth is as great a part of spiritual life as anything else. I love the idea of the 'awakening' process – a lifelong path of awakening, attention, surrender and commitment. Spirituality as a way of life. A happiness that is not dependant on any of the changing conditions of the world but comes out of one's own difficult and conscious inner transformation.

"So much of the male interpretation of spirituality has been a head trip," said Janette, "projected outwards – up there, in the sky, out of us. A woman's is much more internal – wombs, orgasms, childbearing, breast-feeding. Everything we do, as women, can be a spiritual experience. A man sees the world as an extension of himself. In *his* image. God looks like him. For a woman that's not so important. It's more individual and personal. She can accept that each has their own way – that spirituality is more about who we are than what ideal we pursue. In fact I think the growth of consciousness and the interest in conservation is coming about because of the strengthening of the feminine principle. The woman has the babies. She's thinking about what we are leaving for future generations. She's more centred, more down-to-earth, holistic, connected. Men have trouble making connections in the same way. They can only see straight ahead. The thrusting thing – shoot an arrow, lead with their dicks. Women see a rounder, more continuous, cyclical way."

I agree. Not so much an 'out-of-body experience' as an 'in-the-body experience' – making certain, in Jack Kornfield's lovely phrase, that "our path is connected to our heart". Only in *this moment* can we discover that which is timeless. Only *here* can we find the love which we seek. Spirituality is both ordinary and awakened. It allows us to rest in the wonder of life. It allows the light to shine through us. Once again, perhaps the secret of life on earth lies with something so simple as learning to enjoy sufficiency rather than excess. How can spirituality be truly integrated into *every* aspect of life? Not served up once a week as a ready-made, off-the-peg formula but truly integrated.

"I've found what I've been looking for all my life," said Janette. "My spiritual way lies within siddha and hatha yoga. I want to continue to grow and deepen with that. There are lots of principles and teachings that I'm not quite living *yet* but I want to. There's a lot to learn!"

Janette is another example of a courageous woman with a warrior's heart who has had to swim against the stream to re-define spirituality for herself, to live her truth. Now she is studying anatomy in preparation for developing the remedial side of yoga and moving toward her true vocation as a healer.

November brought a welcome invitation to travel with Gemma, another healer friend, to Ireland. I have Irish blood in my veins and I find myself drawn back again and again to that wonderful country. Mary Aver had said to me before I left home, "The Goddess is alive and well in Ireland. You'll meet her in many guises." Meanwhile, where else in the world would you see scrawled on the wall of a pub Ladies loo, in place of the usual obscenities: 'PILGRIMAGE! Meet on the steps of the Church of Our Lady of Drogheda. Sunday. Cost £12'. As we drove through the valley of the River Boyne there was another sign: 'DANGER! DEEP WATERS. DANGEROUS CURRENTS.' A metaphor for Ireland itself. And now it is a bright, cold dawn as we wake after a night's sleep with hot water bottles in Fania Mahony's grand old house in County Louth.

Chapter 9

'If we could read the secret histories of our enemies,
we should find in each person's life
sorrow and suffering enough
to disarm all hostility.'

LONGFELLOW

Fania, whose brother was murdered by the IRA, is bone-weary, as so many Irish women are, of the terrible violence that has riven this beautiful land for so long. Sensitive to the sufferings on both sides, she is also very sensitive to the needs of the poor earth to be listened to and for healing rituals to be performed. To this end, Fania leads groups of people (mainly women) on pilgrimages to ancient sacred sites and stone circles – there to feel and absorb the spirit of place and to do consciousness-raising work in the form of chanting, ritual, dance and prayer. She is very knowledgeable about Irish history and legend and has very kindly offered to be our guide this week to some of her favourite places.

I want to find out more about the role of the goddesses in ancient Ireland, about the veneration of the Mother Goddess and the gradual transition from polytheistic paganism to Christianity. I also want to explore the significance of the feminine and the concept of 'divine marriage' in Celtic culture, myth and religion. What happened? Why, as in so many other places all over the world, did the baby get thrown out with the bath water when the monotheistic religions gained the ascendant and the sacred and divine became exclusively masculine. In the Celtic world, as in the Native American, the Aboriginal, the Yoruba – the Divine Feminine was of equal importance. Spirits dwelled in the landscape, their all-pervading sacred presence presided over all human endeavour. Respect for animals, for all living things, for the living body of Mother Earth went hand in hand with a feeling of intense intimacy between ourselves and the Divine Presence. There was a creative, conscious synergistic relationship between humans and nature, a harmonious co-existence with the environment. At least this is what we would like to believe and to me the question is not, 'was it really like that?' but, 'can we make it right now what it always should have been?'

There are multiple reasons, apart from my Irish blood, why I find myself drawn here. The roots of the Western wisdom tradition, the art of pilgrimage, personal and planetary healing, understanding 'landscape temples', exploring our developing consciousness – I think these are some of them. And to look at the ways Irish women are restoring the sacred feminine to her rightful place in the divine marriage as part of the work we are all doing. It seems no accident that this is the year my two littlest grand-daughters were born: Freya – named after the Great Goddess of the northern European tradition and Zoë – named after life itself.

Our first day was fully taken up with pilgrimages to two of the great 'land temples' of Ireland; The Hill of Tara and Uisneach (pronounced Ushna), the place where the five provinces meet. The morning had dawned bright but by the time we'd driven to Tara it had become cold, windy and overcast. We bundled up in hats and scarves and Fania introduced us to the sacred geometry of the site – the great horizontal body of the Goddess laid out on the ground in a series of straight avenues and curvaceous mounds – suggesting that its original construction had been made with an understanding of the 'chakra' system of energy centres in the body 5500 years ago in Neolithic times.

Tara, the domain of Gods and Goddesses, a sort of Celtic equivalent to Mount Olympus in Greece, was the ancient Bronze-Age capital of Ireland – or rather of the four realms of old Ireland – Ulster, Munster, Leinster and Connaught. From the highest point there is a spectacular vista over the Central Plain of Ireland. Here the bards and Druids assembled every year for the festivals. It was also the royal court, seat of the old heroic, semi-divine kings of Ireland. It's all shrouded in the mists of myth, of course, but it is thought that in early Ireland there were several orders of priestesses and the legends tell us about the Goddess Medb who was the guardian and protector of Tara. She conferred prosperity and fertility on the land by mating with the king in a sacred marriage that sanctified his reign as part of the Feast of Tara. She was the goddess who slept with many kings and in the absence of any suitable candidate for the kingship would rule Tara herself until the rightful king was found.

The green, green fields of Ireland welcomed and held us in their ancient embrace. We evoked the Goddess Mebd, and for good measure, Kwan Yin, at the entrance and Fania asked permission of the spirit guardians to allow us access. It is very important to show the proper respect, said Fania. We trudged up hill and down dale, we three grandmothers, walking the sacred body of the land – connecting the chakras, hugging the stones, clearing the energy, loving the earth. Then, as the rain began to seep out of the low clouds, we set off for Uisneach. By the time we arrived it was raining in earnest and we were thoroughly chilled. We donned our waterproofs and, again invoking the Goddess, entered the 'temple'. To the casual rambler it might just appear to be a normal field but not to us. Here the sacred flame was kept. Here the initiates learned the ropes. Here a sacred pond for purification and there the huge, magical 'Cat Stone' precariously balanced, overlooking the sweep of the valley below. This place, the local farmers will tell you, is lucky farmland. Good crops. A blessed place. The energy did feel wonderful and the whole area must be lovely in the sunshine but for now, three dripping, dippy grandmothers with muddy boots and runny noses reverently walked about the place straining our sixth senses into the ether for visions of past glories. Damply we sang a few goddess songs and danced a little fire dance above the place where Gemma's Tibetan lama, Gen Rinpoche, had buried his precious pot. (Gemma and her late husband, Martin, have been sponsoring some Tibetan monks in exile in Dharamsala. Gen Rinpoche came over to Britain the previous year, at her invitation, to give some teachings and to bury three jars containing prayers, mantras, rice, dried fruit and sacred objects – one in Iona, one in Gemma's garden in Kent and one here in Uisneach).

Uisneach, in County Meath, is one of the most sacred places in Ireland. A place of celebration and renewal. All of us were sure we could definitely feel something special in the energy there but I was well aware how barking mad we must have looked, rain streaming down our faces, holding hands and dancing about the hillside on an inclement November afternoon. As night drew on, the heavens wept and hundreds of starlings rose like an omen in a black cloud from the grass at our feet. The thought crossed my mind, 'If my kids could see me now I'd never live it down'! Cackle, cackle. (Later, when I showed this chapter to Rosanne, my editor, she was indignant and wrote in the margins of the manuscript; "Are you apologising for undertaking women's sacred work? Who cares how it looks? Since when did appearances have anything to do with it?" … and, of course, she is absolutely right. No, I am not for one single minute apologising but I have uncomfortably to acknowledge that by trying to preempt the ridicule this kind of work often provokes, by attempting to defuse the patronising contempt in which it is often held, I myself am guilty of reinforcing the patriarchal prejudices I have grown up with. If I, who believe passionately in its worth, cannot have the confidence to stand tall with it without making it into a joke, how can we ever hope to dismantle those prejudices internally and change the energy around women's sacred work? So I have left this section as I wrote it. Mea culpa.)

We talked a lot in the car, during the two-hour drive back home, about the healing work we are all engaged upon, individually and collectively, whether it be at a personal level, a national level or global/planetary level. It's as if we, along with many other women, are all trying to remember something. That word again – re-member – trying to put back together this fragmented dream of unity and harmony we have, to re-instate the 'Goddess', the Divine Feminine, in order to restore the health of the earth. I must say I feel quite hopeful. Daft as it may look there is a level of seriousness here that cannot be denied or ridiculed. I love the idea of pilgrimage and I love the idea of *embodiment* – taking worship and prayer back out of the head and into the body, out of the church and onto the land. What we were doing was ancient women's business, reverence for life and for our 'Mother' – witchcraft, to put it in plain English – for which, even in these more enlightened times, we could be misunderstood and quite probably reviled. It is sacred work, holy work, if it's done in the name of healing. The legacy of the Inquisition, even all these centuries on, is that such work is treated with fear and suspicion.

Uisneach is actually the very centre of Ireland. And the Cat Stone, also known as the Umbilicus Hibernial or 'mother stone', which we touched today is the navel of Ireland where, as the ancient myth relates, an umbilical cord was attached to the womb of the Goddess. According to Michael Dames' excellent book, *Mythic Ireland,* this was the birthplace of "a Divine Island called by the name of a living Goddess, Eriu (Eire)". It also seems as if Uisneach, like Stonehenge, was the centre of a prehistoric sun goddess religion – the place of the mystic fire from which every chief's hearth was kindled throughout Ireland, the central fire beacon of a radiating ring of Beltane fires. Excavations, said Fania, have revealed a massive layer of ash which would seem to be evidence that a perpetual fire was once kept burning there. In the old Irish language the same word meant sun or divine intelligence.

The next morning the three of us sat around the breakfast table drinking tea and eating our porridge while Fania told us the ancient legend of Macha. She was a warrior-goddess who, disguised as an ordinary mortal, married an ordinary man. Her husband promised never to speak of her superhuman powers but he couldn't keep his mouth shut and boasted to the king and to the men of Ulster that she could outrun the swiftest horse. The king challenged him to prove it so he agreed to have her run in a race against the king's chariot. Macha begged him not to force her as she was pregnant at the time but he didn't dare to retract his boast. While running she gave birth to twins (and still won the race!) but died at the end and with her dying breath she cursed the men of Ulster thereafter to suffer as she had done and to be as weak as a woman in labour during times of trouble.

Well both Gemma and I were struck with the image of this terrible, enduring curse on Ulster and of a net of pain and sorrow engulfing the North of Ireland to this day. We all resolved to use our Crone Power when we reached our day's goal of the Sliabh na Caillighe (pronounced Slieve na Culliuck) or Hill of the Wise Women. We would ask that the curse be lifted and peace and forgiveness come to Ulster. Nothing ventured, nothing gained so off we went, stopping in Kells to admire the wonderful Celtic cross at the crossroads and buy a pair of wellies for me so as to avoid another slosh in wet shoes. As we neared the beautiful hill country of Westmeath the sky cleared. Sliabh na Caillighe is an astonishing place – a green, voluptuously contoured sacred site of sleek, grassy mounds crowned with cairns and stone circles.

We climbed to the top and entered the largest chamber which is shaped like a woman's body and contains a beautiful stone in the 'head' carved with sun eyes and swirls of Celtic spirals. The Mother Goddess as architecture. The decorative quality of Celtic art seems to draw you in to patterns of energy and visions of reality. Like Eastern mandalas they are there to be contemplated. Using Fania's Tibetan singing bowl, we performed our little ritual – spontaneously devised on the spot. We called upon the power of the wise women and the Great Spirit to use us to be of service. We held hands and chanted and prayed and knew for sure that it is still as possible today as it ever has been to encounter the deities in visions and dreams or in moments of inspiration in sacred places. We sat on the mighty throne-shaped limestone boulder (known as The Hag's Chair) set into the periphery of the cairn and could see all the way to Uisneach. The midsummer and midwinter sunsets line up these two sacred sites.

We felt powerful working our crone magic inside the womb of the mother, undoing the curse, sending out light and love. We walked around the vast site in the brilliant setting sun, touching the stones, sitting inside the cairns, raising our arms in supplication. It was very exhilarating. Big black ravens rode the thermals and we sang as we returned to the car, nearly blown off the hillside by the force of the wind. Three rosy-cheeked grannies in our priestess robes of waterproof macs and woolly hats! We would be easy targets for poking fun at but somehow in Ireland, where myths and legends, stories and faeries, fantasies and facts are woven together in a gorgeous tapestry, we are just part of the fabric.

Before coming to Ireland I read for the first time Keats' thrilling poem, 'La Belle Dame Sans Merci':

> *... I met a lady in the meads,*
> *Full beautiful – a faery's child,*
> *Her hair was long, her foot was light,*
> *And her eyes were wild ...*

It was good to be reminded that faery folk still dwell in Ireland in the hearts and minds of many. Fantastical things have always happened here. Curses and blessings thrum in the tangible vibrations that hold the land in thrall. Who's to say that three old grandmothers can't influence the course of history? In our ancient memories are stored vestiges of sacred knowledge and doing this hag stuff rekindles the fires in the depths of our being. Gemma, Fania and I each believe that human beings are due for an evolutionary change as we approach the end of a two-thousand year cycle, that the time has come to release patterns of negativity, of doubt and fear, patterns that are no longer appropriate to who we are and what we are becoming.

Well, it is one thing to intuit all this and quite another to be willing to try to do something about it. My guess is that it is only when we make a real commitment to align ourselves with love, clarity, understanding and compassion that we begin to disempower the impulses toward anger, resentment and vengeance which have cursed Ulster and other epicentres of violence for so long. Our intention and our dearest wish is to use our energy to create something different.

The following day was Brigit's day. The famous figure who so potently straddles the age of mythic goddesses and the age of Christian saints. We three seekers set off to meet up with Fania's friend, May Coyle – a stunning, red-haired Irish woman who is also a Celtic scholar and a storyteller. She took us to Brigit's Well – a clear natural spring said to be her birthplace at Foughart near Dundalk on the border between Northern Ireland and Eire. We anointed ourselves with the holy water and said prayers invoking Brigit to be with us the next day when we were to travel to Armagh. We linked arms and chanted an Irish blessing by the sacred well. Then we went on to Brigit's shrine – a place that exemplifies perfectly her dual identity. A stream with a series of lovely old boulders accords with Brigit's role as ancient divinity, garish statues of her in saintly guise and stations of the cross acknowledge her metamorphosis into Christian icon.

May told us a lot about Brigit – a powerful figure in Irish mythology. In ancient times she was the Triple Goddess (the maiden, the mother and the crone – the model for all subsequent trinities) who has moved effortlessly through many centuries fulfilling different roles in different time periods. Brigit has many links with Juno, Isis, Vesta and Minerva. Her symbols, the vulture, the serpent and the cow were also all symbols of Isis. Her imagery is associated with the sun, the moon, milk and sacred fires. She watches over healing, poetry and the cutting away of the obsolete. She was the Mother Goddess of the Tuatha Dé Danaan (the tribe of Divine Beings who watched over Ireland in

earliest times). Her feast day is February 2nd which coincides with Imbolc, a major feast of the Celtic year, first day of the Celtic Spring when Brigit breathed life into the mouth of the dead winter (and co-incidentally the birthday of my first granddaughter). The milk from Brigit's sacred cow was believed to be an antidote to poisoned arrows.

Even as Brigit metamorphosed into a Christian saint, her role as Mother Goddess was never completely eradicated. Much of her imagery has remained. Flames still come from her head. Milk, fire, sun and serpents figure in the stories of Saint Brigit. Her symbol, Brigit's Cross made of plaited straw is a solar emblem and still used to protect the harvest in parts of Ireland today. Brigit was a form of the Sun Goddess. She is said to have hung her cloak on the rays of the sun. She was whole and complete, one who created herself without a spouse – representing the unity of Irish culture.

A clear policy of the early Christian church, said May, was to appropriate the symbols and feast days of the old religion and convert them to Christian use. Brigit made the transition from Mother Goddess to virgin saint but she didn't go quietly or give up without a fight. Brigit's Cross still hangs in Irish kitchen's (and my bedroom) for luck. Until recent times midwives would mark the four corners of a house with Brigit's crosses and sing:

> *Four angels at her head*
> *Matthew Mark Luke and John*
> *God bless the bed that she lies on*
> *New moon, new moon God bless me*
> *God bless this house and family*

To this sound the newborn entered the world. Michael Dames in *Mythic Ireland* writes; "Brigit's work is nearly done. Creeping secularism is making her visits unnecessary, so she stays away." We must invite her back to dance with us and to help us heal the wounds of this land. She was a healer – the goddess who protected women in childbirth. She was a mediator in battles. She was the Mother Goddess whose main concern was the future well-being of Ireland.

The life of Saint Brigit is steeped in magic and miraculous happenings some of which bear a strong resemblance to the heroic figure of pagan myth. As a baby she was unharmed in a magical fire that glowed but did not consume the house in which she slept. She was associated with prophecy and divination and is the patron saint of poets and seers. She was born at sunrise as her mother straddled a threshold. She was a paradox – both virgin and patron saint of pregnant women, stimulator of fertility and curer of frigidity. The saint like the Mother Goddess was a generous provider of abundance, a gift-giver. The saint retained her namesake's pagan Spring festival – a celebration of the lactation of ewes and cattle. Sheela-na-gigs on medieval churches are none other than Brigit holding her vulva wide open.

Foughart, where we prayed at Brigit's well, is a place of intense and fervent devotion. People come everyday to ask for her intercession. Little rags were tied on the bushes as votive offerings for healing, for wellbeing, for increased milk-production of cattle. The pagan and Christian traditions are so subtly intertwined that it is impossible to disentangle them. Brigit lives on in the myths and folklore of Ireland. I felt her presence today as a great protectress. If we call upon the energy she symbolises, who knows what miracles might occur?

We stopped for tea at a country house hotel and looked out upon the purple hills in the setting sun. Anything seemed possible.

The next morning we set out early for the border, crossing over into Northern Ireland amid a welter of slogans on walls proclaiming 'Free Political Prisoners', 'No Peace, No Surrender'. Gun towers, look-out posts and little village police stations entirely boxed in by barbed wire cages give a sinister war-zone look to the place. The currency changes, the accent changes, the religion changes, the politics change but the land remains the same – beautiful rolling hills and fields, farms and loughs. Birds fly freely across the invisible line in the air. The nonsense of it all seems particularly poignant. Passing through the city of Armagh we went on out to Emain Macha.

This is the site of the ancient capital of Ulster, one of the most important places in Irish history and legend – supposedly marked out by the great warrior goddess, Macha, using her brooch. All kinds of astrological and geometric theories have recently been put forward as to how this miraculous, amazingly accurate pre-historic calculator/compass worked – lining up, as it does, the Earth's energies, phases of the Moon, equinoxes, solstices, seasons and elements. Here we had arranged to meet with Angela and Theresa, two women friends of Fania's who do the landscape temple work with her and a young man called Callum McCann (whose name means Son of the Wolf) – a young warrior with great Irish looks and a living enthusiasm for the myths and legends of the place.

We approached the huge, grassy mound and walked slowly in a spiral around it, entering the sacred site between two towering trees where we paused to ask permission of the guardian spirits and place a few flowers as an offering. We came together at the top in the wind and sun and joined hands in a circle bringing all our sincere prayers for healing to this blighted nation. We stood there in silence, eyes closed, calling on Brigit – the great Mother Goddess and saint – each in our own way asking for guidance and afterwards shared our insights and visualisations. I guess we must all be very imaginative or else very blessed (or very batty) but we were amazed at the power of what happened. ["Why were you surprised?" wrote Rosanne in the margin and, of course, that was just me lacking in confidence again. I *know* this work is powerful.]

Between us we saw visions of angelic beings and spirals of light. We saw ravens and golden crosses. We saw the Goddess with her golden scissors snip the net that held the curse. Wide eyed we sat on the ground feeling rather stunned. I wouldn't have been surprised to hear the Hallelujah Chorus but there was just the sound of the wind. We sang an Irish blessing and asked again for the curse of Ulster to be lifted. We left a rose and a carnation as gifts and stood for a silent moment in the beauty and majesty of that ancient place before walking slowly down – stopping on the way to talk to the old, old man who is the caretaker. We told him what we were doing and he nodded his head. "She'll be glad of your company," he said.

After that it was on to an extraordinary site not far from Draperstown where a complex of stone circles has recently been uncovered in a peat bog. A joyful, dancing place of lovely energy lit by a wild twilight sky with distant curtains of rain which kept away long enough for us to walk further off into the heather to a site discovered by Angela herself – possibly another circle or cairn not yet completely excavated.

Angela is an amazing person – a big, sturdy Ulsterwoman, a sheep-farmer with not much education who has found herself on the 'path' of personal development and steadfastly moved along it. She has been learning massage and healing, getting training and qualifications, struggling with the study and the written work. Every year she asks her bank manager for a loan and spends it on travel – the pyramids in Egypt, the Harmonic Convergence on Mount Shasta in California, workshops with spiritual teachers. Her husband, who does not share her interests, is nonetheless very supportive of her and looks after the sheep when she goes off travelling but it has been a lonely road in a small conservative, rural community to be such an odd-ball.

Angela's friend Theresa has been on several of the trips with her. She was a nun for 11 years until her non-conformity and questioning got her thrown out of the convent. She discovered yoga and meditation, studied massage and began to acknowledge all her own extraordinary psychic and visionary powers. She now practices a form of healing called multi-dimensional cellular work. Like Angela, she is deeply involved with the women's peace movement in Belfast. Both of them are at the grass-roots level trying to make a difference, resisting the violence on both sides, working for mutual understanding. They are good, brave, strong women who are courageous enough to march to a different drummer in what has been for so long a patriarchal, church-dominated society.

We walked around amongst the stone circles in the peat bog until our feet were so cold and wet we could no longer feel them then drove back to Angela's remote farmhouse where she invited us to a typical Irish farm supper. The sheep baaaed contentedly in the yard as we sat laughing on Angela's turquoise settee warming our shins by the open door of the solid fuel stove marvelling at our shared interests and enthusiasms. We all *know* we are doing the same work, no matter how different our backgrounds, coming together from all over the place to love and heal the Earth, to encourage and support each other. There has been so much tragedy here as the Irish 'troubles' have dragged on and on – so much grief, so many deaths on both sides, so much pain. It is time for an end to it. Time for forgiveness, peace and healing.

The next day Fania fixed a meeting for me with a remarkable young woman called Podragín Clancy who is currently writing her Master's thesis on Irish folklore and Celtic spirituality. Podragín grew up in an Irish-speaking house-hold steeped in traditional tales side-by-side with a Catholic upbringing. She sees no conflict now in the weaving together of her love for the Goddess and her love for "J.C.", as she calls Him. Podragín lived for several years on the Aran Islands, the furthest outpost of Ireland where the folklore, mythology and customs are still living traditions. The experience fuelled her love for Irish culture and Celtic spirituality and formed the basis for the post-graduate work she is doing now.

An exceptionally bright and articulate person, Podragín was invited recently onto the most popular chat show on Irish television to talk about Halloween – its origins and its importance in the Celtic calendar. She arrived with a broomstick and a flashing pumpkin and talked with erudition about the Goddess and the *calliaghe* – the hag or wise woman figure – which is pretty daring in Catholic Ireland. She discovered a flair and a taste for this brilliant way of disseminating her passion and the phone hasn't stopped ringing since with further broadcasting invitations.

Podragín is a woman of absolute integrity with an attractive blend of con-fidence and modesty. Her appearance on such a popular show will have reached an audience of thousands. She just feels a sense of wonder that the plot of her life is unfolding as it is. Her childhood was full of pain, violence and alcohol abuse. She knows about anger, helplessness and brutality. As a teenager she was militant, chaining herself to the railings of the British Embassy, attracted to the I.R.A. but by some miracle she began, instead, to do some work on herself – healing the hurt, understanding the power of love and the peaceful path. I can see her becoming a beacon. She has all the qualities and the knowledge and the passion to lead people to a celebration of everything that's most wonderful about this country.

I asked Podragín if she could define Celtic spirituality and how it differed from any other kind. She said it had much to do with the Irish language and much to do with 'immanence' – the sense of God in everything, in every greet-ing, in every action, in the place names and the landscape, the blessings and the prayers. Celtic religion was first and foremost associated with the sanctity of the land and the power of certain particular places.

The entire landscape was alive and hummed with power, she said, the spirituality was in the elements and the seasons and the cycle of the year. It was in the Celtic calendar (Imbolc; Beltane; Lughnasa; and Samhain). It was to do with divination, healing, superstition, spirits and faery folk, animals that speak, ravens, transformation. In pre-Christian Ireland the Druids and Druidesses were powerful spiritual leaders, like shamans in other parts of the world. They func-tioned as intermediaries between the tribes and the spiritual realms. According to the beliefs of the Celts, the Divine pervaded every aspect of life and spirits were everywhere – in ancient trees and sacred groves, mountaintops and rock formations, rivers, streams and holy wells. The earth was regarded as the source of all fertility.

I could see many parallels with the Native American world view or with the neo-Pagans who, I suppose, are none other than the Celts brought up to date. Parallels, too, in the way the ancient stories have lived on in the belly of Christianity – adapting and blending (in the same way as have the deities of the Yoruba religion or Our Lady of Guadaloupe).

Following a lead from Podragín, I travelled to Inishmore, the largest of the Aran Islands off the west coast of Ireland, to visit Tess Harper, Podragín's friend, who has made her home on this remote, forbidding chunk of rock which has always been a holy place, made so by whatever force caused it to soar upwards from the ocean's floor. The journey across the Galway bay was perishingly cold but spectacular with rainbows flinging themselves from sea to sky. Something in the meteorological makeup of the place means there are more rainbows to be seen here than anywhere else on earth. I got a ride from the port to Teample Ciarán and walked the couple of hundred yards down to Tess and Dara's half-built house. They are a gorgeous couple and immediately welcomed me with invitations to eat with them and stay the night. People come and go here a lot, attracted by the loose-knit spiritual community that has gathered around their nucleus.

Dara, until six months ago, was a Catholic priest increasingly unhappy with the rigid forms and hierarchies of his job so he has left Catholicism to become a priest of the Celtic Church. He can see now, he says with hindsight, that what he would have loved to become in his youth was a shaman – a person versed in the magical healing arts and in ritual – but of course no such vocation existed for a young Irish man so he joined the priesthood and became, as he says himself, institutionalised. Not any more.

Dara and Tess are expecting their first baby and building their house by themselves from scratch (it's been five years in the making so far). They publish *Aisling* a non-profit-making, bi-lingual quarterly magazine 'rooted in the Celtic', dedicated to spiritual matters, to living in right relationships and working for transformation. They do not borrow money from commercial banks, they do not advertise commercial products, they do not accept sponsorship from church, state or commercial bodies and raise all their funding through share-loans. The paper is chlorine-free and recycled, the printing press is in their living room. While Dara is up in the rafters, working all day on the plumbing, Tess is tending her goats, baking bread, growing all their own organic vegetables and studying Irish spirituality and folklore. She loves this place and the unique culture of the islands. They are both determined that their child's first language shall be Irish. Living with them for a year and helping out is a young French girl who ran away from home when her family broke up. She followed her dream of living on an island and just turned up here.

All night long the wind screamed and hurled itself against the window behind my head like a demented animal trying to get in and I felt completely exhausted the next morning. I watched the sunrise illuminate the strange, stony landscape and marvelled at the patchwork panorama of pocket-handkerchief fields divided by hundreds of low stone walls painstakingly constructed to keep the scant layer of soil from blowing away. It is not a place for the fainthearted. Life is hard here. Only the most resolute would attempt to cultivate such unforgiving ground. I don't think I could live here even for a week although there are things of incomparable beauty – the rainbows, for example, pouring out of the sky onto the sea or onto the cliffs like bridges to another world.

I went with Tess to feed her goats which graze by the remains of a 6th century Celtic Church, impregnated with prayer, slumbering the years away in a field down the hill. Older still are the megaliths – solitary standing stones still bearing their StoneAge witness. The sun lit up the sea and the intense green fields and I caught a glimpse of the magic.

Tess wrote in a Samhain issue of *Aisling*: "There are days here … in winter – deep sky, sea blue days when the light is crystal, clear, magical. It makes everything vibrate from within. Days for a brisk walk down the lane to the seashore – that small piece of ocean that knows me – Teampal Ciarán neatly nestled behind; church, well, standing stones all pulsing their power – land power to sea swell … This place carries its own benediction … Even on those other days – moody, wet, dark days. Going out at dusk, especially, under a really mean sky before it rains, the wild intensity of grass and grey stone needs to be seen to be believed."

I asked Tess about her love for this strange, wild place and her spiritual path which has brought her here to share her life with Dara.

"Dara is attracted to and immersed in the New Testament Celtic Spirituality – that is to say *from* Christianity onwards", she began. "There certainly was a time in monastic history when it was less patriarchal than it subsequently became – a time when they got certain resonances right, but I'm drawn to the *pre-Christian* spirituality of the Irish people. I like the line of continuity that reaches back through to the older spirituality. They say that Ireland was the only place where Christianity came without bloodshed. To me, that's very significant. The early Irish spirituality was open to the teachings of Christianity. Christianity was an augmentation, a refinement, it offered something new and for a certain time in history the old and the new complemented each other – creating something very powerful in the process. This was what the Irish church offered the world.

"Gradually, though, it became eroded – worn down by the Roman influence and the whole patriarchal social structure that came with it – which was a shame. You see, I like Christianity! I'm not a very good Christian in the standard sense but I really love Christ and I love his message when it's seated into the old spirituality in a healthy way. The big thing about the old spirituality is that it recognised a feminine base to everything. The primary deity was feminine and the Earth itself was feminine. After that came a pantheon of Gods and Goddesses honouring the fact that life is this incredibly complex interplay of energies. I see the 'gods' and 'goddesses' as personifications of these different energies.

"Another thing that interests me very much is the Jungian way of describing the inner world – the collective unconscious in which the gods and goddesses appear as archetypes. The role of religion in those early societies was to balance the energies. It helped people live a psychologically more balanced life. In modern society we have lost these healthy balanced containers and found ourselves in a kind of chaos – floundering in a lack of meaning where the onus is on every individual to balance their own psyches. Many of us don't know how to do that."

But would it not be true to say, I wondered, that people in those early societies way back then weren't conscious of all this? That everything may well have been imbued with spirit but people lived under the yoke of a lot of fear and superstition?

"Definitely," she answered. "In terms of human consciousness, it was the infant stage. The primal female deity was The Big Tit. Early societies worked *because* they were unconscious. They worked at the level of the magical. Every-thing was One. Everybody had a role to play. But because human consciousness keeps moving and developing it was essential for it also to go through the patriarchal phase. Linear, masculine, it was the conscious mind pulling away from this devouring feminine immersion. It was about standing your own ground, being an individual. Now, at this crucial point in time, we're at another transition. There's a need to grow up – to approach this same immanence as adults so that we understand the symbolism of the deities rather than just accepting them blindly. That phase of linear thinking brought us to the edge of the precipice and now we need to re-incorporate some of the wisdom of the magical – re-integrate the feminine – but from a *conscious* point of view, if we're not going to destroy everything. It's make or break and that's what I find so exciting. I don't envisage a return to some mythical matriarchal paradise because there probably wasn't one. I imagine it was a nightmare! I have a terror in me of an all-woman, all-mother mind set."

Me too. And I love the 'otherness' of men. I like the difficult challenge of living with them. One of the disturbing trends in Western society in recent times has been to denigrate and marginalize the role of men, particularly in family life. Many things would not be in conflict at all if it hadn't been for the disempowerment of the 'feminine'. Let's not now disempower the 'masculine' and replace the present tyranny with another.

"I believe we can create a new paradigm which is a mixture of magic and consciousness, subliminal and rational," continued Tess, "but we haven't fully extracted ourselves from the patriarchal yet. There is a terrible homesickness for that part of ourselves that has been lost – so many manifestations of *longing* for the feminine, for a greater connectedness, for nature. I see it in my own psyche – just how entrenched the patriarchy is and how damaging. It's a lifelong journey to heal ourselves. I know that the land is my healer. This is the beginning of a wholesome reconnection to the feminine, to the Mother. I'm finding it in nature. That is the real source for me – going down to my goats, sitting with them, milking them, minding them, just being with them. Or sitting in a field and just watching or walking across the craig. I've developed a love affair with this island. For such a small piece of land there's a huge amount of diversity once you become familiar with it. This land knows my name."

Tess is captivated by the prehistoric mythology of old Ireland, the invasions, the waves of peoples who came to these lands before the Celts, and by the tales of the Tuatha Dé Danaan – gods and goddess figures, divine, magical beings who never really went away.

"Even now they'd be the faerie folk," she says. "The story is that they lost the battle against the Celts because their magic wasn't as powerful. They agreed to go underground as a race while the victors took the upper world. From that moment on that's what we still live with in this land: The *Underworld* where the Tuatha Dé Danaan reside, the primal deities and the feminine spirit; the *Middleworld* for humans and animals; the *Overworld* for the cosmic gods of the sun, moon and stars. The tree would have symbolised the three-tiered concept – the connection between the worlds. It's why a lot of trees were planted around holy wells and why people still hang their little rags onto the branches of those trees as a petition.

"Unfortunately", she went on, "there was a break in the connection with the past and faerie folk tradition lost its root. It became a dump-all for the shadow stuff. Faeries became merely the tricksters. I'd much rather they'd remained the land spirits, the animal spirits which are still a hugely important part of Irish folklore, thought and culture (and overlaps in so many ways with all that I've read about African and Native American traditions).

"I'm interested in why sacred mounds and sites were laid out according to astrological principles – probably totally unconsciously. People were just that much more connected to their instincts. There was a built-in 'knowing'. And I've seen it here on the island with the older people who still have it particularly in relation to how they plant their gardens and work the land. When they wake up in the morning they know their name and what the needs of the land are today. They know what has to be done according to what season of the year it is. They don't sit down with a pen and make a list. It's so much more a part of their bloodstream – a beautiful kind of harmony in relation to the land and to food and to eating. Organic gardeners like us have had to learn it from a book. We're getting there now but it's taken 12 years."

Tess rails against the way modern Western society has become so split apart, so alienated, so compartmentalised. "We've had visitors turn up their nose at goat that has been reared here. I've had kids from Dublin saying, 'I'm not eating those potatoes, they've got mud on them.' The fact that they grew in the soil in a field and had to be washed hadn't occurred to them. I find that tragic because it spells out disconnections and dislocations all through their psyches with echoes right into their emotional lives and into their whole physical experience of themselves in a body."

I reflected that, in the wake of this disconnectedness from reality, it is easy to see how the lure of altered states and 'virtual reality' can be so seductive. Whether with drugs or computer games, youngsters are in danger of losing touch with real life. So it is enormously encouraging to come across little pockets in the world where a human balancing mechanism is asserting itself and people such as Tess and Dara and other members of their community are committed to learning from the old people and rescuing the things of value to be found in the ancient indigenous ways before they are completely lost. "There is a deep pleasure and humility in watching and knowing that systems can right themselves. We are coming into reaping the fruits. Things are definitely loosening up," said Tess.

So how is their community, here on Inishmore, constituted? I wanted to know. Is it a manifestation of a new kind of tribalism?

"I wouldn't use the word 'community' to describe what's happening here," she answered, "because, for me, community spells an older model. Too many hopes were hung on it that fell through. Living with other people is a bitch and everyone knows it is! I've no illusions around that. We have to go back to units that *work* – organic units. Man and woman, child and family works. Then it's finding out what is the next relationship that could support that unit – not damage it or cut it off. People here are consciously choosing to look at what they need in terms of friendship or support. You don't have to live with people to get that. It can be anywhere – across countries even – a web of connections.

"Personally I need that strong soul relationship between a man and a woman. I need to be actively, spiritually worshipping as well. To come together with other people in nature to worship really does nourish me. Every week we have a liturgy on a Sunday – a Eucharist. Weather permitting all our services are outside in the open on an old monastic site at Teample Ciarán where there is an old stone church with no roof on it, a well and some ancient standing stones. Or down by the sea. Stunning! There's no comparison. If you're casting a circle, its electric! Or we've a little hut out on the ledge, a simple prayer house. Ideally I'd like to be able to sit down with other people and pray every day and over the years we've been able to do that on and off. It could be a fairly simple affair like a meditation or people just sharing an insight or singing. The true balance for me comes from living in nature, being a part of it, having a lifestyle that's immersed in it and then having the conscious complement of making and marking sacred space with other people. It's like the two wheels of a bicycle and that's 'community'!"

Back at the house Dara joined us at the table for a hearty lunch of home-made soup and bread. He has written extensively on the Celtic revival and speaks passionately about it.

"The Celtic Church was *communitarian,* and locally controlled," he says. "In this model, the people *are* the church and look after it themselves while drawing on the services of the priest, bishop and Pope whereas the Roman model was (and is) hierarchical, patriarchal and clerical. At all levels of church life, the priest, bishop or Pope is in charge. The Celtic church had its finest hour in the 7th, 8th and 9th centuries when the rest of Europe was plunged into the Dark Ages. There were monasteries springing up all over Ireland connected by pilgrim paths. Art, craft and scholarship flowered. But things fell apart as the Roman influence gained the ascendant, the Latin language was universalised and indigenous liturgies were outlawed. The Celtic monasteries began to decline and disappeared entirely in the 16th century. Today, Celtic monasteries are there only as ruins and place names. There is not a single Celtic monk to be seen."

Yet through it all, the rich spirituality traditional to the Irish people has not been totally lost, said Dara. It has been maintained outside the church buildings, in homes and in the landscape. And it is this rich spirituality of home and land which has held the people together as can still be seen expressed in such traditions as the climbing of Croagh Patrick, the holiest mountain in Ireland, and the continued devotion to the holy wells throughout the country.

Dara has left the Roman Catholic priesthood to found a revival of the Celtic church. Irish spirituality, he says, offers a way of expressing faith that is connected to place and time. It is a spirituality that touches the soul of Ireland and connects people to each other. He talked about the huge new revival of interest in many of the traditional expressions of Irish culture – dance, poetry, music, drama, and the new confidence with which Irish people are beginning to reclaim their unique identity. The Celtic church, he says, will come alive when these artistic traditions find integrated expression within the context of faith and worship. Pointing up the enormous gulf between the atmosphere now in a typical parish church at Sunday Mass and the atmosphere the same evening at the set-dancing session in the parish hall, Dara observes, "Until they come together, the soul of Ireland and its people will not be healed."

Dara envisions the rebirth of a beautiful diversity in a world where the Celtic church can achieve spiritual freedom and co-exist in unity but not uniformity with Rome; a church where local groups make the decisions and the clergy are there by invitation; a church in which a local group might invite a married priest (such as himself) to celebrate a Eucharist for them or recognise the priestly gifts to be found in some of their female members. There are already groups in many parts of Ireland, and this is one of them, where a dedicated few have come together in Christ's name, outside of normal parish structure, to dream their vision into reality.

It is a simple, hard life of great integrity and rich rewards.

"The other great source of strength and delight for me," said Tess, "is the language. Folklore, culture and spirituality are deeply encoded in the Irish language. It's taken twelve years of hard slog for me to learn it but it is very important as we want our child's first language to be Irish. It's a very rich language. A language for poetry. For example, when we greet each other we say, 'God be with you', and the response is, 'God and Mary be with you'. Everything is a blessing or an endearment. What does 'hello' mean? Nothing. The Irish language was a covert thing for so long, oppressed, shame-filled and many people have unfortunate baggage associated with it such as self-consciousness and a sense of crushed self-esteem. The people here in the islands speak a fluid, living language – yet they'll deny they 'have Irish' because they use the vernacular and they're ashamed it's not correct. You have to wade through a lot of shadow to get to any clear, light-filled place. It's a miracle what survives in the memory but it seems as if you have to re-experience some of the pain that surrounds things in order to reclaim what's been denied."

Tess has found her place of contentment, here with her lovely man and their little band of like-minded friends. Spirituality, she says, is in everything. It's in the way you breathe, the way you look at things, in your appreciation of the whole of life. It can't be isolated in a separate compartment. Unless it filters through everything it's meaningless and arid. You have to live it, *embody* it.

One hand shading her eyes and the other resting on her growing belly in a timeless gesture of tenderness towards her unborn child, she looks out at a peerless double rainbow. "I can last a week away from this place, she says, "then everything I get from doing what I do – all the threads that connect my soul to my body – begin to cut off. I have a strong affinity with animals so a practical connection with nature is not only very spiritually nourishing for me, it's essential. I love the fact that there's goats out there and they need minding; that we're three minutes away from the ocean and I can go down whenever I like and listen to it. Without all this I begin to shrivel and dry up. Nothing compensates. I need to come home."

I walked down into the town, hitching a lift part of the way, had a Guinness in the local pub and bought a cosy woollen rug in the quayside store. "The health of the salmon to you!", called the old man I was passing the time of day with and he raised his hand to wave goodbye as I boarded the ferry for the mainland – a spectacular journey across the Galway Bay accompanied by a blood-red sunset that lasted for an hour, turning the water crimson. Even though it was freezing on deck I hung over the railing transfixed by beauty, unable to drag myself away. Ireland is a place that makes you want to worship the great forces of nature – the moon, the sun, the ocean and the wind. Here mountains were named after the breasts of the Goddess (and still are: The Paps of Anu), forests and oak trees were honoured and used as settings for prayer and ritual, rivers and lakes were the homes of deities who might sometimes masquerade as fish and speak to you from the depth of the waters, a faerie woman from another realm might come to live in your household and caution you never to tell of her magical powers. The natural and the supernatural are inextricably bound. The line between the factual and the enchanted is very soft-focus indeed. Faeries and leprechauns are none other than gods and goddesses gone to ground. Holy wells and healing springs abound. In the words of Mary Wickham's beautiful poem, A Dusk Magnificat;

A hum came
from the earth
through my feet,
right to my heart.
It found my throat
and used my voice
and my hands stretched upwards,
to the sky.

Like so many others who come to this wonderful place, I am beguiled. Someone once said, 'The heart that dances is the innocent heart'. Ireland is a country of many dancing hearts. The health of the salmon to them all.

Chapter 10

❖ ❖ ❖ ❖ ❖

*'Reveal to me that timeless space inside
where the dance has no beginning
and no end'*

I am home again, and for the millionth time, I ask myself the question that I have been asking other women; what do I mean by spirituality? The answer, for me, is becoming clearer: I see it as the place in each of us that is our personal source of great fearlessness, compassion and integrity; the place that inspires us to reach out a hand of comfort or to intervene to prevent suffering or the infliction of pain upon another. I can also see that, paradoxically, some people are able to *find* their spirituality through authentic suffering – people like Mary Aver who have been through the darkest dark to reach the light. Compassion, in its truest form, is born of being acquainted with pain and fear, with grief and loss – born of the ability to *be* in that pain and then transcend it. Spirituality is the place within us that grieves at the sorrow of our world and rejoices in the happiness and love that can be found. For me it is being able to live simply in the spirit of reverence and love. For me it is learning to feel at home everywhere and nowhere.

Someone whose life fits this definition well is Laurie Ross from New Zealand, teacher of Dances of Universal Peace. I had met her enchanted child, the aptly named Blessing – singer and song-writer, last summer on the island of Skyros and kept in touch. Now mother and daughter were making a pilgrimage together around the sacred goddess sites of Turkey, Greece, Egypt, Britain and Ireland and wrote asking if they could stay for a few days. I was delighted. As someone who depends so much on the hospitality of virtual strangers I am pleased to pass it on down the road. The two women arrived in a flurry of backpacks, guitars and drums and their visit turned out to be a real pleasure and an unexpected bonus. It gave me the chance, in the midst of impromptu song recitals and dancing round the living room, to ask Laurie about her work – getting to the universal heart of spirituality through dance.

"The beauty of the Dances of Universal Peace is that they honour the integrity of each religious system through confirming the underlying truth of the Divine love and spirit which is the most important common thread that runs through them all," says Laurie.

The Dances of Universal Peace are a collection of over 400 songs, chants and circle dances based on sacred phrases from many of the world's religious traditions. This includes Hindu, Buddhist, Sufi, Celtic, African, Native American, Zoroastrian, Jewish, Christian and Aoteoroan (the original Maori name for New Zealand). They celebrate nature and reverence for life as well as honouring multicultural spirituality. They are a form of meditation in movement or 'body prayer', as Laurie calls it, using music, breath, and voice to help in the development of higher consciousness. The dances, she says, are a way to affirm our sense of the Divine Spirit and to become part of a dynamic and beautiful living art form which anyone can do. They appeal to a growing number of people who yearn for a collective experience of spirituality but do not want to align themselves with any one religion or set belief system. They also appeal to those already engaged upon a particular spiritual path who want to remain open and receptive to other paths.

It is hard to believe that Laurie, a beautiful, ethereal sprite could be the mother of grown-up children and that she has been a creative spiritual dancer for over 25 years. She is a former co-ordinator of the West Auckland Peace Group, an executive officer of the Tree Council. She remains deeply involved with the environmental movement and is an activist for the rebirth of community festivals. She has always been drawn to the idea of 'peace through the arts'.

"I believe that ideals of peace, both within ourselves and with others, need to be cultivated like a garden in many different ways," she says, "political, social, spiritual *and* cultural. Establishing higher universal values for how we live together, how we manage and protect our natural resources, how we achieve social justice and wellbeing must all be interwoven with this artistic inspiration or cultural ethos. Not just acknowledging each individual culture but creating a sense of what our new emerging *common* cultural spirit is. It is our sacred responsibility."

I asked Laurie if the Dances could be seen as a way to by-pass the differences between religious beliefs.

"What interests me most is how to be a facilitator for awakening an appreciation of the whole *range* of human spiritual experience – pointing out where the truth and the essence lies. We can dig into the roots of each and any of the existing religious traditions and find all the knowledge and wisdom and guidelines that we need. However it takes a great deal of commitment to pursue a particular path and learn to use those tools to become a more loving, wise, good person. One of the simplest ways that can appeal to a large number of people is through the sacred songs and chants within each tradition. Music seems to reach out and touch people very quickly and then the extra dimension which is added through my own work is that of movement."

Is it something to do with the vibrational properties of sound itself having a transforming effect on the body at a cellular level? I asked.

"Yes," she answered. "But it's something that is inherent and not necessarily apparent. If people are able to enter into the spirit of the song, free of the baggage wrapped up in the meaning of the words and their connection with a particular dogma, they can recognise a universal beauty of the soul."

I made the observation that in the West we've mostly moved away from sacred dance as a way of worship unlike more primary cultures such as that of the Native Americans or Maori. Are we going to take to this easily?

"A growing number of people are looking for new and more authentic ways to experience the meaning of spirit – exploring esoteric paths and individual meditative practices", said Laurie, "and quite a leap is needed to embrace the whole spectrum of spiritual expression rather than just one. You become open to the whole mandala, the whole body, the whole voice and it's still early days – still very much a pioneering energy in the world – but, yes, I think we are taking to it. We are discovering our innate ability to sing and dance for joy."

I asked Laurie how she came to be interested in it herself.

"My whole life, as far back as I can remember, I have always been attuned to these sorts of energies," she said'. "I had done some ballet, modern and Balinese dance, developed a good technique and choreographed a number of dances as theatre performances but I had no inclination to become a follower or devotee of anyone. I was my own master and enjoyed the expression of Divine love through dance in my own creative way. You could say that through being divinely guided I have become much more mellow and perhaps more humble in my older years. I was happy to discover the Dances of Universal Peace (first introduced as a practice by the American Sufi master Samuel Lewis). They resonated with me straight away as a meaningful way in which I could share what I love with the world. A way of work, of service that could benefit humanity, benefit the planet. I have been able to work for peace, to express my spiritual understanding and use my gifts. I'm very lucky."

I wondered if Laurie saw a connection between the dances and her political and environmental work. Between the spiritual and the practical.

"They are very connected," Laurie answered, "I balance my teaching with my role as executive officer of the Tree Council for which I put in several days a week lobbying and doing P.R. The big challenge is for me to be able to say, 'I am a teacher of sacred song and circle dance. That's my work.' In other words, owning it properly instead of feeling faintly apologetic that it's not really a way to earn a living. I do feel passionately that the real work that needs to be done in the world is spiritual work, creative work, artistic work, environmental education, social justice work – writing the pamphlets, planting the trees, cleaning up a rubbish site. It shouldn't just be dependent on voluntary work. Full-time passionate people should be doing this. That's a political statement. I want to see a shift in the work ethic and see people being rewarded properly so they can earn a living through doing work which is nurturing to the society rather than feeling that you only do those things in your spare time."

So how can sacred dance be a way to develop the spiritual life? I asked.

"Part of the answer needs to be a definition of sacred dance," said Laurie. "Let's say that it is about exploring, kinaesthetically, the space around you – allowing the body to be very conscious of all the ways that it can move and flow. It is a wonder to have a body – this magnificent body! What a gift it is to be *embodied* and to get in touch with our feelings through exploring movement, space and rhythm in the body. Starting to move the body will then begin to stimulate the heart and the mind. Discovering the archetypal movements and repeating them as a disciplined meditation is of great value because it helps to strengthen consciousness and character. It helps you to become grounded and centred. Also, to engage in certain qualities of movement can be very healing, especially collectively. Learning to move in unison, together, as one, in heart, mind and body – part of a circle of power and magic – is beautiful."

I said that, to me, it seems such a feminine way – *dancing* the spiritual path. Here is a real celebration of the body; a healthy counterbalance to the shabby way the poor body has been treated in the Judeo-Christian and Islamic traditions where it is denigrated as full of sin, designed only to lead us astray; where we are continually urged to deny, transcend, even punish, the flesh.

"One of the greatest problems with many religious teachings is that they have created that split – that duality of body and mind," said Laurie. "I can understand how it came about as part of the process of spiritual awakening when you perhaps don't want to be distracted or enslaved by having to constantly gratify the senses but it should never be taken as an ideal or a goal in itself. The much higher aspiration is to be able to affirm body, heart and mind with spirit and to develop a balance; an integration so that there won't be the tendency towards the bizarre aberrations that we see happening in our sexuality and our society."

What about the Goddess? Where does She come into the picture? I wondered what Laurie's thoughts were especially during this pilgrimage to many of Her ancient sacred sites.

"Certainly in recent years I've turned to affirm the ancient goddess spirituality and, in the process, realised that my natural interpretation of the Divine was always androgynous. It was Being. It was Light. It didn't have any gender. Either one was in touch with Divine love and truth, wisdom and goodness, or one wasn't. There was no sense of a division. I was lucky in that respect. I was never conditioned to 'God the Father'. My upbringing was in the Unitarian Church where everyone was agnostic. As a child, I learned about different religions as being very interesting and valuable *ideas* but there was no strong sense of belief or indoctrination of any kind so I was free to develop my own thoughts on what was the truth and to discard whatever seemed to me superfluous or incorrect. That kind of discernment is usually not allowed to children who are expected to take on board a whole system without question.

I was taught that we can go like bees to the different flowers in the garden. We can marvel and wonder at each one – the colour, the fragrance, the shape – no need to limit yourself to one.

"It was only when I began teaching the sacred songs and dances of all traditions that I knew I wanted to do some work specifically on the Divine Feminine as part of an eclectic approach. So it's been very enriching. However, I do feel that there are a lot of shadows in that ancient past. There is a romantic view that can be blind to what those societies were really like. Rather than idealising the past I think the Divine Feminine is more a projection of what humanity is going towards – a new way, a new form in which it can be manifest in the world. It's lovely to think that there is a tradition we can draw on – imagery, stories, and so on – but I don't want to emphasise that too much. It is more about the creation of a new paradigm. If I'm going to do this work with full integrity, with all my heart and soul, then I do have to own that I'm creating it myself with other like-minded beings.

"Sharing this journey to the Goddess with my beloved daughter Blessing has had for me the added joy of watching her discover, within herself, her own attunement to the Divine Feminine. It was her idea to make this trip. She encouraged and persuaded me. It was such a long way to come from New Zealand. It was going to cost such a lot of money. In fact the time would never have been right but here was my daughter wanting my company, loving me enough and appreciating my work so much that she wanted to help and support me. A blessing indeed! So together we have sat upon the ancient stones and contemplated the sacred spaces that are this incredible expression of the Divine. It has led me to reflect that the greatest gift in all my life is that I have brought two wonderful human beings into the world and they happen to be daughters. My greatest wish is to bestow upon them as much of the gift as I am able and as they are willing to receive at the pace and in the way in which they wish to receive it."

Laurie feels strongly that the role of motherhood is grossly undervalued in our culture – yet another thing that is not considered to be a proper job; that we often become caught up in some outer form of activity and maybe neglect our children too much and maybe it isn't worth it. Not that everyone wants to be a wife and mother, of course, but that sometimes political activism can be a substitute for real love or peace in the heart. In the light of this, I asked her what she felt were the achievable tasks that we, as women, should concentrate on to bring about change in a world poised on the edge of catastrophe. Women of our generation, many of whom may have spent our youth being protest warriors, are we now required to put our energy and our passion into a more nurturing format?

"There'll always be a need for dramatic direct action," she said, "*and* carefully organised, patient, persevering, educated action. The thing that can happen for many of us is we lose heart. We haven't got enough faith or love or passion or enough happiness in our souls. So it seems that to carry on with this struggle for the evolution of human consciousness a woman needs to ask herself, well, what is she most passionate about? And it may be raising her children and that's enough. I think if a person can say; what is most important now? and how can I do this well? and how can I bring more happiness into it? That's the key.

"It was only when I felt I had really understood what it meant to be a wife and mother, when I had things really settled and peaceful, that I could go on to doing something for the community. My advice is: to take out into the world what you know you can do well. Whatever practice you do to heal yourself, whatever you do for your family to nurture them – act from that place and there's hope for the world. Find where your passion lies and do that to the best of your ability, both on a personal, intimate scale and in the wider community. It's not enough just to be fighting for a good cause. You need to be working on yourself in the process – constantly developing the qualities of compassion and understanding. The bigger goal isn't as important as how you're going about it and whether you can bring gentleness or patience or selflessness into the situation because that's what really counts."

So, at the end of the day, does she feel optimistic?

"Oh yes!" answered Laurie lighting up the room with her beatific smile. "There have never been so many people on the planet with awakened consciousness. Of course we mustn't be too complacent. We are in great danger and could destroy everything on this Earth. The power has been growing on both sides – the light *and* the dark. As I see it, the fear, depression and anger are all part of it and we need to own all of it. No use pretending it doesn't exist. Seeing those parts of oneself leads to greater understanding and compassion for others. The most important thing is to keep the mind and heart focused on the light and not to give in to the forces of darkness."

The Dances of Universal Peace seem to me to be a wonderful way to understand those conflicting forces and to keep them in balance; to embody those magnetic pulls in a symbolic way and let them move through you. The late afternoon sun was streaming through the crystal that hangs in my window sending a delirium of little rainbows all over the ceiling. I begged Laurie to teach me one of her sacred circle dances and by coincidence, not knowing anything about the time Femi and I spent with the African-American Yoruba priestesses in New York, she chose a praise song to Yemonja.

And then, in a whirlwind of long skirts, beads and scarves, they were gone – Blessing off to Wales to meet up with other young traveller friends and Laurie back to New Zealand. So now the time has come for me to explore one area of spirituality which gives me some difficulty, where I don't feel at home – Islam. Since such a negative image of Islam, especially as regards the role of women, is usually projected in the West, I am well aware that I have probably ingested many misconceptions and prejudices. In all the books I have read recently about women and spirituality, Islam is barely mentioned. I have a book of spiritual quotations and not one is from an Islamic source – surprising, when

the fact is that Islam is a vast spiritual community consisting of over a billion persons – making it the second most populous religion on Earth and the fastest growing.

We hear a lot, in the media, about fundamentalists and fatwas but that obviously can't be the whole picture. I would like to understand Islam better in order to make up my own mind. I want to know who lives behind the veil. I would like to know if there are Muslim feminists challenging the conservatism and the patriarchal nature of Islam. With my growing understanding that real freedom in this life comes not from the things we possess or the rigid views we hold but from the ability to open to each new moment with humility and wonder, I want to start with a clean slate – non-judgmental, open-minded – and speak with some Muslim women about their spirituality. I want to know if they are Muslims through choice or lack of choice.

Islam is one the great wisdom traditions of humanity – 14 centuries of commitment flowing from the inspired life of Mohammed. It provides a disciplined and harmonious way of life for a large segment of the world's population and as such it is worthy of fundamental respect. But because of the political antagonisms between Islamic culture and the West (the United States in particular), the considerable achievements of Mohammed and the 1400 years of rich Islamic civilisation, including the profundity of the religion itself, have often been obscured. Islam still bears the stigma in the West of a religion of violent fanatics. The Arabic word, *Islam*, simply means *surrender* and Muslims are those who consciously and constantly surrender their lives to The One – the single Source of the universe. An unbiased enquiry is made more difficult by remarks such as I read in the newspaper recently where an Iranian cleric was quoted as saying, "All Muslims hate the United States of America." I can't believe that is true.

I put out many feelers for personal contacts in the Islamic world. One idea was that since pilgrimages to the sacred temples in the Nile valley have become popular with Western women in search of a more Goddess-based spirituality, I might travel to Egypt. I wondered if the reclaiming of the ancient Sumerian and Egyptian goddesses which has been an important part of the women's spirituality movement was an interest that was shared by modern Egyptian women themselves. I wanted to meet Nawal El Saadawi, high-profile, outspoken Egyptian feminist. But somehow that whole line of enquiry didn't work out. Contacts came to a dead end, Dr Saadawi was lecturing in the United States and tourist travel in Egypt became too risky.

Frustrated and ashamed of my basic ignorance, I did a lot of reading about Islam. From Peter Occhiogrosso's brilliantly titled resource book, *The Joy of Sects*, I learned that in the context of the Arab world of the time, Mohammed was a radical and compassionate reformer who did much to liberate and protect women. He outlawed the prostitution of slave women. He established the rights of women to inherit – before Islam a woman was not only deprived of inheritance but was herself considered as property to be inherited by a man. Mohammed proclaimed that women should be educated and that married couples have reciprocal duties and rights. Daughters could not be married without their own consent and polygamy was only permitted if a husband was fair to all. He limited the number of wives a man may lawfully have to four (although he, himself, had nine official ones including two Jewish ones and a concubine – a Coptic Christian slave girl who was a gift from the ruler of Egypt).

With a combination of Divine revelation and great personal character, Mohammed brought to the world a religion that was caste-less in which women and members of foreign clans were to be treated with the respect normally reserved for the men of one's own clan. He called for an end to the common practice of female infanticide and emphasised compassion in a culture largely based on codes of honour and shame. His teachings outraged the Establishment of the day.

So far, so good. After a lot of frustrating false starts that led nowhere, one day I got a lead. I was given an introduction, through a friend, to an Egyptian woman who works at The Great Ormond Street Hospital for Sick Children in London as an interpreter and unofficial Muslim chaplain for any Arab-speaking families who might need her services. I rang Laila Shouman and received a very friendly invitation to meet her at the hospital. This would be a good opportunity to talk to an educated, professional woman about her faith and her spirituality, to counter the very stereotypical view of Muslim women as oppressed, submissive, veiled and voiceless underdogs, to set the record straight, to clear up misunderstandings.

Laila, a gentle, softly-spoken woman, came to meet me dressed head to toe in modest Muslim attire complete with hair-covering head scarf. If I had expected any kind of feminist critique or questioning of the patriarchal nature of the Islamic faith I was soon disabused. A strict adherent to the letter of the faith and defender of an uncompromising traditional interpretation of the words of the Prophet, Laila answered all my questions by the book. Every time she mentioned the Prophet's name it was in the conjunction: 'The Prophet Mohammed-Peace-be-upon-Him'. But Laila was kindness itself and this would, as it turned out, be a different opportunity to the one I had in mind – a lesson in the deep sense of peace and contentment that can accompany unquestioning acceptance.

We sat together in the hospital's little sanctuary – a carpeted room with chairs and prayer rugs set aside, in addition to the sumptuous chapel, for the use of staff or patients' families for prayer and meditation. I was assured that our being there would not be a distraction for Muslim members of staff slipping quietly in at intervals to do their ritual ablutions and make their prayers towards Mecca. The sanctuary is also furnished with a small bronze sculpture of a family group, chosen for its neutral symbolism, but now covered with a piece of carpet by someone who must have been offended by its presence. Islam does not allow any representation of the human form which is seen as idolatry. Whenever the sculpture is uncovered, Laila said, somebody covers it up again.

I asked Laila what the word 'spirituality' meant to her as a Muslim woman.

"My prayers are my spirituality," she answered without hesitation. "Five times daily prayers and ablutions as a psychological preparation. "That is a physical and spiritual cleansing for me – the constant renewal of my relationship with God. If I don't read the Qur'an every day I feel quite heavy. It uplifts me. Allah created mankind for no other reason except to worship Him – to live according to His will. Our existence is entirely dedicated to Him. Everything we do is for His sake. When I wake in the morning I acknowledge that who has got my soul is God. He allowed me to raise from my temporary death. My food is His provision. My health is His blessing. My treatment of others is the way He wants me to behave and I look forward very much to Paradise – to eternal life and happiness. To believe in the Oneness of God, the One Creator and His Messengers, angels and the Day of Judgement – this is our work on Earth."

When I ask her, "What is your idea of God?", she brings out her Qur'an from her handbag and reads me the verse that describes God.

"'The One and Only'," she reads. "'He begets not nor was He begotten'. He is like no one and no one is like Him. We are forbidden to compare or describe Him. He is the light of sky and earth."

"So, to you, Allah is a masculine figure? You always use He. Does that bother you?" I persist.

"It is not about gender. Allah is beyond male or female, beyond description," she answers, patiently. "In the Qur'an it is a sin to think about what He looks like or when did He exist because He is the beginning and the end. Nothing before Him or after Him. In the Qur'an are given the '99 Names of God': The Merciful, The Strongest, The Most Forgiving, The Most Vengeful, The Fairest ...We beseech Him by His names: The King, The Most Compassionate, The Most Loving, The Guider, The Light, The Creator ... it leaves no room for you to imagine Him. Since I can't create one wing of a mosquito how can I imagine The Creator?" She smiles sweetly.

I understand that my line of enquiry is getting nowhere. The certainties and the power of revelation are hard to grasp when you're on the outside looking in. I know that at heart there are minimal differences between the major wisdom traditions. Essential teachings transmitted by prophets and sages stress love, compassion and the interconnectedness of all things – that there is no fundamental separation within the one Reality. The sticking point is the way fallible mortal human beings mess things up. Inflexible dogma makes it easier for tyrants to manipulate the masses and I have spoken to Muslims who feel that The Prophet's revelations have been deliberately misinterpreted; that the Qur'an stresses equality but that men have manoeuvred themselves into a position of dominance by twisting the teachings to their advantage (as they have in Christianity and other religions throughout the patriarchal era). "Islam today is corrupted and does not conform to the Qur'an," said one scholar. Patriarchal interpretations, he told me, have been used for centuries to oppress women, contrary to the intentions of Allah and His Prophet Mohammed, and a new understanding might be a great liberation.

I ask Laila if she thinks the feminist movement and the ecological concerns of our age have brought a more critical interpretation to Islam in any way. I stress that the question comes not just from me but from many Jewish, Christian and Buddhist women who have all been saying; 'Look where this patriarchal domination has brought us. Isn't it time for women to speak out?'

"Men and women are equal in the sight of God," she answers, "but different. We have our different roles. Islam is a whole system. If everyone lived according to the rules we would be in an ideal world. Islam gives women priority to be at home without compromising themselves or their families. It is seen as an unacceptable injustice that a woman should be expected to share the duties of being a bread-winner. Look around you! How many children don't know their fathers? Hardly know their mothers? Homeless teenagers alone in the world. Broken families. Is this good? Is this equality? In Islam the mothers have so much respect. A woman's role as mother and wife is the most sacred and essential one. The Qur'an says, 'Paradise is under the feet of the mothers'. What could be a greater responsibility than bringing up the next generation? Who better than a mother to do it? Yes, a man makes the decisions but only after listening to his wife. The Prophet-Peace-Be-Upon-Him, asked his wife's view and listened to her counsel."

"What about the feminine face of the Divine?' I ask. "A divinity to identify with as a woman. Is that something that interests you?"

"The question makes no sense to me," she says. "The wives of the Prophet are honoured – the Mothers of the Believers. I am interested in the feminine side of my gender – in the examples of the 'best four women' that the Holy Qur'an tells us about: Mary, mother of Jesus; Assiya, martyred wife of Pharaoh; Khadija, first wife of the Prophet and Fatima, his daughter. They are my examples – the most perfect, the most pure ..."

All this leaves scant room for argument, but I persevere; "I know that you are a devout Muslim but, as an Egyptian woman, are you drawn to the spirituality of pre-Islamic Egypt? To the ancient Egyptian goddesses – Nut, for example, the Great Mother Goddess who personified the night sky – arching over the Earth, bringing forth the Milky Way?"

"I am not much interested in all the civilisations that went before, except historically," says Laila, looking a bit exasperated. "For me, anything before Islam has *ended*. It was meant to be there for a brief moment. Look at Pharaoh who persecuted the Jews. When God told Moses to take his people through the Red Sea, Pharaoh's army perished. They were destroyed because they were not believers."

So any notion of pre-Islamic Goddesses, Egyptian or otherwise, is unacceptable. The Qur'an supersedes anything that went before it. It is the Direct Revelation of God. God is One. God begot none, nor was He begotten. None is like Him. Period.

The other issue I am curious about is the controversy surrounding the infamous Satanic Verses. Legend has it that Mohammed had supposedly received a revelation concerning al-Lat, al-Uzza and Manat – three *daughters* of Allah – which permitted some veneration towards these three women. That seems like a fruitful line of enquiry to me in looking for the feminine Divine but the trail goes cold. According to tradition, Mohammed later said that he had been misled by a wily Satan, and the so-called Satanic Verses, were expunged from the Qur'an. Orthodox Muslim scholarship now declares that they never existed in the first place and any mention of them is as a red rag to a bull. The controversy reverberates to this day with Salman Rushdie's book of that name being declared blasphemous and resulting in the fatwa issued by the Ayatollah Khomeini calling for the death of Rushdie who remained in hiding – ten years on.

The only time Laila became flinty-eyed during our entire conversation was when I brought this subject up. She agreed absolutely with the death sentence. Blasphemy was unforgivable. I was beginning to understand the truth of a statement I had read by Islamic scholar, Abdul-Latief S. Al-Khayat. He writes; "There does seem to be a general misunderstanding about Islam – an assumption that it is merely a code of beliefs and rituals and hence no more than a personal affair and a voluntary choice." To the devout, such as Laila, it is much more. No half measures. No questions. It is an unshakeable belief in the total perfection of God whose word has provided a complete, unarguable, comprehensive system for living.

Laila is keen for me to understand that womanhood is a fortunate condition – not the crushed stereotype of Western ignorance. She gives me a rundown of some of the basic rights that a woman is entitled to under Islamic law:

- All family decisions are meant to be taken in mutual agreement.
- A wife is due love, kindness and companionship.
- A woman is entitled to divorce her husband if he abuses her verbally or physically or if he deprives her of education thereby depriving her of learning about Islam and therefore depriving her of an understanding of her rights.
- Motherhood is a noble and vital role which shapes the future of nations.
- There is no decree in Islam which forbids a woman from seeking employment especially in positions which 'suit her nature'. Women, in fact, are encouraged into professions such as medicine because it would be improper for a woman to consult a male doctor for example. Leila herself trained as a dentist.
- A woman's inheritance may be only 1/3 compared to a man's 2/3 but that is for the very good reason that a man has full responsibility for the maintenance of wife, children and needy relatives. This responsibility is neither waived nor reduced on account of his wife's wealth. Her money and possessions are for her alone. Before Mohammed, inheritance was exclusively patrilineal.
- A woman keeps her maiden name.
- She has the right of independent ownership. She can buy, sell, mortgage or lease.
- She has the right to participate in public affairs (but it's better if she does not hold high office on account of the physiological and psychological changes to which she is prone during menstruation and pregnancy and which might hinder her ability to make tough or rational decisions).

When compared to a woman's lot in pre-Islamic times, such rights were good news indeed. However, as another Islamic scholar, Dr Jamal A. Badawi has said; "A lot of these rights have been whittled away by people professing to be Muslims but not adhering to the original and authentic sources." It is impossible, he says, for anyone to justify any mistreatment of women by any decree of rule embodied in Islamic law. "Nor could anyone dare to cancel, reduce or distort the clear-cut legal rights of women."

But they do dare and when I ask Laila for her views on such abuses of power she shrugs and says, "There are bullies in every country and ignorant men in the faith. It is ignorance about their religion that has led to men oppressing women because they believe it is permitted and ignorance on the part of the women for not being aware of their God-given rights."

Laila argues in defence of a couple of rules that I find hard to swallow: that a Muslim man can marry a woman from another faith but a Muslim woman can only marry a Muslim man; that a woman's witness in court is only worth half a man's; a clear distinction is made between the 'rationality' of men and the 'emotionality' of women. None of this, she says, is meant to imply the supremacy of one sex over the other but rather the complementary roles of both sexes in life. The 'weaker sex' is entitled to protection but this should not mean a husband's dictatorship over the wife. It says in the Qur'an, "Men are the protectors and maintainers of women because God has given the one more strength than the other". Then there is the issue of polygamy. The primary purpose, says Laila, is to provide a decent solution to the problem of widows and orphans. Also, since Islam strictly forbids sexual relations outside marriage, polygamy is seen as the only honest solution in cases where a *man* (my italics) wants more than one partner as opposed to the untidy options of either serial monogamy or having a wife and mistresses where the resulting children suffer. "A man has to face up to full responsibility for all the relationships into which he enters." (A woman, on the other hand, should refrain from all deeds and gestures that might stir the passions of people other than her legitimate husband. She is warned not to display her charms or expose her physical attractions to strangers. The veil which she must put on is for the purpose of "saving her soul from weakness, her mind from indulgence, her eyes from lustful looks and her personality from demoralisation".)

Laila is divorced from her first husband and lost the subsequent court battle for the custody of her three children when she re-married. The Islamic custody law states that young children of both sexes should stay with their mother; that after the age of about 7 or 8 boys should go to their father; that girls should stay with their mother until they marry *unless* the mother re-marries in which case she loses all custody. At the time, Laila says, she found it very tough but now accepts the received wisdom that no stepfather could ever feel about another man's child as he does about his own so the proper place for them is with their own father who has the financial responsibility for them. (Never mind that no stepmother could ever feel about another woman's child as she does about her own so the proper place for them is with their own mother who has the day to day loving responsibility for their emotional well-being). Anyrate, now, she says, they all get on well, it has worked out fine, the two families have good relations, the kids – girls of 11 and 15 and a boy of 6 – have a special phone line to her and live close by.

Some of the tenets of Islam go so much against the grain for Western women that it can be difficult even to conceive of such a different mind set but I really want to try to convey the fervent passion with which these views are held and not be guilty of the wilful misunderstanding and misinformation which has bedevilled so much discussion of this issue. Certainly the history of Islam is rich with women of great achievements in all walks of life from as early as the 7th century right up to political leaders of Muslim countries in our own time (e.g. Pakistan, Bangladesh, Turkey).

What about the big deal made out of women's decency and dignity needing to be safeguarded from men's lusting eyes? Women have to pay the price of men's lack of self-control by observing the dress code or *hijab*. Is this fair? I ask Laila.

"Shyness is an attribute of faith," she answers simply. "It is not a penalty or an imposition. We are expected always to lower the gaze and guard our modesty." I notice, during our conversation, that whenever a man comes into the sanctuary to pray he will position himself in front of any woman who already happens to be there. A woman will do the reverse. This is in case a woman's clothing might possibly become disarranged during prostrations, says Laila, thereby causing embarrassment to both. Women have a dignified status and should always be objects of admiration.

The Prophet is meant to have said that the most precious thing in the world and the best treasure a man can have is "a virtuous woman who pleases him when he looks at her, who obeys him when he commands her and who guards herself when he is absent from her."

I confess to balking and bucking like mad when I hear such words but Laila carries on reasonably, "Look around you again. Women display themselves, they walk in the streets nearly naked and then they complain about rape and violence and disrespect. Who is to blame? Islam does not permit the free mixing of men and women outside the close family. This is for the woman's protection."

It has to be said that freedom brings many challenges in its wake – foremost among them, the challenge of personal responsibility. If we are indeed helpless in the face of our lust then we have not evolved much beyond the condition of animals. It also has to be said that the evidence points to a messy state of affairs in the West every bit as destructive as the loss of self-determination endured by many Muslim women. Women are under attack. Our streets are not safe. I have often thought how pleasurable it could be to waft through the marketplace completely invisible. No hassle. There's a lot to be said for it. But still, I would find it very tiresome to have to live in a society where the active achievement of honour is seen as the man's responsibility and the passive defence against shame, the woman's.

Laila gave me a pamphlet to read; *The Rights and Duties of Women in Islam* by Abdul Ghaffar Hasan. Much seemed reasonable enough but there are some things I could never accept. One blood-boiling section concerns the evidence of women in a court of law where the author states, "In criminal cases where only women are the witnesses, the four Imams are unanimous in not accepting the evidence of women. They reason that in cases such as murder and rape, the woman will be emotional and may get confused"(!). He goes on to say, "It is an established scientific fact that women cannot explain intimate details of the events with the accuracy of detail of which men are capable. The Prophet described women as being 'incomplete in reason' and this incompleteness is taken into account in the field of legal evidence."

The certainties of Islam, as with ultra-orthodox Judaism and Evangelical Christianity, are at variance with my own understanding that there are a hundred right ways to travel the spiritual path and a thousand spiritual paths to travel but I really liked Laila (except for her views on Salman Rushdie). She is a person at peace with herself and I learned a great deal from our meeting, not least that authentic Islam is not the intolerant religion that its reputation might have led me to believe. The Qur'an's teachings are very clear on the subject of other religions, recognising the Torah, the Psalms and the Gospels as holy scripture and venerating prophets from the Old and New Testaments such as Abraham, Moses, Elijah, John the Baptist and Jesus Christ. Neither is it supposed to be a proselytising religion.

"We are not here to make people Muslim," says Laila, "only to deliver The Message. My faith is something I would love to share with anyone who wants it but not to impose it. I feel very comfortable with anyone of any faith who has a spiritual life. We women need to work for peace and to understand each other. We are all messengers."

We agree as we say goodbye, that if God is love then that is what we would like for each other. Insh'allah!

Karen English, a writer on spirituality has said, "I don't see Islam as patriarchal at all. I see the *practice* of it as extremely patriarchal. In Islam, men and women have equal value. There is no need to develop a feminist theology. There's a need to put into practice the theology that exists."

These words were to have special relevance on the next leg of my journey – a tangent which began with a letter from West Africa.

My friend Geri, and no one is more surprised than she at this unexpected turn of events, is the new proprietor of a small, 18-room hotel in The Gambia called the Safari Garden. Ever since she fell in love with the country and purchased the hotel she has been urging me to come for a visit. When she wrote to say she wanted me to meet a remarkable Mandinka woman, Isatou Touray – coordinator of the Network of Women Living under Muslim Law – I had the perfect excuse to justify buying a ticket.

Chapter 11

❖ ❖ ❖ ❖ ❖

'A person's true wealth
is the good he or she does in the world'
MOHAMMED

A week later I kiss my honey goodbye at Richmond station and set off for Africa with my little suitcase. Waiting at Clapham Junction where I have to change for the Gatwick Express I notice a woman in colourful African dress standing on the platform at 6.30 in the morning and vaguely wonder if she could possibly, out of all the thousands of Africans living in London, be going to Banjul too. Of course I find myself standing next to her in the check-in queue so we sit together on the six-hour flight and she keeps me entertained with her riveting life story – a great tale of survival and triumph over adversity.

Atsede Maryam Ishe, born in Jamaica, was married first to a Rastafarian by whom she had two daughters. Through him she became very involved in the Rastafarian movement and the Ethiopian church. The guy turned out to be violent however, and she left him – having to run away with her little girls to a monastery. Her second husband – another bad choice – was Senegalese. He alienated her, by now teenage, daughters and spent all her money. Times were hard but now that her daughters are grown and she has become a grandmother Atsede is on her own again and running a very successful textile and dress designing business. She has converted to Islam which she finds to be a very open, generous faith which incorporates aspects of other spiritualities and, far from being restrictive, has been her source of strength and emotional security. Atsede is a great travelling companion and I plan to meet up with her again in Banjul but, sadly, we manage to lose each other in the mad luggage scrum at the airport.

Geri is there, however, with a welcoming bouquet of hibiscus flowers and we drive to her hotel, the Safari Garden – a delightful place with little bungalow-style rooms around a swimming pool and tropical garden. A flame tree in all its raucous vermilion splendour guards the entrance flanked by avocados, mangoes, limes and bananas. The rainy season is just beginning. It is hot and humid with overcast, thundery skies and flashes of lightning illuminating the horizon. When rain finally comes it falls in curtains from the tin roof and steams on the hot paths, dramatically washing across the compound in gusty waves, bending the bamboo almost to the ground, pattering the dust with big, splotchy drops, cooling the fevered air. It's lovely to be back in West Africa, in this friendly, sleepy, place. It feels like a time warp and reminds me of Nigeria back in the sixties.

Quite a few women on their own come to The Gambia to start up businesses or to work. Geri's dream is gradually to transform the existing regular tourist trade at the hotel into a unique type of holiday experience where guests can come to learn skills and crafts such as batik and pottery, to participate in workshops on African drumming or dance – a place where local people have a role as teachers and mentors, instead of servants or performers. Geri's is a vision of tourism as a real exchange – a more responsible, appropriate, authentic experience for the visitors and from which local people can actually benefit, both in terms of money and of self-esteem.

To this end I have brought with me the address and telephone number of Malamini Jobarteh, the internationally renowned *kora* player and traditional storyteller whom I met at a storytelling festival in Wales last year. I loved his music and I had luckily kept in a safe place the card he gave me along with an invitation to come and visit if ever I happened to be in The Gambia. Little did either of us expect to meet again so soon!

I particularly want Geri to meet him. I dial the number. His son answers, says his father is at home and that we would be welcome to call in this very afternoon. We chance the bush taxis – a cheap, efficient method of transport if you don't mind being a bit squashed and waiting around until enough people want to go in the same direction. The rain has left the unpaved streets awash in a sea of red mud through which we paddle, marvelling at the local women who manage to look spotless and elegant like galleons in full sail in their white broderie anglais and ruffled-sleeved, multi-coloured print, traditional African dress.

The final taxi drops us outside Malamini's compound which everyone knows because, apart from Malamini's own immense reputation as a classical musician, his eldest son, Tata Dindin, is The Gambia's most famous and adored pop star. Malamini, sitting on a straw mat outside his house, receives us with a great display of pleasure and hospitality. The house is a cacophony of music practice. We meet the famous son, Tata; also Pa, his younger brother, a talented kora player himself; Malamini's three wives and several other members of this family of musicians including a brand new grandson born this very day.

The senior wife asks me to take a photograph of the baby, so I have an excuse to visit the women's quarters. The nativity scene is as exquisite as a Renaissance painting. In the dim half-light of the darkened room veils of red and gold cloth lightly drape the young mother nursing her tiny son. She is spent but content. The Goddess incarnate. The other women attend her like handmaidens to the

Virgin all cloaked in their spice-coloured wrappers. A tableau of warm jewels. The baby, a little ebony miracle, may well be the one to carry the Gambian troubadour tradition into the second half of the twenty-first century, keeping alive the ancient tales of warriors and kings. We bless him and kiss him.

Today is also Pa, the younger son's, wedding day so great preparations are going on for a disco in the young family members' compound adjacent. No sign of wealth or status. No standing on ceremony. A huge enamel washing-up bowl filled with rice and chicken is brought in and Geri and I are invited to eat with Malamini. The women and children all sit round another large bowl and the lads round another. A little ball of food is deftly formed with the fingers, dunked in the chilli sauce and in it goes. Pa brings his kora and plays us a few traditional songs – very intricate, sweet, tinkling music – a vibrant tradition of praise songs, laments, and tall tales with all the oral history of the tribe and deeds of the ancestors kept alive in the countless re-tellings. The kora, the king of African musical instruments, is a magnificent harp-like affair with a big-bellied body made from a gourd – richly decorated with a pattern of metal studs. It is played by plucking the tuned strings. Theirs has been a dynasty of musicians for many generations. It would be unthinkable for the sons to do otherwise.

Pleased at the prospect of becoming involved in Geri's venture, Malamini insists upon driving us, at the end of the day, in his elderly Mercedes, back to Brikama. Geri and I, loaded with cassettes of Gambian and Senegalese music from a roadside kiosk, exhilarated with how special the day has been, make the long journey home to Serrakunda.

The next day, Isatou Touray, the person I have come to The Gambia to meet, turns up at the hotel and we quickly recognise in each other a kindred spirit. Once again I thank my luck as I embark on a friendship and a dialogue that expands my horizons and validates the seemingly random way that life's tides carry me along.

Isatou is a powerhouse woman – sticking her neck out at some considerable risk to herself – trying to change the lot of women in the Gambia where 90% of the population are Muslim. Her main focus is on health issues, education, Islamic oppression and, above all, the widespread practice of female genital mutilation, or circumcision (FGM). She herself is a victim of FGM and has refused to allow her daughters to suffer the same fate. She is married to a Western-trained doctor who supports and encourages her work.

Isatou was a delegate at the 1996 Beijing international women's conference which gave her, if nothing else, a much-needed sense of belonging to a wider, global network of women, an international framework of support. Hers is a lonely road. She meets opposition at every turn. Her organisation GAMCOTRAP (the Gambian Committee on Traditional Practices) has been banned from broadcasting their message on national television. They were hoping for some positive endorsement from the new President of The Gambia but he is young and the powerful old Imams who have his ear also have a vested interest in maintaining the patriarchal status quo. Isatou's appointment for an audience with the President was abruptly and unaccountably cancelled. She says passionately that she loves Gambian traditional culture and has never had the smallest intention of trying to undermine the society or its customs – only to strengthen the good and question the bad. I am invited to visit their offices and meet her colleagues.

At the campaign headquarters I am introduced to Mary Small who runs the office – a very impressive and experienced Gambian nurse/midwife who gives her services voluntarily because she has seen so many terrible instances of the suffering of women who have been circumcised. The office is loaded with teaching materials, posters, drawings and models of what female genitalia should look like and the terrible mess that can be made with a botched circumcision. It makes grim viewing – infections, haemorrhaging, scar tissue, complications in childbirth – the whole thing is an abomination.

"The resistance to our campaign comes from the religious leaders who fear woman's liberation and have a vested interest in keeping them powerless," says Mary, a feisty fighting spirit. "In the rural areas, women have been warned off and frightened from associating with us because we teach them about what they are capable of changing and doing. Women should be seeing themselves in government, as policy makers, as leaders, as forces for change, as contributors. We know that over half the population of our country are women and we are trying to teach them how to empower themselves."

Is it possible to do this within Islam? I ask.

"Yes, it is," she answers. "It all depends on the approach. We have to be mindful that we have very religious people in our midst. Wherever we go and whatever we talk about we look at the religious injunctions and ask, 'Is this in compliance? Are women supposed to be subservient? Are women told to be silent?' We have to present this clearly and plainly and separate out religious issues from cultural and social ones. Whenever we talk to women at grass roots level on their own and in their village settings, they begin to exchange personal stories about money problems, health, oppression. Women themselves are never resistant to our campaigns. It may be the first time they have ever had the opportunity to be listened to by anyone who takes them seriously. They have been silent for so long. We encourage them to speak anonymously and this is how we are gathering our information and getting all this feedback that they would like to see big changes. They are curious and enthusiastic because some-one is actually appreciating their problems."

So what does the Qur'an actually say about female circumcision? Nothing. Allah does not endorse it. Nowhere is it mentioned. In fact only one *hadith* (oral sayings of the Prophet, written down after his death) refers to it: 'circumcision is my way for men, but is merely ennobling for women'.

"Ennobling? How?" asks Mary passionately. "For men to assert control over women's sexuality and guarantee a tight orifice for their own sexual pleasure – that's how!" She is in full flood. "The religious leaders who try to justify these practices are talking rubbish!" A rite of passage? I've heard that argument too. It doesn't make sense. I have seen baby girls as young as one week old going under the razor. I have seen a little girl of 8 years old crying piteously all night and bleeding to death the next day – a vein pierced by the circumcisor. What do they understand of initiation? This is a distortion. This is sacrilege. We have to go on with our campaign. Fortunately this is a small country where it is easier to reach people than, say, in the Sudan for example. Gambian women must understand that they have been kept in ignorance. It is possible for them to be observant, devout, and still make the changes. We travel with victims who tell their own stories. We travel with Imams who have been won over and that is our main strength. Whatever the religious problems and queries we can supply an answer."

It is a long uphill struggle because the whole subject of 'women's reproductive health' has been shrouded in silence, taboo and secrecy and never been openly discussed. GAMCOTRAP workers have had threats against their lives. They know what they are up against and it has made them more deter-mined than ever – but, as Isatou says, they really need the network of support, both moral and financial, that Western women can give them.

With a few days to wait until I can meet up with Isatou again I give myself permission to be a tourist. There are many things to see here. Geri and I hail a bush taxi to Bakau and make our way through the maze of muddy, rain-flooded back streets to a sacred crocodile pool – a heaving, seething green pond with dozens of menacing snouts barely protruding and mosquitoes jumping like raindrops all over the surface. The crocs are inert, fed daily with fish by the custodian, and just lie around the edge like logs patiently allowing people to approach them. Since ancestral times, washing or immersing yourself in their putrid water is supposed to bring fertility to barren women. The air is heavy with silence except for the monkeys calling and leaping through the trees and the disconcerting rustle of baby crocs, malevolent extras from Jurassic Park, lurking in the undergrowth. As in the Florida Everglades I get the distinct feeling that this place and the wild animals who live here are only biding their time. One slip-up and there would be nothing left of you but bleached bones.

As night falls we go down to a bar on the beach enticed by the electrifying sound of wild drumming. A group of about 10 young men with a variety of drums are playing up a storm – not a show, as such, just talented amateur musicians hanging out. For the price of a beer we listen, spellbound, for two hours. It is wonderful to see such a concentration of potent male energy harnessed to a creative, peaceful purpose. As someone said, 'If you can bring that warrior energy into the heart of the community, its fire will warm the village. If it stays outside, it will burn the village down.'

Another day we go to an eating place built on stilts out in the creek in the middle of the mangroves. Pirogues slide by as we feast on a plate of creek oysters with lime juice. The whole place looks like a fantasy from a Bacardi adman's storyboard – old mamas with gold teeth sitting around shelling oysters, furniture made out of salvaged ship's timbers and rope, slippery children's bodies silhouetted against the sun, splashing in the water and paddling hand-made dug-outs, an old man singing because he caught a fish. Some days are just perfect and this is one of them. The sacred can be right there in the simplicity of life being authentically lived.

It's the quiet season. Geri is having some repairs done to the hotel. She can afford to take a few days off so we plan a trip to the interior. Next morning our Crocodile Safari jeep arrives at 9am and we set off for our up-country expedition heading east up the southern bank of the great Gambia River for five hours non-stop until we reach Georgetown. After the crush and squalor of urban shanty-town poverty, rural African life looks so much more tolerable, preferable. The immaculate villages with their swept compounds, neat fields of peanuts and corn, shady baobabs and round, straw-thatched huts of baked-earth bricks are pleasing to the eye and harmonious to the spirit.

At the ferry crossing to Georgetown, a flight of achingly beautiful little children scramble onto the tailgate of our vehicle each trying to thrust a scrap of paper with their name and address into our hands – begging for us to be their 'special friend'. Each one an S.O.S., a message in a bottle, from a hopeful little individual marooned forever in anonymity and obscure rural poverty. It's no use taking one or ten or a thousand for out of the shadows come a thousand more. 'Send me a postcard. Give me a pen, a dalassi, an empty plastic bottle, a banana. Choose *me*.'

The motorised ferry no longer runs so passengers have to .haul the craft across the wide brown waters by a steel hawser. And there is the tiny town with its long and dolorous history as the capture and holding place for slaves on their way down river to the waiting ships. A weighing scale, a streaked and filthy building full of bats is all that remains; and an underground cell where trouble-makers, rebels and ring-leaders were shackled – their food thrown down through the one small ventilation hole, their only drinking water a sink hole that filled with river water at high tide. At the far end of the dungeon are two airless punishment cells – one for men, one for women.

We ask the guide to leave us alone for a while and take the candle with him. He looks at us strangely but does as we ask. As the light recedes and the suffocating blackness closes in, Geri and I sit in the dirt in the women's punish-ment cell and hold each others' hands; thinking about what happened here; meditating on the terrible suffering, the fear and the despair that is stored in these walls – suffering that is borne to this day by their Caribbean and African-American descendants, people like Iyalu Opeodu, priestess of Yemonja, in New York whose roots were so cruelly pulled up and transplanted half a world away. The grief is palpable and hangs in the fetid air like an ectoplasm. Nothing can undo the abominations that took place in this hell hole but we offer our prayers for forgiveness and healing.

Georgetown is actually on an island – Macarthy Island – in the middle of the mighty river. To get to Jangjangburreh Camp where we are to spend the night we have to cross on another ferry to the north bank. The camp looks like a film set. There is a poignant irony in Europeans spending hundreds of pounds to come to Africa to stay in a hotel cleverly disguised as an African village so they can enjoy the fantasy of not being tourists; of tasting the real thing; of returning to a once-upon-a-time communal society – whereas the reality is that most Africans would give their eye teeth to live anywhere else and the children beg you to take them away.

About an hour from the camp is one of the most mysterious sites in the whole of sub-Saharan Africa – the Stone Circles of Wassu. I have had an obsession to visit them, feel them, experience their energy ever since I first saw a photograph. This is one of the great unsolved anthropological and archaeo-logical riddles – only partially excavated – of our time and as yet the only stone circles to be found in Africa. Nobody knows why they are there or what they were used for. To me, they were remarkably reminiscent of the stone circles I went to with Fania's friends near Draperstown in Northern Ireland. Experts assume the existence of an earlier, sophisticated, African culture. Skeletons have been found buried in the centre of some circles, as well as tools, pottery and ornaments. My fantasy, based on nothing but wishful thinking, is that their origins may turn out to have been in an earth-worshipping, life-loving, non-violent, goddess-oriented matriarchal civilisation that will yet reveal itself to us and teach us a thing or two.

In the middle of a flat, arid wilderness far from any village is the sacred site; several circles made from massive megaliths of laterite – heavy red stone – some over six feet tall and probably once much taller. Luckily we have the place to ourselves so we can do some 'women's business' in the peace and quiet of the late afternoon light. We sit. We sing. We chant and pray. We praise the Goddess and pledge ourselves to her peaceful, healing work. I wish I had thought to bring flowers but searching in my bag, the only thing I have to leave for a gift is a single Ricola herb throat lozenge.

The next days are a mixture of relentless jolting over rutted roads so dusty that our throats seize up and rare pleasures it is worth everything to experience – a dawn bird-watching safari into the Kiang West National Park in the company of two knowledgeable bird connoisseurs we meet on the way. They lend us their powerful binoculars and show us what to look out for and where. It is a revelation. We see kingfishers, Abyssinian rollers, West African eagles, hornbills, herons, Senegal parrots, long-tailed glossy starlings, a wonderful yellow and brown swallow, hammerkops and many more.

We spend a night at Tendaba River camp where there is more drumming and dancing galore in the firelight – the wonderful, bonkers Mandinka dancing where the women challenge each other, arms going like windmills, knees pumping up and down. You can so clearly see the origins of tap-dancing and Brazilian street carnival dancing – carried like seeds from these shores during the sorrowful years of the great African Diaspora to spring alive again in the genes of their descendants as soon as they found their feet.

We are dragged into the arena and although I think I'm too tired to dance, the music of Youssou N'dour and Jaliba soon fires my blood. In fact, I can't sit still. "Whoa! Mama can dance!" yell the delighted off-duty waitresses and teach me some steps. I dance with them. I can do it. I never feel overweight in Africa. I feel like a woman. In fact my bottom feels pitifully small by comparison. Under-endowed, by local standards, in the rear department I can only marvel at the rotating moons around me.

Riding home through the frangipani and jasmine-scented tropical night, Africa breathes its hot breath on us. Past the roadside markets where a thousand little lanterns like a sprinkling of fireflies illuminate the family groups sitting around – selling little screws of peanuts, roasting a fish on a charcoal brazier, cradling a sleeping child, bedding down for the night as they live their lives on the roadside. This evening Isatou has invited us to supper. It is an all-female occasion with mountains of African food – fried chicken, benachin, couscous, mangoes. Once the tea has been served and Isatou can relax her role as hostess she expands on the topic for which she has such a passion – the emancipation of women.

Isatou loves her country and chose to come back here after university to put her considerable skills to use (she speaks, fluent English, Mandinka, Wollof and

French) when she had every opportunity to remain in Europe which is what most Gambians dream of. She came home on the day her exams finished and cried with joy as the plane touched down. For all its problems and poverty, these are her people, she says, and this is where she can be truly effective as a role model and an activist for women's rights.

Isatou's house is cool and welcoming with big ceiling fans stirring the humid air as we relax – African and European, Jewish, Christian and Muslim. Like my time with Fania's friends in rural Ireland there is a lovely feeling of women's friendship, shared purpose and sisterhood. There are so many things I want to ask Isatou about her life and her experience of growing up as a Muslim child in an African society.

"I was born into a Muslim community," she says, "and given what we call a 'Muslim education' – in other words: learning the 5 pillars of Islam[1] learning to recite the Qur'an and memorising a few *suras* (Qur'anic verses) to pray. I would have loved to have gone further but because of the norms and cultural expectations for women we were not encouraged to aspire beyond a particular *sura*. The expectation was that you should be, above all else, *respectful*, honour your elders and, once married, obey your husband, provide everything for him and never question his rights or practices. You are taught not to question anything. In fact, it is *disrespectful* and *unreligious* to question. We were taught to believe that heaven lies under the feet of your husband. He alone has the key to your happiness. Education should only be to a certain level and beyond that it is dangerous to educate a woman. That was the traditional belief."

I ask Isatou if she minds talking about her own circumcision.

"Not at all. My own experience is what I can share. I am a victim of Female Genital Mutilation. The operation that was done on me was excision and clitoridectomy. So I lost my clitoris and my labia minora. In fact I wrote my Master's thesis on the subject and also a prose poem entitled, *The Lamentations of a Victim.* I was 11 years old so I have a very clear, strong memory of the event ...

"The preparation for the ceremony was so exciting I could hardly wait for the day to come. The night was so full of dances and fanfare I wanted it to be morning straight away so when I went through the experience it was a terrible shock. *Nobody is ever told the truth of what will happen.* No one knows about the mutilation. The type of preparation is all about making you want to take part. The elders tell you, 'you are going to be given bananas, you are going to be given oranges. We are going to dress you in gold and jewellery. We are going to buy you clothes.' *Nothing about being cut.* Even my older sisters never told me. When I went into the initiation I was told, 'there are songs we will teach you and you must never, never tell what your eyes have seen or your ears have heard'. You are sworn into a secret society.

---

1 These are: 1. The Statement of Belief ('There is no god but Allah, and Mohammed is His Messenger'); 2. The five-times-daily prayer; 3. The compulsory annual charity or *zakat*; 4. The Ramadan fast; 5. The *hajj* or pilgrimage to Mecca.],

"The information which is being passed on is all encoded in the initiation songs and it is all geared to protect male supremacy. They include education about sexual practices; how to entice your husband, aphrodisiacs for women, what you are supposed to submit to in intercourse and expectations. In my day women were not taught anything about these matters except during such ceremonies. There are also songs of revenge: "They have done something to me and if I am not dead I will do the same to somebody else". It is all part of the process of induction. You are told you are going to learn a trade but that is a lie. The trade is being a wife. I saw a trade as learning to develop a skill but you are really being taught how to be a subservient woman in the culture of men.

"It was a woman, who did this to me', says Isatou shaking her head in sorrow. "The circumcisor. Her African name means 'mother of the initiates' and she is paid per 'rose'. It was not done with my consent nor with the consent of any woman. The process is such that you are suddenly grabbed, blindfolded. They hold you down, sit on your chest, open your legs and ... whuff!" she holds an imaginary razor blade between her fingers and makes a swift, slicing motion. "Everything goes. You are placed in water as the blood billows around you then concoctions of crushed leaves and herbs, wood ash and cow or donkey dung – are put on the wound. The whole procedure is horrifying. No woman could ever forget the agony. It is there in your head for evermore. For the rest of your life you will associate sex with fear and pain and you are not supposed to talk about it ever. No matter what.

"I thought it was a normal religious ritual which every Muslim woman has to go through but now, through my own exposure and subsequent education and reflection about what FGM can do to the sexual and reproductive health of a woman, I know I have been fooled.

"One of the worst things was that if any complication arose it was never attributed to the practice itself. It was seen as diabolical. Someone among us must be a witch. When one of the initiates in my group died of her wounds – bled to death in the night – a rumour started that she was being eaten up by witchcraft and I believed that too. That's what our elders taught us to believe and a girl I knew, in fact she lived with us and slept next to me, was duly accused of witchcraft and blamed for the death. She was beaten so badly that she, herself, also died."

The period of initiation lasts for four weeks and during this time all the initiates are kept away from the rest of the village in a special hut lying on mats on the floor. "You have your food there" Isatou continued. "The place is not hygienic. It's full of flies. You are not allowed to wash your hands, only to sit in some water that has been boiled with herbs. They say that is what brings you luck. Whilst we were there in the bush my wound became infected. Maggots and worms were coming out. I will never forget it." She shuddered in horror at the memory.

But why did your mother consent? Why does any girls' mother consent? I asked.

"Because it was part of her culture, part of the tradition. Nobody questioned it. Every child that is born within that culture has to undergo it in order to become a member of the community and to *fulfil the religious injunctions of Islam*. And anyway you feel proud to be initiated. It gives you a sense of self–identity. We used to ostracise those who had not had it done. It becomes like an elite club. It cuts across class boundaries, educational background or anything else. It's only now with education, awareness and developed sensibility that I am trying to question, 'what's going on? Why can't we have a rites of passage initiation into womanhood without this terrible mutilation?'"

So when did she begin to question the practice? What changed her view?

"My husband, as you know, is a medical doctor. It was *he* who refused to allow our daughters to be circumcised. He said, ' Look at yourself. You have been having problems all your life. Don't you know? There is not a single line mentioning it in the Qur'an. The Prophet Mohammed didn't do that to his daughters. This is nothing to do with Islam. It's bad for you. Would you inflict something bad on your daughters?'

"I didn't resist but I had a big problem with his family who thought it was my 'urban' influence on my husband. I was afraid his parents would insist on a divorce but he said, 'Don't worry. You talk to your people and I'll talk to mine'. We had to prevent our daughters from going to the village on holiday because here the practice is that an auntie can snatch her brother's child for initiation and feel proud for taking the responsibility if she thinks the parents are failing in their duty. I trusted my husband because he came from the same culture as myself. I knew there had to be a good reason for him rejecting the practice and I started getting inquisitive about the whole issue.

"In the beginning I was not easily persuaded because I thought FGM was a religious matter too so I went back to the Qur'an. It was not there. It was not in any of the authenticated *hadith* so now I *know*, not only from my husband, but from my own studies that it is not a Divine injunction. There is no going back. Gradually a committee began to form under the auspices of the Women's Bureau and I became the first organiser and decided to use my research experience to find out more. Meanwhile, when we have debates or go into villages and meet resistance I reflect on myself and remember what I used to believe and how much I needed convincing."

No one seems to be able to say for sure when the practice of female circumcision began. It seems to pre-date Christianity and Islam. Some say that mutilating women was a way of controlling their sexuality when their menfolk went off to war. Now in The Gambia opinion is divided between those who say traditions must not be tampered with — that they are the very backbone of society — and those who say there is nothing wrong with change. A lot of traditional practices such as piercing and scarring for example have disappeared.

"Once ordinary women understand that FGM is not a religious injunction they will tell you we should stop it." Isatou went on. "The main problem we are having now is *men* — particularly the influential religious leaders. They tell us they are quoting from 'sources'. If that were true we would dissolve the committee immediately because we all want to go to heaven but we've gone through the two Holy books that guide the people of Islam and we know it is not in either of them. So what is going on? How can an Imam stand by in a community and tell you things which are not true? How can it be to men's advantage to mutilate their own women? I will tell you. The belief is that a circumcised woman is more obedient, more submissive, well-mannered, faithful. These are the qualities encoded in our initiation songs. It is to promote male control over female sexuality. He can have his satisfaction but she will have none. Also the culture of silence runs very, very deep. We know that men are exploiting women sexually, socially, economically in all its ramifications and they don't like anyone drawing attention to these things. They have got women where they want them."

Isatou goes to her filing cabinet and fetches a copy of the leaked policy document her organisation managed to get their hands on: an internal memo sent from the Director of Broadcasting Services to the Manager of Radio Programmes; the Manager of TV Operations; the Principal Producer of Programmes and others. This is what it said:

Policy on Media treatment of the FGM issue:

> *The broadcast by Radio Gambia or Gambia TV of any programmes which either seemingly oppose female genital mutilation or tend to portray medical hazard about the practice is forbidden, with immediate effect. So also are news items written from the point of view of combating the practice. Gambia TV and Radio Gambia broadcasts should always be in support of FGM and no other programmes against the practice should be broadcast. All programmes must therefore be previewed to ensure compliance with this directive. The Manager, Radio Programmes and the Principal Producer, Programmes should bring this to the attention of all producers and programme-makers.*

"So you see what we are up against," said Isatou laconically. "These are the decision makers in our society. Because female literacy is so low, we need the media in order to raise awareness. We need a forum to debate the issues, to understand the historical reasons, to ask ourselves if we want to continue, to speak for ourselves instead of men speaking on behalf of women about things that affect *our* bodies."

In addition to her work with GAMCOTRAP, Isatou is the representative and co-ordinator in The Gambia of The Network of Women Living Under Muslim Laws – an organisation which embraces 26 countries in Asia, the Middle East, Africa, France and the Caribbean. Her particular hobbyhorse is the issue of inheritance laws about which she has published a paper.

"It is not Islam, it's the male stranglehold that keeps women down. We are concerned with social justice and equality and the *blasphemous* way the Qur'anic injunctions have been misinterpreted. Women need land. They need financial independence and security in a society where you can be divorced on a flimsy excuse. You can be left, irrespective of how many children you have, with nothing. We need to find out, as women, what God intended for us"

I ask Isatou about her personal concept of God.

"Something I am thinking and cannot touch," she says. "Something I am feeling and cannot see. Something divine I am trying to live with and who manifests as a guide in my struggles. I cannot stop. I cannot give in. I must keep on and that something behind me, telling me I am going in the right direction is the Lord – a genderless being, neither male nor female; greater than anything I could imagine; beyond my comprehension; superimposed over my will; God is the *thought* I communicate with.

"Sometimes I have a feeling that God could be a woman. It is women who have brought love and gentleness into the world. They are the life-giving force not the life-taking force. Who are the perpetrators of coups, genocide, war, fights, killings? Who are they? One man will sacrifice a whole generation just to stay in power. That is the male manifestation of *dominance*. Is that what God is? Or is God the love and gentleness of women? When I look at Gambian women and see how even a woman selling peanuts in the street is making something out of it. Despite all the difficulties of their lives they make something beautiful out of the smallest thing. That is the feminine face of the Divine.

"And as to the concept of Holy War! That is nothing but political ideological, selfish manoeuvring. What God said about war is what we, as women, are trying to define. It should be a war against ignorance and poverty and injustice. That is Holy War.

"In the ancient African religions the earth was venerated as a mother, the trees, the sea, *everything* had spirit in it. Can't we learn something from that? Amongst the symbolism were realities. Look at the baobab tree. It provides us with everything we need to survive – seeds, roots, fruit, leaves, bark, shade. Nothing is wasted. Within our celebration of these natural wonders we can say God exists."

I offer the thought that in my own culture there has been a lot of reflection on the pre-monotheistic societies who seemed to live more in harmony with the earth and on how much we have thrown away and are now busily trying to retrieve before it is too late.

"I absolutely agree with you," says Isatou. "If you read the Qur'an, God said, "Reflect, reflect in the name of thy Lord." To me, religions have been manipulated so much by men that people are beginning to lose faith. It is a disrespect for Divinity. If you went by the true teachings you would have a peaceful world. Why should I go and pray behind an Imam who is blasphemous when I think I am closer to God than him? Why waste my time? I make an individual decision to communicate with my God in my own special and personal way with my five daily prayers. Why should I trust our religious leaders? I try, as much as possible, to abide by the divine injunctions. I don't have to tell anybody.

"I don't pray behind an Imam because I have <u>lost faith</u> but I am a more spiritual person than ever. The God in my heart is stronger than ever. I know I am not perfect but I am not going to listen to people who I know are just there to perpetuate themselves. This domination has gone on far too long. Things have got to change. Women have to come out to define and share their own religious perspective. We share stories in the Network. When it comes to issues of real power and choice – such as land ownership; what age you want to marry; how many children you want to have – that's where the trouble starts but I am no longer ignorant of the Qur'an and I know, for instance, there is nothing about birth control in the Qur'an so women must take the initiative. The population is exploding. Resources are finishing. Rains are not within the control of the State. Proper planning has to take place."

So you are not in the business of rejecting religion or spirituality but rejecting organised travesties? I say.

"Look, God said 'Support the Poor' so if you come together with that purpose you are performing one of the fundamentals of Islam," said Isatou passionately. "I try to be a good Muslim in the eyes of God. What *are* the important things? In fact many of us are beginning to question why a woman cannot become religious leader. We have been told it is because we are impure, unclean – that we cannot hold the Qur'an especially during our menses and so on. We shall see. There is a long road to travel but we have started."

And what about her own daughters? What aspirations does she have for them?

"I want them to grow up here – proud to be African women – in my society, in my country, embracing every aspect of my culture except the negative practices that disempower them like FGM, leaving school early, becoming a child-bride, learning to be submissive and not to question. I want them to be educated, to contribute effectively to our Gambian society, to stay here and be role models. I have given them the knowledge of everything I was never supposed to talk about. They know about the trickery. They have seen their father's video. Certainly we should have rites of passage but not with *cutting*. A new celebration without injury. That is what GAMCOTRAP is trying to initiate."

I tell Isatou of the reluctance many Western women feel about interfering in other peoples cultural traditions. Feminist friends have said to me that it is none of our business and yet another example of colonial arrogance to presume to criticise ancient customs, that we should keep our noses out of things we don't understand. Hasn't our meddling done enough to hasten the disintegration of indigenous cultures?

"No," she cries. "We want you to join us in our struggle. We are not trying to condemn our culture and it is very important for Western women to know that we need support both financial and moral. Don't leave us to face this alone. It needs to be outlawed."

At the end of the evening our little group of women spontaneously form a circle with our arms about each others' shoulders in a warm embrace, giving thanks, feeling sure that it is no accident we have been brought together. We each, in our different way, have a vision – a spiritual network of women supporting each other's work.

Next day, with a head full of things to think about, I meet up with Geri for a last walk along the beach and a dip in the tumbling Atlantic breakers as warm as maple syrup. We attract a little band of charming rogues. They're all hoping for some sugar mummies and can't understand what we are doing here without our husbands. They drum for us, dance for us, try to persuade us to go with them to a palm wine/jungle juice joint ... It's all very good-humoured and non-threatening. We joke and laugh and slip away to watch the sunset – shades of apricot and silver turning deeper and deeper and a perfect crescent moon appearing like an omen in the sky. Everywhere in the cool of the evening young athletes are training – running, doing squats and press-ups, playing football. I am moved by the beauty, the grace, the dedication. Despite all the poverty and deprivation they are rich in many of the things we have lost – close families, uncontaminated natural food, unpolluted air, low instance of drug and alcohol abuse (a big plus for Islam), an open, friendliness, good manners, hospitality, generosity. Geri is right when she says we have a such lot to learn from the Gambians if only we have ears to hear. Someone once said to her, "The white man came to Africa in search of healing only he just didn't know it." The bad things might be terrible but there are many good ones. Isatou is one of the best.

Before my journey back to England Geri and I plan a blessing ceremony for Safari Garden – that her dreams for it becoming a place of real cultural exchange and learning will come true. Late at night we take a lantern, a little chalice of water, a shell from the sea, a seed-pod from the flame tree and the wooden carving of 'Unity' (my gift to the hotel) and, beginning in the eastern corner of the compound we invoke the powers of the four directions, the four elements, and the Divine Presence. We sprinkle the water, rattle the seed pod and ask for a blessing. In each corner of the grounds we set up the carving with the lamp in the centre, illuminating the faces of the intertwined wooden figures all carved from a single block of wood. We acknowledge the shadows, the distractions, the discouragements and intolerances that will have to be faced and dealt with and, finally, at midnight, under a clear, starry sky we stand in the middle of the garden by the newly-planted frangipani tree and Geri recites an American Indian prayer:

I stand at the centre and the light shines all around me
And now I know that my spirit glowing makes this light
I come into power with the sun, for I am like the sun
I am my own light.
Here at the centre I see the meaning of things, all things
And now I know that I am the meaning. The whole meaning
The four directions come together in me
I am the centre. Everything flows from me, returns to me.
I am that which they call Great Mystery.
I am that which each one calls Wakantanka before coming.
Before seeing the light.
I am here and so I know. Here I know everything.
Here I know myself.
I am thought and will and nothing sits above my will.
I am pride and joy and nothing sits above my joy.
I own my life and only mine
And so I shall appreciate my person
And so I shall make proper use of myself.
I stand here in the light of my own presence
And I recognise my power.
I am reason and nothing sits above my choice.
I am truth and so I live in the spirit.
And so I live forever.
I am the oneness of the whole and whatever happens
Happens in me.
I am Ahbleza. I own the Earth. Hanta Yo.

We are joined by some of the hotel's African employees whom Geri has been firing with her vision. (She holds 'team-building' days when everyone from the gardener to the manageress is invited to contribute). Quite spontaneously, without a word, feeling the specialness of the moment, we link hands, replicating the 'Unity' symbol of the carving and in that sacred space a blessing is said in Wollof in which I recognise the words Allah and Maryam. We also say a prayer for the night-watchman's wife who is trying to hold onto her pregnancy after many miscarriages[1] and we all feel very hopeful in the tropical night.

On the plane back to London I reflect on what an unexpected bonus it has been to see, in action, the courage of Geri, trying against all the odds, to run her little hotel on ethical, spiritual principles. A determined woman with a deep-seated belief that we are all one, a quiet example of someone who empowers others, whose motives are clear and pure, whose heart is trusting, who is willing to learn and grow. She is modest and self-effacing and always sees the good in everyone. In the face of massive cynicism she is quietly moving mountains. All around her jaded gloom merchants shake their heads and say, on the one hand, yes, how lovely The Gambia is, how nice and friendly and, on the other, of course Africans are lazy and only work when white people are watching. They have no initiative. They are like children. I can hardly believe that attitude still exists but I heard one would-be foreign entrepreneur use the very phrase. What is he doing wanting to live here if that is how he feels?

The Gambians are 'nice and friendly' because they have strong cultural traditions of hospitality and generosity. They have deep-seated values of neighbourliness and family responsibilities. They love their children. They take care of their old people. They were possibly the earliest human society. They built beautiful villages – models of simplicity and aesthetic grace – which stressed-out Westerners try to recreate when they come here to play-act a simulated African village experience. Yes, the people are poor and there are many problems in contemporary African society but how different might things have been had they never been enslaved, colonised, infantalised? Initiatives like Geri's – restoring self-esteem, treating people as responsible, decision-making adults, as co-workers and profit-sharing partners is a way towards healing.

---

[1] I later heard that she gave birth to a healthy baby daughter.

Chapter 12

❖ ❖ ❖ ❖ ❖

*'The heart that breaks open
can contain the whole universe'*

In 1996 Roshi Bernard Glassman and the newly formed Zen Peacemaker Order of New York organised an interfaith meditation retreat in the Nazi concentration camp of Auschwitz-Birkenau. They called it *Bearing Witness* and when I read about it, even though it tugged at old childhood memories of denial, dread and panic, I knew that if it were to be held again I wanted to be part of it. So in the winter of 1997 I found myself in Cracow – my courage boosted by the presence of my beloved Israeli friend Levana – to meet up with other retreat participants coming from all over the world.

It's such a strange feeling to be standing on Polish soil, the land of my ancestors, for the first time in my life. Slavic currents in my bloodstream quicken and pulse. I remember Tess Harper's lovely phrase. Something about this land knows *my* name. My father had always promised to take me to Poland, to introduce me to the land of his birth, to share with me the Polish sausage and chocolate memories of his childhood, to show me the woods and farms of the country he never ceased to love. We planned, at regular intervals, to make this trip together but he died before we ever got round to it and suddenly 20 years have passed.

For reasons that are easy to psychoanalyse but somehow I never have, this last, missing piece of my own personal jigsaw has been the most difficult to fit. Poland is not that far – a couple of hours by plane from London – and yet the distance seems vast. I am travelling not only through space but backwards in time through an immeasurable distance of sorrow and longing. It has taken me so long to make this journey. I've kept on putting it off. What impels me now like an invisible force shoving me between the shoulder blades is the profound understanding that stepping into the past – this bit of my ancestral and personal past – with my eyes and my heart fully open, will release me to move on.

Our plane touches down in Cracow on a freak mild, sunny November morning and we find ourselves sweltering in our layers of sweaters and thermal knickers – suitcases bulging with woollies in the anticipation of snow and bitter winds. I don't know quite what I expected but it certainly isn't this untouched, undamaged medieval city of cobbled streets and graceful buildings, the most beautiful Renaissance covered market I've ever seen, well-stocked shops and people thronging the squares, shopping and sitting outside in cafés. Cracow Old Town is absolutely ravishing in the sunshine.

Amongst this loveliness, though, statistics sit insistently at the edge of my mind: In 1939 a quarter of the population of Cracow were Jews. 70,000 Jews lived here – a continuous presence since the 12th Century. Their homes, synagogues and schools throbbed with an exuberance that made Poland the centre of world Jewish culture. Now there are *less than 100*. Tasteless little carved wooden caricature figures of Jewish 'Klezmer' musicians in traditional long black coats and wide-brimmed black hats sit jauntily on the tourist stalls – hollow and tragic reminders of a once vibrant community.

I have come here in the knowledge that a precipitous emotional roller-coaster ride awaits me – joy at seeing the beautiful country of my father's birth, horror at the reminders of what happened here. Like a deer on the edge of a wide open meadow I step gingerly, my senses on red-alert, ready to flee. The sudden sound of shouting and running boots as a posse of Polish police arrive outside our hotel freezes me in my tracks – a chilling flashback to ghetto days which sends a shudder down my spine. They have merely been called to deal with a drunk disturbing the peace but I find myself trembling. I never experienced the pogroms personally but I must carry the fear in the rivers of my DNA.

I know how important it is for me to make this pilgrimage. I need to collect the last scattered bits of me that are mirrored in the faces of the Poles I see in the street, that are buried with my grandmother's bones, that lie with my cousin's ashes in the ruins of the gas ovens of Auschwitz. I am terrified of going to Auschwitz but I also know that many of those people who came last year have called it a holy place where the work of contemplation, remembrance and peace can be carried out – a place of transformation and pilgrimage. I have brought with me a few special tulip bulbs to plant somewhere here, given to me by my daughter, Francesca, and a few acorns from my son, Ben. Seeds from us, the descendants, to return to the soil of our origination.

To me it seems a way that I can begin to draw together the threads of my long, rather eccentric, spiritual journey – my Ladder to the Moon. For what does 'spirituality' mean if not a way to live with the big questions of life and death, love and evil, compassion and suffering, mystery and understanding? Buddhists are coming, Sufis, Christians, Jews, monks, priests, nuns, rabbis, teachers and seekers to be together in communion and intention – to sit together for a week inside the barbed wire, to walk, meditate, *be* with the fact of Auschwitz. The names of those who died here and in other places during the Holocaust will be chanted and midnight vigils kept. When I began this quest I had no idea it would bring me here but I trust that I have been brought at the right time to the right place to finish the tapestry.

I am swept along on a switchback. One minute I am a tourist in a pretty town where everything is new and interesting, the next I am engulfed by a wave of sorrow for my father and his pain at losing his family, his language, his country. These look such nice, ordinary streets. Could neighbours have informed on Jewish families *here*? Could people have been dragged from their homes in *this* quiet square and forced to live like rats in a squalid ghetto? Could the local citizens really not have known about the extermination factory one hour up the road? And those who murdered or turned a blind eye were 'civilised' people, not barbarians. They were Poles and Germans – ancient cultured peoples, people like us.

"Religion is for folks who are trying to keep out of Hell. Spirituality is for those who've already been there." I am talking to Siddiq Khulwati, a black American Sufi Imam who has come to take part in the retreat and lead the Muslim services- a beautiful, courageous man who has been in recovery for two years from alcohol and drug addiction. Siddiq is a wonderful talker – full of stories and humour and good conversation. He had reached rock-bottom, he tells me, lost everything – wife, children, friends – through his dependency. Many detox efforts were attempted but ended in failure when the pain of life crowded in on him again. On the way addiction hooks you again and again he quips, "If you're up to your ass in alligators you're inclined to forget the reason you wanted to drain the swamp!" It was only when a brother, an ex-addict, stretched out a hand to him in the gutter and took him to A.A. that he began to understand that he wasn't a bad person who needed to become good but a sick person who needed to become well. And now he is positively incandescent with the life force and his unique gifts of experience and wisdom enable him to help others. "We cannot free another being", he said, "but we can show the way and we can show love. Freedom is contagious." Siddiq has learned to teach and serve by being who he is and listening deeply with an open heart. Suffering, he says, can be a way to learn about freedom – words to be used with care in the context of Auschwitz. They would sound unacceptably trite and smug uttered by most people. Maybe, like him, you have to earn the right to use them. Something about reaching rock-bottom and losing everything before you learn that, as long as you can still breathe, you have the power to change. I think of George, the Vietnam veteran I met scrubbing floors in Massachusetts and know I have met yet another free man.

It was the end of a long day. Levana and I had walked miles, beginning in Cracow Old Town, buying delicious poppy-seed rolls from a street vendor, looking round the ancient market, strolling past the Wawel Castle – home of Polish kings for 500 years. Then, suddenly, there we were in Kazimierz where most of Cracow's 70,000 Jews had lived. It was another sunny day – a shock to see it all in colour with a few golden autumn leaves still on the trees. Poland,

to me, has always been a black and white place – my interior landscape constructed of old newsreels and stark photographs of displaced people with fear
and shock in their eyes. Even the film, *Schindler's List* was shot in black and
white. What I am seeing now and what I know do not sit easily together. My
mind keeps slipping back and forth disorientatingly from, 'What a lovely old
city this is' to 'Oh my God, what happened here!' The sleepy main square, full
of parked tourist coaches, was once alive with old men playing chess, children
running about, women going to market, vendors selling. There has been an
attempt to re-habilitate the area in the light of the recent, post-*Schindler's List*
tourism boom but the place is full of ghosts, the wind brings echoes of voices
and images of the past keep bleeding into the present.

We sat outside at Ariel's Café to eat borscht and herrings in sour cream for
lunch. How my father would have loved it! He often spoke nostalgically of the
food of his childhood and would try, for the main part disastrously, to re-create
his mother's dishes for us. At the bookshop we engaged a young student as a
guide. She took us walking over the River Vistula to the ragged remains of the
ghetto where the people were packed into a few square blocks, several families
to a single room, for two years before they were 'liquidated' anyway or transported to the death camps or forced labour camps. Nazi soldiers, said Margaret,
our guide, used to play a game, the objective of which was to try to kill four
children with one bullet by making them stand in a line. If one should happen
to survive he would be put in the next line. For another sport, they threw
babies from balconies for their comrades to catch on their bayonets while the
mothers screamed in horror. Remnants of the ghetto wall still stand, built in
the shape of a row of Jewish tombstones – a little Nazi jest to remind those
within that they were as good as dead already and would never come out alive.
The synagogues were desecrated and used as stables for their horses, the ancient
cemeteries plundered for gravestones to use as paving slabs. Every humiliation
and cruelty that can be imagined was perpetrated here in this beautiful city by
people from the land of Beethoven, Bach and Goethe. It is hard to grasp the
enormity of it all.

All these things one can know as historical facts. I've known them for as
long as I can remember but somehow walking these cobbled streets, hearing
the spectral voices of the lost souls who died here, seeing what someone once
called "the tears of things", brings it into sharp focus. Clearly, I can never begin
to know what it must have felt like to have been Jewish in Poland back then.
I can only say that not to try would be worse. Many Jews of that generation,
like Levana's parents who survived, have never been able to talk or even think
about what happened. To have survived, to have found the strength to go on
into the future, to emigrate, to start new lives, to build the state of Israel you
couldn't afford the time or the energy to mourn. We are perhaps here to do their
mourning for them – the strange overlap of personal and collective mourning
– to process it through our own bodies as an exorcist does. We are far enough
removed from the pain to allow ourselves the luxury of thinking about it.

Maybe. I don't know. It's almost too huge to take in. I am just here, for what it's worth. I can say, 'I hear you' to those little children lined up to be shot by a single bullet. I can be a witness. There is an old Jewish saying, "It is on the breath of our children going to school that our world is founded". This is where that world, my father's world, disintegrated. Meanwhile the moon shines down and the birds fly, the clouds scud across the sky and the quiet River Vistula flows on by, murmuring in Yiddish, as they say, to those who listen.

When I was a child I didn't want to hear about any of this. My father had terrible shouting nightmares all his life and my mother tried to tell us why. She talked about babies being thrown alive into incinerators and such like horrors because she thought it was important we should know. But she became so emotional that I couldn't stand it. I used to cover my ears and run out of the room. Their pain was too much, too bottomless, I couldn't bear it. There was an excess of darkness, too dense for light to penetrate. I was never able to talk with either of them about what happened here but the long shadows cast by this early knowledge have always haunted the deepest recesses of my imagination and now, of course, I wish they were here to ask.

In the beautiful Old Synagogue, the oldest Jewish religious building in Poland dating back to the 15th Century, miraculously still standing, there is an exhibition of devastating photographs showing the gradual erosion of human rights, the gathering horror – 'Jews Only' buses, armbands with yellow stars, notices forbidding Jews from this and that, photographs of executions, transports, brutality. So as night falls we are as prepared as we will ever be and board the buses taking our group on the 60 km trip to Oswiecim, better known by its German name, Auschwitz. It begins to rain as we drive. The unseasonable mild weather has come to an abrupt end. Cold and fog envelop us like a shroud and a mysterious cough takes hold of my throat. I am glad it is too dark to see anything. There will be time enough.

At the camp there are three places offering accommodation. Levana and I are billeted in the Centre for Dialogue where we will sleep five to a room and eat breakfast and dinner. The rest of the time will be spent inside the wire. There are 130 of us on the retreat. I am the only English person and it all seems quite daunting. We have a brief introductory meeting that first evening and Roshi Bernie Glassman advises us to begin from a place of 'not-knowing', with no expectations – giving up any fixed ideas about ourselves and the universe; to share our own processes and to allow our own healing and that of others. We are all here for our different reasons.

"You are entering a place of unimaginable horror and tragedy", says a sign at the entrance to Auschwitz but nothing can prepare you for the scale of it. I had seen the films and read the books, but until you walk through those gates with the cruelly cynical inscription; 'Arbeit Mach Frei' – work makes you free – and feel the oppressive silence of the spirits of the dead vibrating in the very air you breathe, it is impossible even to begin to imagine it. The Nazi's tried to blow up the place to destroy the evidence of their crimes and it has been left exactly as it was. The 30 surviving prison blocks house the museum of what was found here after the liberation of the camp by Soviet troops in January 1945. The exhibits lead you ever downward to the depths of human depravity. No photograph can really give an accurate impression of the mountain of shoes taken from the dead – 10, 15 feet high on both sides of the room – or how much space 70 tons of women's hair takes up or convey the impact of seeing the bolts of lining material for German soldiers' uniforms that was made out of it. No film could make you catch your breath and stare in disbelief as can the actual sight of the tangled pile of artificial limbs or the little baby clothes.

I had brought with me the *tallit* (Jewish prayer shawl) I found, neatly folded inside a hand-embroidered maroon velvet bag, forlornly displayed in a London junk shop before I left home. I bought it for £1 and it symbolised for me all the anonymous Jews, un-named, unknown, who died here. Now I put it round my shoulders as I entered the museum and sometimes the horror was so over-whelming that I had to put it right over my head and hide inside its protective tent. Each person in our group had their own flashpoint when the grief en-gulfed them, when the sobs and the tears could no longer remain inside. Mine was the sight of a little grey plait, which could have been my mother's, lying amongst the mountain of shorn women's hair. Shattered and shivering, Levana and I clung to each other in the gas chamber only able to say, Oh my God, Oh my God over and over. Into this dank basement filed 2,000-strong groups of men, women and children expecting hot showers but getting instead a cloud of Zyklon B gas that took 20 minutes to kill them as they clawed the walls. The fingernail marks are still there.

Outside again in the open air, hardly able to breathe for the heaviness in my chest, we held a heartrending *Kaddish* (memorial) service at the terrible 'execution wall'. We placed candles on the blood-soaked earth and the Rabbi in our group recited the ancient Jewish prayer for the dead which was then spoken in translation by a representative of every language amongst us – Japanese, Polish, Spanish, Hebrew, Portuguese, French, German, English – each speaker in turn wrapped in the Rabbi's rainbow-striped *tallit* while the awesome sound of the *shofar*, the rams horn, tore open the sky with its defiant call to awaken the dead. The woman who read the German language translation faltered and broke down but carried on bravely as Rabbi Singer stood with his hand on her shoulder to steady her. The Buddhists bowed, the Muslims prostrated, the Catholics crossed themselves and the Jews put tiny pebbles in the cracks in the wall. Then we just stood in silence in the raw air, in that grey place inhabited by so many ghosts as the dozens of tiny flames flickered at our feet.

A 45-minute walk away is Auschwitz II or Birkenau – the purpose-built killing factory – the extension camp with the machinery for murdering and incinerating 60,000 people a day. This is where the cattle trucks arrived; where those railway lines converge at the 'selection point' – that infamous image of dread and despair – the place where Dr Mengele or some other honourable member of the medical profession stood and pointed to the left or the right as each dazed, exhausted person got off the train. His job was to assess whether you were fit for work or not. Reasonably young and strong? This way, slave labour until you drop. Pregnant or old or holding small children by the hand? That way, instant death.

The vastness of the place is shocking enough – a scale which defies comprehension – and then there is the duplicity, the trickery, the meticulous planning, the chilling documentation, the gas chambers cunningly constructed underground so people wouldn't guess the fate that awaited them and panic before being herded in. We were shown the gruesome, sturdy gallows from which 12 people could be hanged at once; punishment cells where people caught trying to escape were slowly starved to death or suffocated 40 to a tiny cell with no ventilation or crammed four to a dog kennel where there was only room to stand all night.

I heard the one (maybe there were more but not many are documented) heroic story of Father Maximilian Kolbe, the Polish Catholic priest who volunteered to take the place of a family man condemned to the starvation cell. The Gestapo accepted his offer and locked him away without food or water until he died but the man whose life he exchanged for his own, survived and lived into his nineties visiting Auschwitz to give thanks and bring flowers every year from the end of the war until his death two years ago.

All of us were left wondering about the nature of courage, the disintegration of decency, the hardening of conscience, the numbing of feeling, asking ourselves: what would be my breaking point? When would I become an animal? When would my own survival become more important than all the ethical and moral precepts that I try to live my life by? When would I have lost the will to live? Broken in body and spirit, lost in a sea of suffering and helplessness with everyone I loved murdered, could I have gone on? Could I have given my life to save another's? There is, of course, no way of knowing how I would have behaved and I can only hope I am never forced to find out.

The hush here makes your skin crawl. It reverberates in the air like the silence after a scream, invades you with the shock waves. The walls echo with desolation and despair. The grey ponds where the ashes of the victims were dumped stare like opaque, blind eyes at the towering ruins of the crematoria. I understand, for the first time, why many survivors were never able to talk about what they experienced or why, if they did, people couldn't listen. It is beyond the range of what a human being can hold. There are no words, there is nothing with which you can compare it. It is the worst, most grotesque thing that has ever happened in the history of the world and it happened right here, in my lifetime, to members of my family.

In a rare moment when the sky cleared briefly we walked along the train tracks as the moon rose in the east. We sang the *Kaddish* again around the ruins of one of the largest gas chambers and the last of the winter sun hung low in the sky. There was a tender wind and a pale light played in the graceful, leafless branches of the silver birches. How bizarre, how obscene that the cold-blooded killing went on regardless even on beautiful evenings like this. Everyone mangled by the impact of the day, we walked slowly back to our accommodation.

After supper we gathered again as we would every evening to share our own stories in the large group. Rabbi Singer talked about the meaning of the *Kaddish* (from the Aramaic: *qaddish*; holy). He interpreted as 'bearing witness' this prayer to sanctify God. It is about being ready to give one's attention, one's ego, one's heart energy to the ideal of peace and the alleviation of suffering. In the language of poetry the *Kaddish* expresses the idea of the Great Name and the desire for good. In the Jewish tradition the response to mourning is to recite the *Kaddish*. The sorrow and the mourning draw our attention and we struggle to express in words the great themes of life and death, the tragedies, the love. The *Kaddish* expresses the idea that all of life is *now* and that 'Now' is one of the names of God. It is about saying 'yes' to life. It is about being a witness. It was very moving to see so many non-Jews finding meaning in the *Kaddish* and it filled the heart to hear the poetic words translated into half a dozen languages at the execution wall where so many died a wretched and terrified death.

We begin each day, typically, at 6 am and meet in small groups of six or seven before breakfast for an hour. I am lucky to be in a group facilitated by Seisen Fletcher, a shaven-headed Zen woman priest who leads us skilfully into feeling safe enough to talk openly. Also in our group is Roshi Bernie Glassman, the wise teacher and founder of the Zen Peacemaker Order; Paul a quiet, devout American Christian who lent me his gloves when my hands were freezing one day; passionate, brilliant, articulate Levana and gentle Margaret with the over-flowing china-blue eyes. We are asked only to listen to each other attentively without commenting or judging and when it's my turn to speak I find myself talking about the place in me where hatred lies, where unforgiveness, where the murderess. Out of the blue in an unstoppable outpouring comes my rage towards my youngest daughter's partner who is a violent and disturbed alcoholic. Only recently did we discover that he has been hitting her and hurting their baby. The first step, of course, was to assist her in getting a legal injunction to stop him from harming her again. But now that she is safe, I hate him. I want him dead yet I also know what pain he must be in to do what he does and I don't know if I want to help him or kill him. I don't know anything except that I, too, am capable of base thoughts and actions, prejudice and intolerance. My mother felt exactly the same hatred and unforgiveness towards all Germans. Being here in this place is the time to ponder these things and each of us, in our own way, must wrestle with questions of good and evil.

We tell our stories, have breakfast and walk to Birkenau through the wintry fields. On the way we have to cross the dolorous railway tracks near to Oswiecim station and each day, at the same point, a long goods train with box-cars trundles past, creaking and clanking, making that iron-wheels-on-iron-rails sound so ominous in this context. It rains all day, every day, sometimes drizzly, sometimes pouring. Quite a few of our people, expecting snow, are not prepared for wet weather. We are wrapped in dustbin liners and flimsy plastic capes, our jeans are soaked and our boots not waterproof yet it all seems as nothing compared to what the prisoners here were made to endure − forced to stand barefoot in the snow, sleeping eight to a bunk in damp rags under a leaking roof, the appalling medical experiments, the row of 200 concrete latrines with no privacy where people had to shit all together, allowed a maximum of 45 seconds each and only twice a day. The humiliation, the fear, the stench ...

We gather inside the camp to participate, if we want to, in any one of the four daily religious services on offer. I choose the Christian service on the first day because Father John has readily agreed to combine his Catholic Mass with Danuta, a dramatic, raven-haired Polish witch who has offered a Native American dance and blessing for the Earth. She drapes the communion altar with Our Lady of Guadeloupe and smudges us all with sage smoke. We take Communion − something I have never done before − of bread and wine, and say the beautiful prayer of St Francis beside the forlorn, murky pond where the ashes from the crematorium were thrown. Then we circle the pond dancing the Earth healing dance to the four directions. The Earth has a heartbeat. She is alive, says Danuta, she needs our love and our feet pound to the rhythm of her pulse. The music sustains us, lifts us. Even in the rain it is a joyous service and we can hear the *shofar* sounding its ancient call to awakening from the Jewish service and the drums from the Buddhist one floating across the barbed wire from other locations around the camp.

The rain plasters our hair and runs down our noses as we return to sit together in meditation by the railway tracks, the final disembarkation point for over three million people from all over Europe. While the sky weeps, four people at a time, one at each compass point in our circle, begin a continuous chanting of the names of those who died here. We have each been given three pages of closely typed names and will have a turn to read them out along with any personal ones. I have brought the names of my family, the Honigs and Tennenbaums, and those of Jewish friends in London whose parents and relatives were also murdered in the Holocaust. It is very powerful just to hear them spoken aloud and to pray that the souls of those who perished will be released. If I and my husband and all our children had been exterminated I think my anguished spirit would be glad if one day in the future someone, perhaps not yet born, remembered us: Richard Taylor, Allegra Taylor, Ben Taylor, Tim Taylor, Femi Taylor, Matthew Taylor, Francesca Taylor, Harry Taylor, Maddison Taylor ... This is what it sounds like − each death a horrible murder, whole families wiped out – turned to ashes. As it sinks in the effect is devastating. You can still feel waves, gusts of fear in the air everywhere here. The fear of death and that no one would ever know what happened; that no trace would remain; that no one would remember your name. Well, they are not forgotten. May they rest in peace.

A young Dutch woman has come on the retreat with the main purpose of making a memorial ritual specially for the children who died in Auschwitz. As the mother of an eighteen month-old daughter herself it is the calamity most particularly close to her heart. We walk to the barracks where the children were incarcerated and make a Star of David out of candles on the floor. The rain falls and falls as if the heavens will never stop weeping and we stand holding hands in a circle. We call on the spirits of the poor little things to come into the light so that we can offer them the comfort and the tenderness and warmth that was denied them as they cried for their mothers in terror and pain. Someone reads two poems, extraordinarily mature and prophetic, written by a cousin of his who died here at the age of 14. Then people just sing or speak as they are moved to do so.

In a cracked and watery voice, I find myself singing the Skye Boat Song which my own children used to love when they were little and I see each of their precious faces, one by one, appear in the candlelight. A young German man sings, 'Schlaf Kinderlein Schlaf' and breaks down into convulsions of grief, falling on his knees, sobbing, pounding the earth with his fists. People sing lullabies in Hebrew and Polish and offer visions of happy, normal childhoods to the unquiet ghosts of those whose own had been snuffed out. Someone reads a list of some of the children's names and the ages at which they died: Sarah Rosen, age 6 years; Daniel Isaacson, age 5 months; Rebecca Moisewitz, 2 years; ... 8 years; ... 1 month ... it goes on and on remorselessly, unendurably. Although we are all moved to tears it isn't just about grieving it is also about healing. Perhaps the very grieving itself is the healing factor. With streaming faces we embrace these spirit children and each other and leave the guttering candles burning in the darkness. The silver birch trees look on and the last of the migrating geese fly overhead in ragged V's. The forgiving Earth is still there and holds us in her arms again.

We disperse to be alone with our thoughts – the clouds lower and darker than ever. Had they not been murdered, those children, they would be my age. They were my contemporaries. They would be men and women in their fifties and sixties with grandchildren of their own. "When I get home I will kiss my children's feet!" vows Levana passionately. "Never again will I grumble at them about anything."

In our evening get-together people are overflowing with the emotions of the day and many get up to speak in the large group. The main theme is the extreme pain and guilt carried by the Germans of today. Just as the children and grandchildren of camp survivors still carry the suffering of the victims so the Germans have a terrible burden of shame and sorrow to bear for their parents and grandparents. All of us are children who have lived our lives in the shadow of our parents' stories. "We felt horrible to be Germans," said one man. "German was a bad word. Nation; father; were bad words. I am a peaceful man but I feel contaminated, unclean. To be the children of the perpetrators is a terrible thing."

"I have spent most of my life trying not to feel," said another man. "I *felt* today from being here, from being with the spirits of the children and I am a different person. I don't know anything but I can feel."

Gabriella spoke in an anguished voice about "being a German when so many people find it hard to be around Germans." Her father had been a fighter pilot. When he came home from the war he retreated into a depression that lasted for the rest of his life until eventually he died of cancer. "I am also here for him," she said. "For the man I never knew." I saw her today at the Jewish service. She held her umbrella over the Torah while the rain soaked her to the skin.

A young Polish woman told about her parents. "All his life my father seemed only to want power over people and I hated him. I was afraid of him. I saw him as a bully and my mother as weak but today, in the children's service, I got close to them for the first time. *They* were children in the war. My mother had documents hidden in the plaits of her hair as an 11-year-old child. She was forced to smuggle forbidden sausage in her clothes. The punishment for such 'crimes', if you were caught, was severe. She must have been in constant terror. My father hid in a bush when the bombs were falling on his village. He was six years old, afraid he would die because his feet were sticking out. How must they have suffered? Their pain was constant. It hibernated in them and was passed on to me. It infected our lives like a deadly disease. If I don't find a way to express it I will pass it on again."

"I am German," said another woman, and those words were enough to cause her voice to catch in her throat. Her eyes filled with tears. "I never could cry as a child. It was not allowed. My parents were very harsh – authoritarian, in the Germanic way of parenting in those days. 'You've got nothing to cry about,' they would say, 'shut up!' And now I feel stupid for crying, embarrassed, crying for nothing. What is my pain compared to those who suffered and died here?" And yet as she talked we learned that her own father, a Nazi Naval Commander, committed suicide after the war and she tried to kill herself just to be close to him. She was saved and now she is here with us, weeping for the first time. "Yesterday was so heavy I thought I couldn't bear it," she said, "but today in the Muslim service we danced together and I am on the way to my healing." As she sat down kind hands reached out to her in tenderness and empathy.

And I thought of a line from Anaïs Nin:

> *"And the day came when the risk to remain tight in a bud*
> *was more painful than the risk it took to blossom."*

I was so admiring of the courage of the Germans and Poles who spoke. It was very brave to come here to be with so many of us Jews and to work on this old wound together. Until we set about finishing unfinished business, taking responsibility, learning from each other we can never move on. It takes tremendous guts to expose the places of fear, hatred, intolerance and prejudice in ourselves but if we don't own them no true healing can ever take place. It came to me that the most important thing we can offer anyone in distress – perhaps the only important thing we can ever offer – is our *mindful presence* without agenda or expectation. Then, as we work with others, we have a profound means of working on ourselves. Or maybe our work on ourselves gives us the means of working with others.

"It starts from the heart, from opening the heart and being aware," said Bernie. "We need to look with self-awareness at what sort of strategies we employ for our own survival in everyday life. Do I neglect my own children so that I can become enlightened? Am I sometimes unkind? Thoughtless? Do I withdraw? Do I not listen well enough to others?"

"This is the strongest place I have ever been in my life," said a young Pole, fervently. "I vow from this day to be open and to love."

An elderly African–American Buddhist monk spoke up, "My promise to the millions of people here and around the world who died so horribly is that we must become the watchdogs of the Earth. Coming from the South in the United States, I learned very early in my life that we all have red blood and salty tears," he said. "Part of my practice, my vehicle for the rest of my days on this planet is to be ever watchful of people in power so that nothing like this should ever happen again."

In the course of the following days the pattern of morning service, sitting meditation, chanting of names, walking meditation and recitation of the *Kaddish* in different parts of the camp is repeated many times. I participate in a different religious service each day. Nearly everyone does the same. It is one of the most profound aspects of the retreat. There are so many ways to wisdom and to the heart. As Bernie observes, the deeper he goes into the heart of Buddhism the more Jewish he becomes. At the centre the differences disappear – each of us being drawn, in one way or another to the same great vision. It is more than a vision. It is the next step in our evolutionary journey – transcending religiosity and finding our own authentic spiritual voice. No doctrine, theory or ideology is definitive. We have only the gift of sharing perceptions that hopefully can help others on their journey. All systems of thought are guiding means, they are not the absolute truth. They are an opportunity to connect with the bigness. I can dance in a circle of drumming women. I can enjoy my Jewishness in a *chavorah*. I can sit zazen with the Buddhists. I can love Jesus and his Jewish mother. I can chant *La Illa Ha Illa La* and *Allah Hu* with the Sufis. They're all wonderful but they're not 'it'. 'It' is being present moment by moment.

On one miserable freezing cold day, mud everywhere and puddles reflecting the dripping skeins of barbed wire we chant the names of the dead in one of the barrack buildings that had been used for the quarantine of typhoid prisoners and then say the *Kaddish* in the terrible latrine block where we place candles and sing. Amidst the tears that flow every time we gather for such ceremonies there is something thrillingly defiant about hearing the raw blast of the *shofar:* "We are here!" it cries, "We are alive", and to those who died here in despair and desolation, little thinking that the beautiful Hebrew melodies would ever be heard soaring through the rafters in this hell on Earth, it shouts, "We remember you!"

Bundled up to the eyes in my waterproofs I walk the train tracks alone. This morning I have been reading an extract from the notes of a Jewish inmate found in the camp after the war. He writes about his arrival at Birkenau:

> 'It is already dark in the yard. An electric lamp shines in the distance, casting a faint light. The only strong illumination comes from a big floodlight mounted above the gate, visible from far away. We stumble along the soggy, clayey ground full of fear and exhaustion ... Before we drew in a breath of air, some of us had our heads clubbed. Blood was already flowing from split heads or injured faces. This was the first welcome for newcomers. All of us are bewildered, looking around the place where we have been brought. Now they inform us that this is a sample of camp life. Iron discipline reigns here. We are in the death camp. It is a lifeless island. A man does not come here to live but to die, sooner or later. There is no room for life here. It is the residence of death. Our brains are dulled, thoughts are numbed, this new language is impossible to grasp. Everyone is wondering where his family is. Where were they taken and how will they manage in the new conditions? Who knows how their terrified children will behave when they see how their mothers are mistreated? Who knows how these thugs will treat the sick, the weakened mothers and the sisters they love? Who knows what human grave received their fathers and brothers, or what they are going through? They all stand helpless, full of anxiety, in despair, lonely, wretched, broken.'

I am standing on the very spot where the trains arrived. The old photographs show the same buildings in the same places. Nothing has changed and then I realise with a shock that I am walking the exact route along which the newly arrived sick, old and mothers with young children were herded straight to be gassed. Along that via dolorosa the images crowd in on me. I allow them to come. Alone in the twilight, I hear what sounds like the cry of a wolf, a wild and piercing howl, and realise it is coming from me. I feel small, trusting hands in mine and in the silence the anguish rises from my guts to rend the air. Those mothers had to keep up a pretence of calm to comfort their little ones. I can howl for them.

I howl, I wail, a torrent of tears pouring down my face, as I walk with those long lost souls to the gas chamber and stand by the ruined crematorium and the pit of ashes watching the drops of rain spread their ripples outwards – a one way journey for hundreds of thousands. At the height of the madness they were gassing and burning day and night – 14,000, 15,000 people a day. I can walk back. They couldn't.

Rudolph Hess, the Commandant of Auschwitz, recalled coolly in his auto-biography his amazement:

> *"I noticed that women who either guessed or knew what awaited them nevertheless found the courage to joke with the children to encourage them, despite the mortal terror in their own eyes. One woman approached me as she walked past and, pointing to her four children who were manfully helping the smallest ones over the rough ground, whispered:*
> *'How can you bring yourself to kill such beautiful, darling children? Have you no heart at all?"*

Surely that detachment, that inability to identify with the 'other' is where the seed of evil is sown.

Our regular morning and evening group sharings continue to be full of moments of revelation – of profound opening. In that place of not-knowing – allowing judgements and assumptions to drop away – we bear witness not only to what happened here 50 years ago but to each other, all of whom carry the legacy. In the intensity of these moments I am totally present. The barriers between self and others melt. Nearly all of us grew up in families swamped by sorrow or guilt or hopelessness. Listening to each other we could look anew at our own stories and see them reflected in the stories of others, see more clearly that the heart of love, forgiveness and grace lies within each of us. In that place of openness and not-knowing, people felt able to abandon their defensive, self-protecting reflexes in favour of striving towards a clearer and more balanced understanding.

"I saw the mandala of my life not in words but in pictures," said one woman. "My childhood was haunted by the shadow of the gas ovens, soundless faces coming one after another. Now I know we can become either wounded killers or wounded healers. I want to make a spacious home beyond the barbed wire and invite my parents to my heart."

"As a German and a Christian I have experienced my whole life a profound speechlessness in myself, within my family and within my nation," said one man.

"At this place I have felt so strongly that I need to overcome this speechlessness and that the best way to do this is by speaking. I want to learn how to bear witness by my words and not remain silent."

"Another word for 'bearing witness' is listening," said Siddiq. "If I am to do anything for humanity I must first change myself. I must look at my fears and recognise them. If I stay in a state of fear I am useless. If I stay in a state of hatred I am useless. If I stay in a state of anger I am useless."

"In Auschwitz I found the place where I saw the rags that are myself sewn into a beautiful garment," said another.

"My experience was like a shower of blessings," said yet another. "A merging of my Jewish path and my Buddhist path."

Roshi Bernie spoke, "We all have many strategies for getting away from facing our pain – planning to solve all the problems of the world, for example! I had to come and sit here to learn how important it is just to be in the moment, to abide in stillness, to listen with the heart and speak from the heart. If we can talk to each other as if this was all the time we had and be able to live in the moment of our truth, that is the Tao of Auschwitz. You can't understand it. You can't fix it. But you can learn from it." These are wise words and reflecting on them has been helpful to me in living with the knowledge of my daughter Francesca's cancer.

At the heart of this whole retreat, although never labelled or stated as such, was the principle of the Great Fourth Noble Truth of the Buddha – the Eightfold Path which does not avoid or deny suffering but allows for a direct confrontation with suffering as a means to overcome it. By practising mindfulness, it teaches, you can develop a concentration which enables you to attain understanding which, in turn, is meant to liberate you from the shackles of suffering and give birth to peace and joy.

Sometimes we just sat in silence and there was benediction in the moments of stillness. How acutely important it is to live as awake, compassionate human beings. As people told their stories our hearts opened to acknowledge the courage that it took to stand there so nakedly. Heartbreak and grief are not the sole territory of any single era.

Levana expressed her thoughts in a powerful poem:

> *From my first breath*
> *I received a silver tray, dripping with my ancestors' blood …*
> *Never forget, never forgive.*
> *These words were engraven on my heart …*
> *This was the legacy that I received.*
> *"Amen", I said, vowing to avenge,*
> *virtuous with the pain;*
> *righteous with the horror …*
> *For hundreds of moons*
> *my ancestors' foes lodged in my heart –*

demons, human vultures, monsters,
turgid in my people's blood;
my people, the scapegoat of the world,
the Chosen, the people of the Torah ...
With my soldier's heart
I stood at Death Wall ...
My steel heart dissolved
in the fire of pain and love.
The children of my foes were there with me, bearing witness.
They sat with me, and prayed.
They held me in their arms ...
They told their stories – I heard.
I wept; bore witness to their suffering ...
I am becoming one with darkness,
with light
with the victims
with my foes.
All in the spaciousness of my heart.
Who am I now? ...

In my walking meditations I think about this constantly: Auschwitz presents us with a challenge – to meet our own darkness, because only then may we find another kind of ground into which to plant the tree of life. Also, if there is no compassion for those who abuse and oppress – for those who have no compassion – do I not become like them? Do I not then enter the darkness myself? A compassionate heart is the most effective way of challenging the power of evil. It can bring light where there was none. This understanding helps me to see that I must examine my choices each moment in terms of whether they move me toward the light or away from it. It shows me that the place to begin the task of eliminating evil is within myself.

I also think about the profound metaphors in the Sumerian myth of Inanna which embodies the ancient vision that humanity can only be awakened through an entry into the deepest darkness. It conveys, beyond the confines of space and time, that humans cannot develop unless we have the courage to die to a vital part of ourselves (the ego), become willing to risk utter nakedness protected only by our trust and hope that we will be safeguarded by that within us which is humble and faithful, which has the capacity to weep and to stir into compassionate action those aspects of self which are prepared both to be troubled and to *act* in order to enable the mysterious rebirth of our will to life.

Following on the grey, sombre days of mourning, witnessing and remembering came Shabbat – ravishing, ecstatic, filled to overflowing with a wild joy. Moments of beauty seeped through the cracks of the seemingly impenetrable sadness like a healing miasma – restoring us and reaching out to surround the ghosts of those who were broken here.

It is Friday night and we squeeze into the refectory of a nearby convent to have a special Shabbat dinner. There is soft, plaited cholla bread and wine. We light the candles to welcome the Sabbath Bride, the Shekhina, the indwelling spirit, the breath of God – bringing her into our eyes, inviting her into our hearts – that gentle, timeless ceremony which I love so much. To be singing Jewish Sabbath prayers in Auschwitz is a glory and a triumph. They couldn't shut us up! After the meal we find that we can dance and sing in a rapture of love and delight. We are happy after so many tears.

The final day of the retreat and I am one of the last to chant my list of names, placing them when I have finished along with all the others in a beautiful wooden box in the centre of our circle. Then we all remain sitting for another half hour and repeat the bleak mantra, "Name Unknown" over and over again for all those who were never documented. Only those prisoners deemed fit for work had their details recorded, most did not, including all those mothers holding their tired, stunned little ones by the hand as they were led away to die. A Puerto Rican woman in our group who, since coming here, has asked herself quite a few times in astonishment, 'what on earth is a Puerto Rican doing in Auschwitz?' hears the voices of the dead answering her. "Alcun me recuerdo", they whisper. "Alcun recuerdo mi nombre." Someone remembers me. Someone remembers my name. "Now I know why I am here", she says.

On the last evening, Rabbi Singer lights the multi-wick Havdallah candle for the end of Shabbat. It represents, he tells us, all our differences braided together to make one fire. It is the Light of Creation, the indivisible wisdom of the heart, the best of dreams. We pass the candle from hand to hand around the circle looking into each others' eyes and observing the light and shadow cast by the tiny flame. We stand in the radiance of our own compassion. It is very hard to find words for any of this. It is vastly different from what I had expected. Yes, there was grief and yes, there was anguish, but I hadn't anticipated so much joy and laughter, so much wisdom of the heart, so much to learn about one's own shadow and the possibility that the old might be discarded and a transformation achieved. One Catholic nun said, "I never expected Jewish songs to sing in me! It is a resurrection!"

The experience of the Auschwitz retreat was a rite of passage, a crucible of healing and learning. Not just a trail of tears but an unparalleled opportunity to go into the heart of the fire to the alchemy of change. We heard words etched in pain and beauty, a passion play of human stories simply told from the place where no more hiding was possible. And suddenly it is all over and the dear people who came together to share this unique experience all go off in different directions – back to their everyday lives. My head and heart still full of the richness of the Bearing Witness Retreat, I will stay on for a few days in order to make a pilgrimage to a little town in central Poland called Tomaszchow-Mazowiecki – my father's birthplace. The Director of the Centre for Jewish Culture in Cracow has kindly arranged a car and an interpreter to go with me

as English is not widely spoken and I have no Polish, alas, beyond *dzien dobry,
dzienkuje* and *do widzenia*.

The way to Tomaszchow passes near to Czestochowa the home of the miraculous painting of the Black Madonna known as the Queen of Poland, the
world-famous Icon of the Monastery of Jasna Gora – place of pilgrimage and
one of the most visited holy sites in the world. I have always loved the painting
of the Dark Mother with the two great scratches on her face (attacked by
vandals in 1430 in one of the numerous invasions of Poland by the Swedes in
the past). I also really wanted to see something of the 'other Poland', a deeply
Catholic country where the people adore Mary as much as the Irish do.

She is definitely the Goddess, this Jewish woman, this Mother of God. Even
on a rainy November day the chapel in the basilica of the Monastery is packed
to the rafters with pilgrims. The halt and the lame flock here in huge numbers
every day of the year in the hopes of a miraculous healing and the walls of the
chapel are festooned from floor to ceiling with votive offerings, little silver legs,
hands, hearts and discarded crutches. This being a Sunday, there were almost
continuous services throughout the day from 6 am till late at night. The painting,
adorned in precious silver and gold cladding so that only the faces peek
through, is unveiled daily from behind its protective screen to the accompani-
ment of a moving and awe-inspiring drum roll and trumpet fanfare. The crush
of people crowding in on the altar means that I don't get a close-up view but
it is quite special to be in the midst of all that fervent devotion. We arrive as
the faithful are receiving Holy Communion. There is some beautiful singing,
then the solemn drum and trumpet music as the Black Madonna is covered up
again and that is that. At least I have seen her and said hello.

The much-loved Cracovian Jewish writer and thinker, Rafael Scharf, in his
book, *Poland, What Have I to do With Thee …* tells of a visit he once paid to the
Church of the Holy Virgin Mary in Cracow where he got talking to a sympathetic young man at the end of the service. After a congenial conversation
the young man confided in him, "I know, and it no longer causes me any
difficulty to accept this, that Our Lord Jesus was a Jew. But in no way am I able
to accept that Our Holy Virgin Mary, the Queen of the Crown of Poland, as
we like to call her, was a Jewess …"

'I didn't know what to say,' writes Scharf. 'To understand these things, on a
level which does justice to the depth and complexity of these predicaments, is
too difficult for me, for most of us.' For me too.

Then on through the foggy drizzle to Tomaszchow, the fabled, much
imagined home of my beloved Dad – that clever, studious, curious, inquisitive
child who grew up to be my father. Any romantic notions I may have had
about a little Fiddler On The Roof *shtetl* are quickly dispelled. It is a straggly,
unimpressive, strung-out town surrounded by blocks and blocks of concrete

Soviet-style apartment buildings. We arrive at dusk, driving past quite a few dismal and disconsolate-looking hookers plying their trade near the truckstops along the highway, and ask a local taxi-driver to recommend a nice hotel. He directs us to *the* hotel – the only one in town – the glum Mazowiecki Hotel – incorporating the Red Fox Restaurant (a bleak place of wood-grain effect Formica) and the Klub 'PARADISE' on the first floor. Vacancies are not a problem and a glance at the town plan pinned on the wall shows us that Warszawska Street where my Dad grew up is actually an extension of the very street the hotel is on.

We ask the concierge to point out the old Jewish Quarter which, of course, doesn't exist anymore but we drive around in the dark peering through the windscreen wipers at any old-looking buildings which might have been a shop on a corner – the family business – 55 years ago. Nothing to see, town completely dead, so we give up and spend the rest of the evening in the silver foil-clad PARADISE night club. We are the only customers. We sit on swivvley bar stools under the flashing UV lights, bombarded by high-volume, low-grade, disco tunes and watch the National Lottery on TV as our driver, Pawel, has bought a ticket. If he wins he is going to drive me all the way home to London free of charge. He doesn't. Instead he has a beer. Robert, my charming young interpreter, has a tequila and mint syrup with soda in a glass frosted with desiccated coconut and decorated with a paper toadstool. I knock back a couple of buffalo-grass vodkas. It is a surreal experience in this ghost town where 14,000 Jews were transported to Treblinka on two terrible days in May 1942, to be sitting in the Paradise Night Club.

I ask Robert why he, a young non-Jew of 26, chooses to work at the Centre for Jewish Culture and he replies that he wants to help celebrate and revive the incalculable contribution that Jewish life brought to his country's history. He is an exceptionally intelligent and dear young man – very sensitive and good company.

The concierge has also mentioned that there are some Jewish graves over on the edge of the main town cemetery, so next day we go there to see what we can see. We push open a rusty iron gate on the far side and find a vast, ancient, neglected burial ground overgrown with creepers and tree roots with hundreds of Jewish tombstones – mostly fallen down or broken – strewn about in the long grass. I spend a long time looking, but to no avail. Since the inscriptions are all in Hebrew, I would never be able to find which graves might belong to my grandparents even if they were still intact, but I leave a single flower there in memoriam.

Next we try, at the Kafkaesque Town Hall, to make some enquiries about what happened to Warszawska Street. The Town Hall only keep records going back 50 years but at the Town Archive on the far side of town they are very helpful. They bring from the vault some old leather-bound ledgers from the time of the Russian occupation of this part of Poland. Records were kept up to date from the end of the 18th Century until 1917 when the Russians left and, sure enough, there were Elia and Sura Honig – my grandparents – and their only child Rachmil Yitzak, my father, born 1905. My heart leaps. My fingers brush the spidery, faded, brown Russian copperplate and I think of the proud parents coming to register their miracle baby born when my grandmother was 46. Elia, my grandfather, died in November 1915 as I knew, when Daddy was 10 years old, although the book does not record the manner of his death – murdered on the Sabbath in front of his son's eyes. The book, alas, also does not record the family's exact address in Warszawska Street and the trail goes cold.

Next day I study the map of the surrounding area. I am looking for the source of the River Pilica. I have some unfinished business to complete. Anyone who has read my book, *Older Than Time* – which is about wisdom and older women – may remember a description of an uncanny experience in which my grandmother came to me in a visualisation. It took place on the last day of the Mother Nature camp in Wales when Anna led us in a guided meditation as part of her course on 'magic in the European tradition'. The idea was to journey in your mind to a place where you might meet your 'guide' – perhaps a wise spirit or animal that could help you in your life. This is a magical technique, widely deployed in healing and hypnotherapy which assumes that deep down inside ourselves we know a lot more than we think. Spirit guides help us to access this wisdom. Although, of course, we create them, these visualisations can, like dreams, take on surprising forms. So much lies hidden just below the surface of the conscious mind waiting to be summoned up.

I closed my eyes and, following Anna's voice, allowed myself to travel a long way through a tunnel, a gate, along a path, through a labyrinth. I eventually found myself standing by a deep, bubbling pool which looked like a spring at the source of a river. My guide appeared at once and said, 'Lalushka, I am your grandmother Sura.' Only one person ever called me Lalushka and that was my father – her son. As she spoke, mists swirled around her and her face disappeared from view. 'It will not be easy for me to reach you or for us to communicate because I am very far away but I will find ways. Know that I love you, care for you, watch over you.' Then the mist covered her up and her voice grew fainter. 'Before I go I will give you a gift, a token of faith,' she said, and put into my hand a very unusual shell carved into a spiral. A distinctive cone-shaped, smooth, beige shell. Then she was gone. The scene faded, the meditation was over and I returned to everyday consciousness – to my body curled up under a blanket.

I was puzzled by the incredible clarity of the setting, the message and the gift. Puzzled, yet suffused with contentment. It really felt as if I had made contact with her – the grandmother I had never known who perished in Poland before I was born. The next day was wild and windy but I took a walk along the cliffs by the sea. There was nobody about and I shouted and sang in a cheerful mood. After about an hour's walking, I descended to a dreary little seaside village where I warmed myself with a cup of tea in an empty café which doubled as the village shop. I absently looked at the tacky souvenirs and postcards of sunnier days. Suddenly I saw it, unmistakable, lying there on a shelf – a smooth, beige shell carved into a spiral, the only one in the shop – the very one my grandmother had given me! I bought it for a few pence and it now sits in a basket on the floor of my healing room.

A few months later, when I was trying to trace an elderly cousin of my father's who survived the Holocaust, I went to Israel. I took with me my father's manuscript of his unfinished memoirs, *The Wonderings of a Wandering Jew* which I had skimmed through years before when I was too young and too preoccupied with the present to be interested in the past. This time I read it avidly in the hopes that it would bring me closer to him and to my grandmother. On my last day in Tel Aviv I walked along the shore to the old city of Jaffa where I watched the sun go down and read the last bit of the memoirs in which my father describes going with his mother to her favourite place – a famous local beauty spot on the outskirts of Tomaszchow Mazowiecki, their town. People used to come from miles around to marvel at it:

> *It was a walk through the woods,* [he wrote]*, to the River Pilica and its blue, effervescent source … A place called Molieskie Zrodla where you could look to the bottom of the clear sky-blue water several metres down and see the very place, deep and mysterious, where the water bubbled up out of the sand.*

When I read that my heart pounded. The source! The very setting of the visualisation where I had met my grandmother and received from her the shell. And now I am here in Tomaszchow looking at the town map on the wall of the hotel and there it is, a nature reserve called 'Blue Sources' a little way out of town. Pawel and Robert drive me there then leave me. It is a cold, overcast, winter's day with nobody about, luckily, so I am able to be alone with my thoughts and do what I need to do undisturbed. The Blue Sources does not look very blue today but it is a majestic, quiet place – really a series of inter-connected ponds studded with mossy, tree-covered islands. I follow a winding path around the water's edge through a birch forest until I come to a particu-larly lovely spot. I know that my grandmother and her family would have come here to this exact place – maybe even when she, herself, was a girl. She certainly would have brought my father here for picnics with his cousins and friends. I imagine the sound of their childish laughter as I walk in their footsteps on the land of my ancestors – starkly beautiful on this grey day with the black, leafless winter trees reflected in the still waters.

In the rich, loamy soil under a silver birch by the riverbank I plant my daughter Francesca's five red tulips. I gently place my son Ben's acorns into the shallow silt with the hope that one day four English oak trees from Richmond Park may take root somewhere here. I throw a beautiful amethyst crystal onto the nearest island as a gift to my grandmother. I talk to her and tell her that I love her and that she is not forgotten. Finally I light my floating candles, one for each of my six children, and send them off among the little islands carrying the light of life and remembrance. I have come to rest in the present moment. I have found life in the place of death. I stand and watch, in the darkening day, the miniature beacons like fairies dancing, drifting silently out, carried by the faintest of breezes, reflecting their tiny flames in the water. A very satisfying healing ritual and a fitting culmination to this spiritual quest – a rite of passage which has necessitated separating from the known and familiar, crossing the threshold of the new/old/timeless truths and embodying my own spirituality. 'L'Chaim!' I whisper, 'To life!' I feel whole and peaceful.

Further Reading List

ADILAKSHMI – *The Mother* – Mother Meera Publications, (1987)

ANDERSON, Sherry Ruth and HOPKINS, Patricia – *The Feminine Face of God* – Bantam, (1991), ISBN 0-553-352-66-0

ANDREWS, Valerie – *A Passion For This Earth* – Harper Collins, (1990), ISBN 0-06 250068-6

ARTRESS, Dr. Lauren – *Walking a Sacred Path* – Riverhead Books, (1995), ISBN 1-57322-007-8

BARSTOW, Anne Llewellyn – *Witchcraze* – Pandora, (1994), ISBN 0-06-251036-3

BENDER, Sue – *Everyday Sacred* – Harper San Francisco, (1995), ISBN 0-06-251289-7

BOLEN, Jean Shinoda – *Goddesses In Everywoman* – Harper and Row, (1984), ISBN 0-06-091291

BOLEN, Jean Shinoda – *Crossing To Avalon* – Harper Collins, (1994), ISBN 0-06-250272-7

BROWN, Mick – *The Spiritual Tourist* – Bloomsbury, (1998), ISBN 0-7475-3667-8

CAMERON, Anne – *Daughters of Copper Woman* – The Women's Press, (1981), ISBN 0-7043-3946-3

CHRIST, Carol P. and PLASKOW, Judith – *Womanspirit Rising: A Feminist Reader in Religion* – Harper Collins, (1979), ISBN 0-06-061377-7

CHRIST, Carol P. (Ed.) – *Diving Deep and Surfacing* – Beacon Press, (1990), ISBN 0-8070-6207-3

CRAIGHEAD, Meinrad – *The Mother's Songs* – Paulist Press, (1986), ISBN 0-8091-2716-4

CROWTHER, Patricia – *Lid Off The Cauldron* – Weiser, (1985), ISBN 0-87728-629-9

DAMES, Michael – *Mythic Ireland* – Thames and Hudson, (1992), ISBN 0-500-27872-5

DOWNING, Christine (Ed.) – *The Long Journey Home* – Shambala, (1994), ISBN 0-87773-937-4

Du BOULAY, Shirley – *Teresa of Avila* – Hodder and Stoughton, (1991), ISBN 0-340-51864-2

El-SOHL, Camillia Fawzi and MABRO, Judy – *Muslim Women's Choices* – Berg
Publications, (1994), ISBN 0-85496-835-0

FAMA, Chief – *Fundamentals of Yorùbá Religion* – Orúnmìlá Communications,
(1993), ISBN 0-9644247-0-3

FOX, Matthew – *Original Blessing* – Bear and Co., (1983),
ISBN 0-939680-07-6

GALLAND, China – *Longing For Darkness: Tara and The Black Madonna* –
Penguin, (1990), ISBN 0-14-012184-6

GLASSMAN, Bernard and FIELDS, Rick – *Instructions to the Cook* – Bell Tower,
(1996), ISBN 0-517-70377-7

GOLDENBERG, Naomi R. – *Changing of the Gods* – Beacon Press, (1979),
ISBN 0-8070-1111-8

GREEN, Miranda – *Celtic Goddesses* – British Museum Press, (1995),
ISBN 0-7141-2303-X

HALIFAX, Joan – *The Fruitful Darkness* – Harper San Francisco, (1993),
ISBN 0-06-250313-8

HARDING, M. Esther – *Woman's Mysteries* – Rider, (1955),
ISBN 0-09-150061-3

HARVEY, Andrew – *The Return of the Mother* – Frog Ltd., (1995),
ISBN 1-883319-07-2

HOPMAN, Ellen Evert and BOND, Lawrence – *People of the Earth* – Destiny
Books, (1996), ISBN 0-89281-559-0

HOUSTON, Jean – *The Search for The Beloved* – Tarcher/Putnam, (1982),
ISBN 0-87477-476-4

KAUFER, Nelly and OSMER-NEWHOUSE, Carol – *A Woman's Guide to Spiritual
Renewal* – Harper San Francisco, (1994), ISBN 0-06-250882-2

KING, Theresa (Ed.) – *The Divine Mosaic* – Yes International, (1994),
ISBN 0-93-6663-10-3

LERNER, Gerda – *The Creation of Patriarchy* – O.U.P., (1986),
ISBN 0-19-505185-8

LONG, Asphodel – *In a Chariot Drawn By Lions: The Search For The Female in
Deity* – The Women's Press, (1992), ISBN 0-7043-4295-2

LOUDON, Mary – *Revelations* – Penguin, (1994),
ISBN 0-14-024456-5

MARLOW, Mary Elizabeth – *Handbook for the Emerging Woman* – Donning,
(1988), ISBN 0-89865-672-9

MARIE-DALY, Bernice – *Ecofeminism* – Teilhard Studies No. 25, Anima Books,
PA

NICHOLSON, Shirley (Ed.) – *The Goddess Awakening* – Quest, (1989),
ISBN 0-8356-0642-2

OCCHIOGROSSO, Peter – *The Joy of Sects* – Image, (1994),
ISBN 0-385-42565-1

PAGE, Dr. Christine – *Beyond the Obvious* – The C.W. Daniel Co. Ltd (1998),
ISBN 0-85207-322-4

PETERSON, Brenda – *Nature and Other Mothers* – Ballentine, (1992),
    ISBN 0-449-90967-0

PIRANI, Alix – *The Absent Mother* – Mandala, (1991),
    ISBN 1-85274-099X

PURCE, Jill – *The Mystic Spiral* – Thames and Hudson, (1974),
    ISBN 0-500-81005-2

RAE, Eleanor and MARIE-DALY, Bernice – *Created in Her Image* – Crossroad
    Publishing, (1990), ISBN 0-8245-1013-5

RANCK, Shirley Ann – *Cakes for the Queen of Heaven* – Delphi Press, (1995),
    ISBN 1-878980-10-6

ROOSE-EVANS, James – *Inner Journey, Outer Journey* – Rider, (1987),
    ISBN 0-7126-1431-1

ROOSE-EVANS, James – *Passages of the Soul* – Element, (1994),
    ISBN 1-85230-708-0

ROTH, Gabrielle – *Maps to Ecstasy* – Crucible, (1990),
    ISBN 1-85274-086-8

SCHARF, Rafael F. – *Poland, What Have I to do With Thee?* – Judaica
    Foundation, Krakow, (1996), ISBN 83-7052-415-X

SNOW, Kimberley – *Keys to The Open Gate* – Conari, (1994)
    ISBN 0-943233-63-1

STARHAWK – *Spiral Dance* – Harper and Row, (1979),
    ISBN 0-06-2250814-8

STARHAWK – *Dreaming the Dark* – Beacon, (1982),
    ISBN 0-8070-1001-4

STARHAWK – *Truth or Dare* – Harper and Row, (1987),
    ISBN 0-06-250816-4

STEIN, Diane – *The Women's Spirituality Book* – Llewellyn, (1992),
    ISBN 0-87542-761-8

THICH NHAT HAHN, – *Being Peace* – Parallax Press, (1987)
    ISBN 0-938077-00-7

WALKER, Barbara G. – *The Woman's Encyclopaedia of Myths and Secrets* – Harper
    and Row, (1990), ISBN 0-06-250925-X

WASKOW, Arthur – *Seasons of Our Joy: A Celebration of Jewish Renewal* –
    Beacon, (1982), ISBN 0-8070-3611-0

WILLIAMS, Cecil – *No Hiding Place* – Harper Collins, (1992),
    ISBN 0-06-250988-8

WOOLGER, Jennifer Barker and Roger J. – *The Goddess Within* – Rider, (1990),
    ISBN 0-7126-3934-9

Index